# Praise for *Unspeakable Love*

'This is a compelling read. It captures with detail and with disturbing accuracy the difficulties and dangers facing lesbians and gay men across the Middle East. It helps us to understand the social pressure, the sense of isolation, the anxiety and fear and trauma. And through it all we glimpse also the possibility of hope, of remarkable courage, and perhaps even in the longer term, the chance of a more open and accepting society.'

**Lord (Chris) Smith, former UK Secretary of State for Culture**

'This is an important, timely book, and lucid to boot – a must-read for anyone who believes in human rights.'

**Rabih Alameddine, author of *Koolaids* and *I, the Divine***

'A fascinating insight.'

**Ben Summerskill, Chief Executive, Stonewall**

'Brian Whitaker has given us a moving analysis of the hidden lives of Arab homosexuals. This genuinely groundbreaking investigation reveals a side of Arab and Muslim culture shrouded by the strictest taboos. Arab societies can no longer contain their cultural, religious, ethnic or sexual diversity within their traditional patriarchal definitions of the public sphere. Anyone interested in reform in the Arab world must read this book.'

**Mai Yamani, Research Fellow at Chatham House and author of *Cradle of Islam***

'It is high time this issue was brought out of the closet once and for all, and afforded a frank and honest discussion. Brian Whitaker's humane, sophisticated, and deeply rewarding book, *Unspeakable Love*, does exactly that.'

**Ali Al-Ahmed, Director of the Gulf Institute**

'I enjoyed and learnt much from Brian Whitaker's book, which is excellent. It was inspirational to me on the challenges to international law, and the uses of nationalism to suppress dissent within countries.'

**Professor Fred Halliday, London School of Economics, and author of *100 Myths about the Middle East***

Brian Whitaker

# UNSPEAKABLE LOVE

## Gay and Lesbian Life in the Middle East

**SAQI**

ISBN 10: 0-86356-819-X
ISBN 13: 978-0-86356-819-0

This edition published 2006 by Saqi Books

A full CIP record for this book is available from the British Library

Manufactured in Lebanon

**SAQI**
26 Westbourne Grove
London W2 5RH
www.saqibooks.com

# Contents

# Introduction

DEPARTURE GATE, Damascus airport: a young Arab man in jeans, T-shirt and the latest style of trainers is leaving on a flight to London. He passes through final security checks, puts down his bag, takes something out and fiddles furtively in a corner. No, he is not preparing to hijack the plane; he is putting rings in his ears. When he arrives in London the tiny gold rings will become a fashion statement that is unremarkable and shocks no one, but back home in Damascus it's different. Arab men, real Arab men, do not wear jewellery in their ears.

This is one small example of the double life that Arabs, especially the younger ones, increasingly lead – of a growing gap between the requirements of society and life as it is actually lived, between keeping up appearances in the name of tradition or respectability and the things people do in private or when away from home.

For many, the pretence of complying with the rules is no more than a minor irritation. Men who like earrings can put them in or take them out at will, but sometimes it's more complicated. Arab society usually expects women to be virgins when they marry. That doesn't stop them having sex with boyfriends but it means that when the time comes to marry many of them will have an operation to restore their virginity – and with it their respectability. There is no medical solution, however, when a boy grows up too feminine for the expectations of a macho culture. When he is mocked for his girlish mannerisms but can do nothing to control them, when his family beat him and ostracise him and accuse him of bringing shame upon their household, the result is despair and sometimes tragedy.

This book was inspired – if that is the right word – by an event in 2001 when Egyptian police raided the Queen Boat, a floating night club on the River Nile which was frequented by men attracted to other men. Several dozen were arrested on the boat or later. The arrests, the resulting trial, and the attendant publicity in the Egyptian press (much of it highly fanciful) wrecked numerous lives, all in the name of moral rectitude. It was one of the few recent occasions when homosexuality has attracted widespread public attention from the Arab media.

Some time afterwards, while visiting Cairo as a correspondent for *The Guardian* newspaper, I met two people intimately connected with the case: a defendant who had since been released and the partner of another defendant who was still in jail. At that stage I was thinking of writing a feature article, but later I met a young Egyptian activist (identified as 'Salim' elsewhere in this book). As we chatted over lunch, our conversation moved on from the Queen Boat case to questions of homosexuality in the wider Arab world. He seemed very knowledgeable and I remarked casually: 'You should write a book about it.'

'No,' he said. '*You* should write one.'

I mulled this over for several months. It was clearly time for someone to raise the issue in a serious way but, as Salim had indicated, it was difficult for Arabs – at least those living in the region – to do so. Foreign correspondents such as myself often write books about the Middle East, though they tend to be about wars or the big, newsworthy events: Palestine, Iraq, and so on. I had no desire to follow that well-worn path, but this was one topic that would break new ground as well as some long-standing taboos. Homosexuality is a subject that Arabs, even reform-minded Arabs, are generally reluctant to discuss. If mentioned at all, it's treated as a subject for ribald laughter or (more often) as a foul, unnatural, repulsive, un-Islamic, Western perversion. Since almost everyone agrees on that, there is no debate – which is one very good reason for writing about it.

I did have some qualms, though. One was the possibility that Arab and Muslim contacts on whom I depend for my daily work might take offence. Another was that in today's political climate any critique of Arab/Islamic society tends to be interpreted in the region as serving American designs. In the end, I decided these were risks worth taking and struck a deal with 'Salim': I *would* write the book, if he would suggest people to interview.

There are twenty-two countries in the Arab League (if we include Palestine), and to try to give a country-by-country picture would be both impractical and repetitive. Instead, I wanted to highlight the issues that are faced throughout the region, to a greater or lesser degree, by Arabs whose sexuality does not fit the public concepts of 'normal'. Most of the face-to-face research was done in Egypt and Lebanon – two countries that provide interesting contrasts. This was supplemented from a variety of other sources including news reports, correspondence by email, articles in magazines and academic journals, discussions published on websites, plus a review of the way homosexuality is treated in the Arabic media, in novels and in films.

One basic issue that I have sought to explain is the reluctance of Arab societies to tolerate homosexuality or even to acknowledge that it exists. This has not always been the case. Historically, Arab societies have been relatively tolerant of sexual diversity – perhaps more so than others. Evidence of their previous tolerance can be found in Arabic literary works, in the accounts of early travellers and the examples of Europeans who settled in Arab countries to escape sexual persecution at home. Despite the more hostile moral climate today, however, same-sex activity continues largely undeterred. This is not quite as paradoxical as it might seem. As with many other things that are forbidden in Arab society, appearances are what count; so long as everyone can pretend that it doesn't happen, there is no need to do anything stop it. That scarcely amounts to tolerance and the effects, unfortunately, are all too obvious. People whose sexuality does not fit the norm have no legal rights; they are condemned to a life of secrecy, fearing exposure and sometimes blackmail; many are forced into unwanted marriages for the sake of their family's reputation; there is no redress if they are discriminated against; and agencies providing advice on sexuality and related health matters are virtually non-existent.

A point to be made clear from the outset is that Arabs who engage in same-sex activities do not necessarily regard themselves as gay, lesbian, bisexual, etc. Some do, but many (probably the vast majority) do not. This is partly because the boundaries of sexuality are less clearly defined than in the West but also because Arab society is more concerned with sexual acts than sexual orientations or identities. Although it is generally accepted in many parts of the world that sexual orientation is neither a conscious choice nor anything that can be changed voluntarily, this idea has not yet taken hold in Arab countries – with the result that homosexuality tends to be viewed either as wilfully perverse behaviour or as a symptom of mental illness, and dealt with accordingly.

A further complication in the Middle East is that attitudes towards homosexuality (along with women's rights and human rights in general) have become entangled in international politics, forming yet another barrier to social progress. Cultural protectionism is one way of opposing Western policies that are viewed as domineering, imperialistic, etc, and so exaggerated images of a licentious West, characterised in the popular imagination by female nudity and male homosexuality, are countered by invoking a supposedly traditional Arab morality.

To portray such attitudes as collective homophobia misses the mark, however. They are part of the overall fabric and cannot be addressed in isolation: they are intimately linked to other issues – political, social, religious and cultural – that must all be confronted if there is ever to be genuine reform. One of the core arguments of this book, therefore, is that sexual rights are not only a basic element of human rights but should have an integral part in moves towards Arab reform, too. There is little hope of developing sexual rights except within a framework of broadly-based reform, and only when Arab societies start to debate sexuality in a rational way will it be possible to regard them as serious about reform in general. Not only that. Open discussion of sexuality can bring other reform-related issues into sharper focus.

Many of the Arabs that I interviewed were deeply pessimistic about the likelihood of significant change, though personally I am a little more hopeful. In countries where sexual diversity is now tolerated and respected the prospects must have looked similarly bleak in the past. The denunciations of sexual non-conformity emanating from the Arab world today are also uncannily similar, in both their tone and their arguments, to those that were heard in other places years ago ... and ultimately rejected.

A number of Arabs and others have helped with this work by offering their time for discussions, providing contacts, reading drafts of the text and suggesting improvements. For obvious reasons, most would prefer not to be thanked by name but I am grateful to them all, nonetheless.

Since the main object of this book is to stimulate debate, readers who wish to take part in further discussion can do so by visiting the relevant section of my website, www.al-bab.com/unspeakablelove. The footnotes are also available there in an online version which provides easy access to web pages mentioned in the text.

*Brian Whitaker*
*August 2005*

# A Note on Terminology

One of the problems when writing about same-sex issues is choosing terminology that is accurate and acceptable to the people concerned but does not become too cumbersome when used repeatedly. Many English-language newspapers treat 'gay' and 'homosexual' as more or less interchangeable. The style guide of *The Times* newspaper advises that 'gay' is 'now fully acceptable as a synonym for homosexual or lesbian', while *The Guardian* says 'gay' is 'synonymous with homosexual, and on the whole preferable'. Guidelines issued by the BBC for its broadcasters in August 2002 state:

> Some people believe the word 'homosexual' has negative overtones, even that it is demeaning. Most homosexual men and women prefer the words 'gay' and 'lesbian'. Either word is acceptable as an alternative to homosexual, but 'gay' should be used only as an adjective. 'Gay' as a noun – 'gays gathered for a demonstration' – is not acceptable. If you wish to use homosexual, as adjective or noun, do so. It is also useful, as it applies to men and women.

In the context of Arab and Islamic societies, however, proper use of 'gay' is more complicated. The word carries connotations of a certain lifestyle (as found among gay people in the West) and it implies a sexual identity that people may not personally adopt. 'Homosexual' – describing a person – may not have the same westernised connotations but can be equally inappropriate, especially where homosexual acts are an occasional alternative to those with the opposite sex.

Arabic itself has no generally-accepted equivalent of the word 'gay'. The term for 'homosexuality' (*al-mithliyya al-jinsiyya* – literally: 'sexual same-ness') is of recent coinage but is increasingly adopted by serious newspapers and in academic articles. The related word *mithli* is beginning to be used for people who are gay or homosexual. Both these terms are neutral and generally approved by Arabs who consider themselves to be gay. Meanwhile, the popular media continue to use the heavily-loaded *shaadh* ('queer', 'pervert', 'deviant'). The traditional word for 'lesbian' is *suhaaqiyya,* though some argue that this has negative connotations and prefer *mithliyya* (the feminine of *mithli*). Arabs also have a variety of more-or-less insulting words for sexual types (e.g. effeminate men) and those who favour certain kinds of sexual act. Arabic terminology is discussed more fully in chapter 7.

For the purposes of this book, the following English usage has been adopted:

Homosexuality: Acts and feelings of a sexual nature between people of the same gender, whether male or female, and whether or not the people involved regard themselves as gay, lesbian, etc.

Homosexual: Behaviour, feelings, practices, etc, directed

towards people of the same gender. It is used adjectivally in the text but not as a noun (e.g. 'a homosexual').

Lesbian: Applied to women who have adopted this as their sexual identity.

Gay: Applied to men who have adopted this as their sexual identity. In some contexts (e.g. 'gay community') the term should be regarded as shorthand which includes various other non-heterosexual identities: lesbian, bisexual, transgender, etc.

Gay rights: A shorthand way of referring to all sexual rights of a non-heterosexual nature. Not restricted to gay men.

Transgender: Refers to people who for physical or psychological reasons do not consider they belong to the gender originally assigned to them.

The usage outlined above applies to the author's text; quotations reproduced within the text may contain different usages.

# ONE

# A Question of Honour

FACED with the problem of a son who shows no interest in girls, the first instinct of many Arab parents is to seek medical help. Salim was twenty when his family asked if he was gay. He said yes, and they bundled him off to see the head of psychiatry at one of Egypt's leading universities. Salim told the professor that he had read about homosexuality and knew it wasn't a mental illness, but the professor disagreed. 'An illness,' he replied, 'is any deviation from normality.'

The professor offered Salim a course of psychiatric treatment lasting six months. 'He told me he couldn't say what the treatment would be until he knew more about my problem,' Salim said. 'I asked how he knew it would take six months, and he said that's what it usually takes. I turned it down.'[1]

Six months' psychotherapy may be pointless, but there are far worse alternatives. Stories abound in Egypt and other Arab countries of sons with homosexual tendencies being physically attacked by their families or forced to leave home. Ahmed[2] told of a friend whose father discovered he was having a homosexual relationship and, after a beating, sent him to a psychiatrist. 'The treatment involved showing pictures of men and women, and giving him electric shocks if he looked at the men,' Ahmed said. 'After a few weeks of this he persuaded a woman to pretend to be his girlfriend. His father was happy for a while – until he found a text message from the boyfriend on his son's mobile phone.' The beatings resumed and the young man fled to the United States.

Ali, still in his late teens, comes from a traditional Shi'a family in Lebanon and, as he says himself, it's obvious that he is gay. Before fleeing his family home he suffered abuse from relatives that included hitting him with a chair so hard that it broke, imprisoning him in the house for five days, locking him in the boot of a car, and threatening him with a gun when he was caught wearing his sister's clothes.[3] According to Ali, an older brother told him: 'I'm not sure you're gay, but if I find out one day that you *are* gay, you're dead. It's not good for our family and our name.'

A year on, having left home and found a job in a different part of Lebanon, Ali seemed remarkably phlegmatic about his relatives' behaviour. 'They are a Lebanese family and they didn't have enough information about gay life,' he said. 'For my dad, being gay is like being a prostitute. He would say: 'Is someone forcing you to do this?' My family would ask: 'Why are you walking like that?' My sister suggested going to a doctor. She said it's time to get married and have sons and daughters. I thought something was wrong with me, then I met a guy who told me about gay life and I started to understand myself more.'

The final break came when Ali's father seized his mobile phone and found gay messages on it. 'My dad told me I couldn't go out any more – I had to stay at home 24/24. After two hours I just put all my things in my bag and said I'm leaving. My brother said, "Let him leave, he's going to come back after a couple of hours." That was a year ago when I was eighteen. For the first three months I lived with my boyfriend.'

Asked if he thought the conflict with his family was over, Ali replied: 'No. It will come back when one of my parents dies.' Out of concern for his safety, friends recorded a detailed statement of his experiences and deposited it with a lawyer. They also urged him to leave the country but he was unable to retrieve the necessary papers from his family's home in order to get a visa.

The threats directed against Ali by his brother, and the accusation that he was besmirching the family's name, reflect a concept of 'honour' that is found in those parts of the Middle East where old-fashioned social values still prevail. Preserving the family 'honour' requires brothers to kill an unmarried sister if she becomes pregnant (even if – as has happened in some cases – her pregnancy is the result of being raped by one of her own family). Although deaths of gay men in 'honour' killings have been suspected but not confirmed,[4] at least one non-fatal shooting has been recorded.

A Canadian TV documentary highlighted the case of a gay Jordanian, the son of a wealthy politician.[5] At the age of twenty-nine he was forced into marriage by his father when rumours spread about his sexuality. The man, identified by the name 'al-Hussein', said he had told his fiancée the truth but she went ahead with the marriage because of his family's social standing. They later had three children by artificial insemination.

Al-Hussein continued to have discreet same-sex relationships but, after ten years of marriage, he fell in love with a member of

Jordan's national judo team, separated from his wife and moved to a house on the outskirts of the capital, Amman, to spend more time with his male lover. One night, his brother saw the two men kissing and pushed al-Hussein down the stairs. He spent three months in hospital recovering from the injuries, with an armed bodyguard outside the door. Later, his brother found him in the hospital lobby following a visit from his lover, and shot him in the leg. His brother, a Jordanian civil servant, was never prosecuted for the attacks because they were considered a family matter.[6]

On his discharge from hospital, al-Hussein was not allowed back to his own house but became, in effect, a prisoner in his brother's home, confined to a tiny room with bars on the window. A sympathetic aunt who was living in Toronto persuaded the family to let him join her in Canada and he was eventually allowed to go in return for signing over all his possessions – his house, his interior design business, two cars and his inheritance rights – to the brother who had shot him.

'I don't approve of what my brother did,' al-Hussein told a Canadian newspaper, 'but I understand why he did it. It was about preserving the family's honour.'[7]

* * *

WHETHER a gay Arab is considered mad or bad – as a case for psychotherapy or punishment – depends largely on family background. 'What people know of it, if they know anything, is that it's like some sort of mental illness,' said Billy,[8] a doctor's son in his final year of studies at Cairo University. 'This is the educated part of society – doctors, teachers, engineers, technocrats. Those from a lesser educational background deal with it differently. They think their son was seduced or lured or came under bad influences. Many of them get absolutely furious and kick him out until he changes his behaviour.'

A point made repeatedly by young gay Arabs in interviews was that parental ignorance is a large part of the problem: the lack of public discussion about homosexuality results in a lack of level-headed and scientifically accurate newspaper articles, books and TV programmes that might help relatives to cope better. The stigma attached to homosexuality also makes it difficult for families to seek advice from their friends. Confronted by an unfamiliar situation, and with no idea how to deal with it themselves, the natural inclination of parents from a professional background is to seek help from another professional such as a psychiatrist. In Egypt this is a common middle-class reaction to a variety of behavioural 'problems'. One (heterosexual) Egyptian recalled that his parents had sent him to a psychiatrist because he regularly smoked cannabis. The treatment failed, but he went on to become a successful journalist.

Psychotherapy in Egypt doesn't come cheap.[9] There's also no evidence that it 'cures' anyone. Contrary to the prevailing medical opinion elsewhere in the world, the belief that homosexuality is some form of mental illness is widespread in the Middle East, and many of the psychiatrists who treat it do nothing to disabuse their clients.

In the West, sexual reorientation ('reparative') therapies are rejected by most mental health organisations but supported by some evangelical Christian groups. Treatment is not permitted in Britain, though it is offered by some therapists in mainland Europe. In the United States, the only treatment approved by the American Psychiatric Association is 'affirmative therapy', which aims to reconcile clients with their sexuality. For other forms of treatment, clients must sign a consent document acknowledging the APA's view that sexual reorientation is impossible and that attempting it may cause psychological damage.[10]

In Egypt, treating gay men is a 'not very prominent and very under-developed' branch of psychiatry, Billy said. Treatments described by interviewees, either from personal experience or that of their friends, range from counselling to aversion therapy (electric shocks, etc). Futile as this may be in terms of reorientating the client, it is not necessarily a total waste of money: Billy cited several cases where failed therapy had helped to convince parents that their son would not change, and thus persuade them to accept his sexuality.

In contrast to their perplexed parents, gay youngsters from Egypt's professional class are often well-informed about their sexuality long before it turns into a family crisis. Sometimes their knowledge comes from older or more experienced gay friends, but mostly it comes from searching the Internet.[11] This of course requires basic computer literacy, access to the Internet and fluency in English (or possibly French), and is therefore only available to the better educated. 'If it wasn't for the Internet I wouldn't have come to accept my sexuality,' Salim said, but he was concerned that much of the information and advice provided by gay websites is addressed to a Western audience and may be unsuitable for people living in Arab societies. Many of these sites carry first-person 'coming-out' stories from Westerners who found the experience positive, or at least not as painful as they expected. The danger of this, Salim explained, is that it encourages Arab readers to do the same – and the results can be catastrophic, especially if they have no access to support and advice when relatives and friends respond badly. The difficulty of finding a sympathetic ear is illustrated by the case of one anguished Lebanese student who, knowing of nobody to turn to locally, sent an email to a professor in the United States who had written articles about Islam and homosexuality. Purely by chance, the professor knew someone in Lebanon who could help.

Having a lesbian daughter is less likely to cause a family crisis than having a gay son, according to Laila, an Egyptian lesbian in her twenties.[12] Her mother had once broached the question of her sexuality by asking: 'Do you like women?' – to which Laila replied 'Yes, of course.' Her mother put the question again: 'I mean, do you *really* like women? Don't you want to get married and have children?' That was the only time the subject had ever come up, Laila said, and even then her mother seemed relatively unconcerned.

Laila suggested two reasons for a more relaxed attitude towards lesbian daughters. One results from a heavily male-orientated society in which the hopes of traditional Arab families are pinned on their male offspring. Baby girls are not particularly welcomed and many parents continue having children until they produce a son. Boys therefore come under greater pressure than girls to live up to parental aspirations. The other factor is that lesbian inclinations remove some of a family's usual worries as their daughter passes through her teens and early twenties. The main behavioural requirement placed on a young woman during this dangerous period is that she should not 'dishonour' the family by losing her virginity or getting pregnant before marriage. A daughter's preference for women at least reassures the family that she won't bring shame on them by getting into trouble with men.

Laila's experience was not shared by Sahar,[13] a lesbian from Beirut, however. 'My mother found out when I was fairly young – around sixteen or seventeen – that I was interested in women, and she wasn't happy about it,' she said. Sahar was being treated for depression at the time and her university-educated mother decided to change the therapist. 'The previous one was sympathetic. Instead, she took me to a very homophobic therapist who suggested all manner of ridiculous things – shock therapy and so on.' Sahar thought it best to play along with her mother's wishes – and still does. 'I re-closeted myself and started going out with a guy,' she said. 'I'm twenty-six years old now and I shouldn't have to be doing this, but it's just a matter of convenience, really. My mum doesn't mind me having gay male friends but she doesn't like me being with women. I've heard and seen much more extreme reactions. At least I wasn't kicked out of the house.'

None of the young people interviewed in Egypt had initiated a conversation about their sexuality with a parent. 'People rarely come out to their family,' Billy said. 'They wouldn't tell their parents directly but might tell an aunt or uncle or a person they really trust.' Even so, it is a high-risk strategy: 'For those that I know [who did tell], it was such a drama.' Parents sometimes raise the issue, Billy said – either because they have noticed their son or daughter mixing with unconventional friends or because they have decided it is time for marriage. In Salim's case, although his parents had been the first to broach the question of his sexuality, he said he had provoked them into doing so – mainly because he feared being pressurised into getting married. 'I kept giving them hints, like laughing whenever they mentioned marriage.'

Marriage is more or less obligatory in traditional Arab households. Arranged marriages are widespread and parents often determine the timing, as well as taking on the responsibility of finding a suitable partner. Sons and daughters who are not particularly attracted to the opposite sex may contrive to postpone it for a while but the range of plausible excuses for not marrying at all is severely limited. This presents them with an unenviable choice: to declare their sexuality (with all the consequences that can entail) or to accept that marriage is inevitable and either try to suppress their homosexual feelings or pursue outlets for them alongside marriage.

Parental pressures of this kind, although extremely common, can vary in intensity from one family to another and are not universal. 'It depends on how you manage your career,' Billy said. 'There is less pressure to get married if you are focused on a career. If you're not doing much and seem to be messing about, parents will start talking about marriage.'

There are also some families where issues of sexuality are never raised, even obliquely, and even when it must be obvious to the parents that their son or daughter does not live up to conventional expectations of heterosexuality. 'Adagio', the only son of an Egyptian army officer, had reached the age of twenty-five without any hints from his family about the need to marry or any questions about his sexuality. They would complain if he stayed out all night without phoning them, but they never enquired too deeply about why he was staying out.[14]

There is surely an element of 'don't ask, don't tell' in this, a feeling that it will be better for the whole family if any suspicions remain unconfirmed. In the absence of confirmation the parents can still hope for a change in their son's behaviour. It is not entirely a forlorn hope. A point made repeatedly by interviewees in Egypt was that to be gay and Arab is often extremely lonely. Adagio said several of his gay friends had gone on to marry or were planning to do so – not because of family pressures but because they feared 'being alone' as they grew older. Their sexual feelings were largely unchanged by marriage, however. One of them, Adagio's first boyfriend who had since fathered a child, complained privately that sex with his wife was not as enjoyable as it had been with Adagio. Two of Adagio's other friends had taken a different route out of the gay life: by killing themselves.

The sense of duty that Arabs in general feel towards other members of their family is extremely powerful. Gay or lesbian Arabs are no exception to this and often they are willing to put family loyalties before their own sexuality. Hassan,[15] in his early twenties, comes from a prosperous and respectable Palestinian family who have lived in the United States for many years but whose values seem largely unaffected by their move to a different culture. His eldest sister is betrothed to a young man from another Arab-American family, and it was arranged in the traditional way, with a meeting between the two families who agreed that the couple were suitable and would marry when they had finished their studies. Until then, they remain apart and do not mix with the opposite sex. Hassan's family were unsure whether to let their daughter leave home to study but they allayed their fears by getting a relative who lives near the university to check on her at frequent intervals.

GHAITH, a Syrian, grew up with his sister in a single-parent family. 'My mum and dad got divorced when we were really young,' he said.[18] 'It was definitely not easy for my mum. She raised us by herself and everybody's eyes were on us. She was always scared of what people would say about how she was a single mother. I feel that in a way me and my sister were like an exam for her – if we screwed up everybody was going to blame her. This was her biggest concern when she heard I was gay.'

In 1999, Ghaith was in his final year studying fashion design in Damascus, where he often hung around with five other student friends. 'We were three boys and three girls,' he said. 'We were like boyfriends and girlfriends, but in Syria boyfriends and girlfriends don't sleep together. They don't even kiss each other or anything, except rarely. Of course, I had known that I was gay for a long time but I never allowed myself to even think about it until I went to college. Then, for the first time in my life I met people who had no problem with being homosexual. Most of them were homosexual themselves – they were fashion teachers.'

Ghaith developed a crush on one of his teachers. 'I felt this thing for him that I never knew I could feel,' he recalled. 'I used to see him and almost pass out every day. One day I was at his place with a lot of guys and girls. We were having a party and I got drunk. My teacher said he had a problem with his back and I offered him a massage. We went into the bedroom. I was massaging him and suddenly I felt so happy. He was facing down on the bed so I turned his face towards my face and kissed him.

'He was like ... "What are you doing? You're not gay."'

'I said: "Yes, I am."'

'It was the first time I had actually said that I was gay. After that I couldn't see anybody or speak for almost a week. I just went to my room and stayed there, I stopped going to school, I stopped eating, I stopped doing everything. I was so upset at myself and I was going … "No, I'm not gay, I'm not gay, I'm *not*." It was very difficult for me at that time. Everything in my life had suddenly changed, but I also felt this happiness too.'

Ghaith decided to entrust his secret to a female cousin. 'She lives in the United States and I really love her. I called her and told her: "I really don't know what to say. I'll understand if you never speak to me again, blah blah blah, but I'm gay."'

'She was laughing and she said: "I will never be upset if you are gay. I'll be happy for you, you're not doing anything wrong." She told me that it's not something you have to be ashamed of. It's who you are and you should be proud of yourself.

'So next day, after a week on my own in my room, I went to school and told my friends. They were mostly cool about it and some of them said: "Yeah, we knew." Then this girl, the one who was supposedly my girlfriend, was so upset she said: "I don't want to hurt you or anything, but I really think you should see a shrink."

'I said I didn't feel I had anything wrong with me but I would do it just because I didn't want her to misunderstand me. She said: "Do it for me." So I told her: "You find me a shrink and I will go."

'So I went to this psychiatrist and before I saw him I was stupid enough to fill in a form with the whole info about who I was, with my family's phone number.

'I told the doctor I had no problem but had come just to prove to my friend that it's not a sickness. He was very rude and we almost had a fight. He treated me like shit. He said: "You're the garbage of the country, you shouldn't be alive and if you want to live, don't live here. Just find a visa and leave Syria and don't ever come back."

'Before I reached home he had called my mum, because I had put the phone number on the form, and my mum freaked out. She gathered all my straight friends and two of my uncles, and my sister and her husband. When I arrived home there were all these people in the house. My mum was crying, my sister was crying, and I thought somebody had died or something. They put me in the middle and everybody was judging me and humiliating me.

'I said to them: "You have to respect who I am, this was not something I chose." I told them everything I had read about homosexuality, but it was a hopeless case. It was a very stupid move when I think about it now. I should have just denied it and everything would have been fine.

'The bad part was that my mum wanted me to leave the college. She was right in a way, because the college had changed me – it had opened my mind. Before that I was a typical Syrian guy but then I stopped behaving like the others. In Syria, everybody has to be a stereotype. If you don't have a big moustache and short hair it's always a problem.

'Anyway, my mother threatened she was going to stop paying the college and I said: "No, I'll do whatever you want." It was my final year and I was first in the class and doing very well. After that, she started taking me to therapists. I went to at least twenty-five different therapists and they were all really, really bad. Really bad. They did all sorts of medical tests, like hormones and things, and they always made you masturbate into this little container.

'In Syria they think the only reason why you would be gay is that you're over-feminine, that you're having problems with your hormones ... that you're transsexual, basically. I told them, "No, I don't want to be a woman, I'm a man." It's very difficult but I totally understand. I used to be aggressive against gay people myself – maybe because I was gay and not admitting it.

'One day we were having a family dinner and I had to go to see another therapist. My brother-in law offered to drive me there. While we were in the car he said, "You know, I married your sister because she's from a good family and she has a good reputation. I don't care about you or what you do, but if I ever hear anyone say my brother-in-law is gay I'm going to divorce your sister." I felt sad for my sister more than anything else, and she would have been stupid enough to blame me for the divorce if it happened.

'My sister was pregnant at the time and I wanted her to feel close to me. I told her: "I hope you're going to have a little girl and I'm going to make dresses for her." My sister said: "Yes, I hope it's a girl too, because if it's a boy I'll be so scared if you touch him." That was mean.

'After what my brother-in-law had said, I decided to stop resisting. I said "*Khallas!* I cannot do this any more. Nobody is remotely trying to understand me." I started agreeing with the psychiatrist and saying "Yes, you're right." I was going there every day and soon he was saying"I think you're doing better." He gave me some medicine that I never took. I have no idea what it was, but he used to charge a big bill.

'So everybody was fine with it after a while, because the doctor said I was doing OK, and because I was lying to the doctor. But I don't think anybody was convinced 100 percent.'

As soon as he graduated, Ghaith left home and left Syria. Six years on, he is a successful fashion designer in neighbouring Lebanon, though he visits his family occasionally. He feels that the experience has affected his mother and sister in different ways. His sister – once very traditionally-minded – has become more understanding, while his mother, who was once a very open person, never talks about his sexuality. 'I've tried to open the subject a few times but it never worked out,' he said. 'My mum is in denial. She keeps asking when I am going to get married: "When can I hold your children?" In Syria this is the way people think. Your only mission in life is to grow up and start a family, then raise your children so they can start their own family. There are no real dreams. The only Arab dream is having more families.'

* * *

EMIGRATION is one option that many young Arabs contemplate – especially those who are gay or lesbian. Khalid, an Egyptian with a British boyfriend of six years' standing, was planning to apply for residence in Britain, while Laila was hoping to go abroad to raise a child. 'I'm a lesbian but I'm also a woman, and women have maternal feelings,' she said, adding that life as a single mother would be just too difficult in Egypt. Acquiring permanent residence abroad, however, is not particularly easy.

Countries that have signed the 1951 UN Refugee Convention have a legal duty to offer protection to anyone with 'a well-founded fear of being persecuted for reasons of race, religion, nationality, membership of a particular social group or political opinion', and it is possible to interpret this as including those who are persecuted, or fear persecution, because of their sexual orientation. In Britain, for example, a legal ruling in 1999 determined that lesbian and gay people constitute a 'social group' under the terms of the refugee convention and are therefore eligible for asylum.[19] The United States takes a similar view.[20] To bring a claim for asylum, applicants have to show that there is a 'reasonable' likelihood of serious harm – extra-judicial execution, physical violence, torture, denial of liberty, etc – if they return to their home country. The serious harm must come from the authorities or other sections of the population from whom the authorities are either unable or unwilling to protect the asylum seeker.[21]

Despite the acceptance of sexuality-based persecution as grounds for asylum in the US, Britain, Australia, Canada and several other countries, the number of successful applications has been relatively small – about thirty in Britain,[22] and most of those in Britain were initially refused but eventually won on appeal.[23] The Stonewall gay rights organisation cautions: 'The vast majority of applications for asylum are refused. This is not an easy route ...'[24]

At least two gay asylum seekers in Britain have ended up killing themselves. Hussein Nasseri, a twenty-six-year-old Iranian, shot himself at Fort Fun, a children's play centre in Eastbourne, in June 2004 – just two weeks after his appeal to remain in the UK was rejected. He had fled from Iran claiming he had been imprisoned because of his sexuality and would be persecuted if he returned. At the inquest into his death, a coroner noted that the refusal of asylum was 'an obvious motive' for his suicide.[25]

In September 2003, Israfil Shiri, another Iranian, poured petrol over his body and set fire to himself in the offices of Refugee Action in Manchester. He had sought refuge in Britain to avoid having his homosexuality exposed but, following the rejection of his asylum application, had been homeless, destitute and unable to receive medical care for a painful bowel condition.[26]

Among the successful cases in the United States was one brought by a gay Lebanese man who had been detained, assaulted and threatened with death by a Muslim militia. His application was backed up by evidence from experts about socio-religious conditions in the country and Lebanese newspaper articles naming people who had been arrested for homosexuality. Another man granted asylum in the US was Mr H, a Jordanian with permanent residence in Saudi Arabia, who had suffered years of ill-treatment because his father suspected he was gay. When the suspicions were confirmed, his father threatened to kill him. An additional reason for granting asylum in this case was that Mr H could not expect police protection because homosexuality is criminalised in Jordan, the country of his birth, and is grounds for execution in Saudi Arabia, where he lived.[27]

On the other hand, Norway rejected an application from a twenty-five-year-old Moroccan whose very religious father had allegedly demanded that he marry his cousin and threatened to report his homosexuality to the police if he refused. An appeal court decided that the risk of imprisonment if he returned home was low and argued that Morocco was a relatively large country where the man would not have much difficulty hiding from his father.[28] The first person to be granted asylum in France on grounds of sexual orientation, in 1997, was an Algerian who had founded an AIDS organisation and another to promote human rights. He had suffered at the hands of Algerian police who had frequently assaulted and arrested him, and had also been pursued and threatened with death by civilians.[29]

The other main route to residence abroad is through sexual partnership with a foreigner – though by definition this only applies to those who can prove a long-standing relationship with someone from a country that recognises same-sex couples for the purposes of immigration. The fifteen that currently do so are Australia, Belgium, Britain, Canada, Denmark, Finland, France, Germany, Iceland, Israel, the Netherlands, Norway, South Africa, Sweden and New Zealand.[30] In Britain, residence is granted under the Unmarried Partners Rule, first introduced in 1999, which applies to both unmarried heterosexual couples and gay couples, granting them the same immigration rights that married couples are entitled to. In the absence of a marriage certificate, the couple must convince the authorities that they 'have been living together in a relationship akin to marriage which has subsisted for two years or more'. This, of course, requires a high level of proof – in fact just the sort of documentary evidence that might get someone arrested in an Arab country. The UK Lesbian & Gay Immigration Group advises couples to prepare a dossier of evidence showing that they live together at the same address, plus other evidence of joint activities and joint financial commitments. Both partners should write a covering letter 'detailing most, but not necessarily all of the following: how and when you met; how and why the relationship developed ... your shared social activities and hobbies; milestones in your relationship ... what makes your relationship special for you; what makes your partner special for you; future plans you may have; how you would feel if you were forced to be apart'.[31]

For Palestinians who face persecution in the West Bank and Gaza, the usual escape route is to Israel, where sexual relations between men have been legal since 1988.[32] The punishment for same-sex acts under Palestinian law is not entirely clear,[33] though in practice this is less significant than the extra-judicial punishments reportedly meted out by the authorities and the threats that gay men face from relatives intent on preserving family 'honour'.

The American magazine, *The New Republic,* described the case of Tayseer, a Palestinian from Gaza, who was eighteen when an elder brother caught him in bed with a boyfriend.[34] His family beat him and his father threatened to strangle him if it ever happened again. A few months later, a young man Tayseer had never met before invited him into an orange grove for sex:

> The next day he received a police summons. At the station Tayseer was told that his sex partner was in fact a police agent whose job is to ferret out homosexuals. If Tayseer wanted to avoid prison, he too would have to become an undercover sex agent, luring gays into orchards and turning them over to the police.
>
> Tayseer refused to implicate others. He was arrested and hung by his arms from the ceiling. A high-ranking officer he didn't know arranged for his release and then demanded sex as payback.
>
> Tayseer fled Gaza to Tulkarem on the West Bank, but there too he was eventually arrested. He was forced to stand in sewage water up to his neck, his head covered by a sack filled with faeces, and then he was thrown into a dark cell

infested with insects and other creatures he could feel but not see ... During one interrogation, police stripped him and forced him to sit on a Coke bottle.[35]

The key ingredients of Tayseer's story are repeated in other published accounts given by gay fugitives from the West Bank and Gaza: a violent family reaction, entrapment and blackmail by the police coupled with degrading improvised punishments. The hostility of families is a predictable response from those who regard homosexuality as a betrayal of 'traditional' Arab-Islamic values and is by no means unique to Palestine, but while it might be possible in some Arab countries to take refuge from relatives in the anonymity of big cities, the Palestinian territories are small, with mainly close-knit communities making it difficult to hide.

A further difficulty for Palestinians is that in the highly-charged atmosphere of the conflict with Israel, their sexuality tends to become caught up in politics. Fleeing across the Green Line into Israel is viewed as a betrayal of the Palestinian cause, while those who stay also come under suspicion. 'In the West Bank and Gaza, it is common knowledge that if you are homosexual you are necessarily a collaborator with Israel,' said Shaul Gonen, of the Israeli Society for the Protection of Personal Rights.[36] Bassim Eid, of the Palestinian Human Rights Monitoring Group, explained: 'In the Arab mindset, a person who has committed a moral offence is often assumed to be guilty of others, and it radiates out to the family and community. As homosexuality is seen as a crime against nature, it is not hard to link it to collaboration – a crime against nation.'[37]

This generalised view equating homosexuality with

treachery[38] makes it extremely dangerous for Palestinians to return home after fleeing to Israel. One man told *The New Republic* of a friend in the Palestinian police who ran away to Tel Aviv but later went back to Nablus where he was arrested and accused of being a collaborator: 'They put him in a pit. It was the fast of Ramadan, and they decided to make him fast the whole month but without any break at night. They denied him food and water until he died in that hole.'[39] There is little doubt that some – though by no means all – gay Palestinians are indeed forced by their precarious existence to work for Israeli intelligence in exchange for money or administrative favours such as the right to live in Israel; both Eid and Gonen said they knew of several.[40] Others, meanwhile, are coerced into undercover work for the Palestinian authorities, and one nineteen-year-old runaway stated in an interview with Israeli television that he had been pressurised by the al-Aqsa Martyrs Brigade to become a suicide bomber in order to 'purge his moral guilt', though he had refused.[41]

Estimates of the number of gay Palestinians who have quietly – and usually illegally – taken refuge in Israel range from 300 to 600.[42] Although Israel is a signatory to the 1951 Refugee Convention and recognises same-sex partnerships for immigration purposes, it does not welcome gay Palestinians – mainly because of security fears. This often leaves them trapped in an administrative no-man's land with little hope of finding a proper job in Israel and constantly at risk of being arrested and deported.[43] Some try to disguise themselves by dressing in the style of Israeli youth, wearing fake military dog-tags and even Star of David medallions.[44]

'The Palestinians say if you are gay, you must be a collaborator, while the Israelis treat you as a security threat,' Gonen told a BBC news programme.[45] But even if they are neither collaborators nor a security threat, they can easily become targets for exploitation by Israeli men. 'They work as prostitutes, selling their bodies unwillingly because they have to survive,' Gonen said. 'Sometimes the Israeli secret police try to recruit them, sometimes the Palestinian police try to recruit them. In the end they find themselves falling between all chairs. Nobody wants to help them, everybody wants to use them.'

# TWO

# In Search of a Rainbow

A LARGE rainbow flag hangs in the Beirut office of Helem, the Lebanese gay and lesbian rights organisation. The flag is unique: you can buy most things in Lebanon, but not rainbow flags. This one was specially stitched together by a Helem member from strips of coloured cloth and, as far as anyone knows, it's the only rainbow flag to have flown in public anywhere in the Arab world.[1] It was paraded through the streets of Beirut for the first time in March 2003 when a small gay contingent joined a demonstration protesting against the war in Iraq. Four Lebanese newspapers[2] noted their presence – recognition of sorts, even if the main point of interest for the press was how weird they looked. 'Ten gay people took part in the march,' *an-Nahar* reported. 'One of them had his hair dyed green and another had piercing in his ears while others wore black T-shirts.'[3]

One of the group agreed to talk to *an-Nahar* – but only after the reporter promised not to describe them as *shawaadh* ('perverts'):

Q: What does your flag symbolise?

A: It's the rainbow, our international emblem ...

Q: Aren't you worried about being harassed?

A: Absolutely not. We have the right to unite and reveal our
   identity just like the others.


For Helem's members, joining the march was part of what they
see as a 'struggle against homophobia through visibility'.[4] Their
black T-shirts carried a one-word slogan, 'Exist', because the first
step towards winning acceptance, they believe, is to assert their
existence. Increased visibility helps to normalise gay people in
the eyes of the public, countering stories in the media that often
link homosexuality to crime, drug-taking, devil-worship and so
on (though whether the green hair helped to make them seem
normal on this occasion is another matter). Compared to the
thousands who attend annual Pride celebrations in other parts
of the world, though, it was visibility on a microscopic scale.
And in the Arab world, even that could only happen in Beirut.

The Lebanese capital is unlike other Arab cities. Ravaged by
civil war in the 1980s, it has an extraordinary mix of Sunnis,
Shi'as, Christians, Druzes, Palestinian refugees, rich Gulf Arabs
and migrant Syrian labourers. As the city recovered from war, it
began to regain its reputation as a playground where visitors can
swim in the sea, ski in the mountains and dance in a nightclub
all on the same day. After the war, Lebanese who had moved to
the US or Europe for safety also returned, often with teenage
families who had grown up abroad and acquired a Western
lifestyle. Today, you can find kids in Bermuda shorts and baseball
caps in one street and robed Shi'a clerics in another. It's a place
of extravagance and extremes but war-weariness has brought a

kind of mutual tolerance which, among other things, makes gay life a little less furtive than elsewhere. A 'Postcard from Beirut' published on a gay website sums up the picture:

Beirut is a city of paradoxes ... clapped out jalopies share roads with sleek new Porsches. Unbelievable wealth and increasing poverty all exist side by side, holding together the delicate fabric of the Lebanese character, each unable to survive without the other. This paradox is no less evident when it comes to homosexuality. Being gay is technically still a crime but is also a lifestyle quietly flourishing in this the most liberal of Middle Eastern societies.

Lebanese culture is firmly based around old family and religious traditions with no room for drastic change. Most gay people are only out to close friends, returning to their families under the persona of model heterosexual, desperate not to bring shame unto the family name. Most gays face a simple but painful choice: admit your sexuality and be ostracised from your family, or continue leading a double-life. Most choose the latter.

Here in Beirut one can find an internationally renowned transsexual artist, a flamboyant openly gay male belly dancer (although his mama doesn't know), and a popular TV drag queen, all celebrated by the masses whose government keeps it illegal. There have been scandals involving government officials and members of Beirut's glitterati found in uncompromising [sic] situations with gay prostitutes. The most famous made global headlines in the mid-nineties, exposing the seedy goings-on of Beirut's 'Velvet Society'. This hypocrisy only serves to sustain prejudice.

Lebanon's men are handsome, womanising and fiercely macho yet nowhere in the world is it easier for a gay man to have sex with one. Even Beirut has its cruising grounds (bizarrely Dunkin' Donuts is one of them) ... There is a gay beach run by a couple of nice Lesbians and even gay-friendly Turkish baths. Things are changing and it is all there as long as you don't give the game away.[5]

The famous Acid club in Sin el-Fil district is a sort of circular concrete bunker, painted entirely in black on the inside and with an amazing array of flashing lights. Its music, ranging from techno to Arab, is reputedly the loudest in Lebanon and dancers have occasionally been spotted wearing cotton wool in their ears. Acid did not set out to attract a gay crowd. At one time men were liable to be refused admission unless accompanied by women. Nowadays, Acid is happy to let them in on payment of 30,000 Lebanese pounds (twenty US dollars), though women can get in free of charge before midnight. Once inside, there are unlimited free drinks and, since the bar stays open until 5 AM, the floor becomes littered with bottles and the dancers' movements become distinctly unsteady as the night wears on. Large men in black jackets labelled 'Security' mingle with the crowd and intervene if male couples are thought to be dancing too close to each other. Kissing is strictly forbidden. These constraints are part of the thrill of Acid, one regular explained: they make you think of all the things you would like to do when, hopefully, you leave with a companion.

Acid has been raided by police twice, though neither raid seems to have been connected directly with the sexuality of its clientele. One was drug-related and the other, in March 2003, was part of a bizarre hunt for 'Satan worshippers'. On that occasion, plainclothes officers arrived at 2.30 AM, when there were about 200 people in the club:

> They dimmed the music, turned on the lights and ordered us to raise our arms and place them behind our heads,' said one eye-witness, a thirty-five-year-old who frequents the club every couple of months. Everyone had to keep their arms raised for about fifteen minutes, added witnesses. 'They were brandishing big rifles, whips and batons,' the thirty-five-year-old added.
>
> Witnesses also said that the security men went around, randomly demanding people's identification and asking some men to pull up their shirts to see if they had any tattoos or body piercings.[6]

According to the *Daily Star* newspaper, detectives at Jdeidet police station had become aware of 'young men between the ages of twenty and twenty-five sporting long hair and beards, who would frequent the Acid nightclub to listen to hard-rock music, drink mind-altering alcoholic cocktails and take off their black shirts, dancing bare-chested.'[7] About ten people were detained for questioning and testing 'for drug use'.

The raid occurred during a widespread and apparently baseless furore about devil worship that had partly been stirred up by religious leaders (both Muslim and Christian). It began when a girl in Tripoli lost her virginity and explained it to her conservative family by inventing a story about being kidnapped by devil worshippers. 'Police and sheikhs were speaking about a sect; there were stories about cemeteries, and sacrificing babies.

There was no evidence at all, and no prosecution,' lawyer Nizar Saghieh said – adding that in any case there was nothing in Lebanon's penal code to prevent people from worshipping the devil if they wished.[8]

Over the last few years Beirut has also witnessed a succession of gay-leaning clubs or bars, which appear and disappear, though their closure seems to have had nothing to do with the gayness of their customers. Rapid comings and goings of this kind are a common feature of Beirut's night-life. Various other establishments in the city have become popular with a gay clientele, but not all welcome this patronage, fearing it will drive more conventional customers away. One of these was Dunkin' Donuts. Exactly why gay men found it so attractive is a bit of a mystery, since most of those who preen themselves at its tables would not dream of eating a doughnut for fear of the damage it might do to their waistline. Whatever the reason for its popularity, Dunkin' Donuts became the subject of a long-running battle after it was accused of banning 'gay-looking' customers. The company put up notices at its branches in central Beirut and the upmarket Achrafiyeh district saying: 'We ask our dear clients to conform to decent appearance and to comply with our supervisor's directions on this matter.' One of the first incidents happened in 2001 when a man named Danny was turned away by a doorman who reportedly said he had strict instructions not to let in 'gay-looking' or 'hippie-looking' people. Contacted by the local press, Dunkin' Donuts said it was a mistake and blamed an over-enthusiastic doorman.[9]

Two years later there were more complaints that the firm was refusing to serve 'gay-looking' customers. This time the company repeated that it was not discriminating against gay people but merely wanted some of its male customers to behave better. 'They talk loudly and invade other customers' privacy,' a spokesman said.

An employee at Dunkin' Donuts who refused to give her name told a rather different story to the *Daily Star*. Gay customers' behaviour went far beyond local social norms, she said. 'In several instances, these customers displayed homosexual affection. They held hands, hugged and sometimes even kissed while they were on the premises. Personally, I'm not offended by such demeanour. But for Lebanese social norms, their behaviour was not acceptable to other customers, who threatened to call the police.' She added that gay customers still had a high probability of getting served if they behaved well, but if they wanted to fight for the 'freedom to come out of the closet', then Dunkin' Donuts was not the place to do it.[10]

Fighting on more conventional territory in Beirut, Helem – an acronym for *Himaya Lubnaniyya lil-Mithliyyin* ('Lebanese Protection for Homosexuals') – is the only specifically gay and lesbian organisation functioning openly in an Arab country.[11] The initials also spell 'dream' in Arabic and members wear red-and-white badges saying '*indi helem*' which echo the famous words of Martin Luther King: 'I have a dream'. Helem's stated aims are to work for 'the liberation of the lesbian, gay, bisexual and transgender (LGBT) community in Lebanon from all sorts of legal, social and cultural discrimination' and to empower them 'through rights and health awareness'.[12] This includes campaigning for the abolition of article 534 of the Lebanese penal code which criminalises 'unnatural sexual intercourse', and engaging in advocacy work and health promotion in relation to HIV.

Because of the difficulty of establishing non-governmental

organisations in Arab countries, Helem was originally registered in Canada as a non-profit organisation but now considers itself legally registered in Lebanon too (on the basis that registration becomes automatic under Lebanese law if the authorities fail to respond to an application within a specified time period, as happened in Helem's case). Besides its Canadian connection, it has support groups in Australia, France and the United States. These international links are important and, in some respects, vital to its existence: they are a source of both funds and expertise. In the field of health promotion, for example, Helem draws on Canadian material and adapts it for local use. International links also give a measure of protection because the Lebanese authorities know there will be complaints from abroad if repressive action is taken.

Helem has one full-time paid worker plus several part-time volunteers, and its weekly meetings are usually attended by twenty-five to thirty people. It has several sub-groups working on specific projects such as creating a manual to help teachers deal with homophobia in schools, another working on women's issues, and a media awareness group which monitors the press.

* * *

IN TERMS of opportunities for gay social life and activism, Beirut is as good as it gets in the Arab world. Cairo, the largest Arab capital with a population of more than sixteen million – roughly ten times the size of Beirut – has far less to offer, mainly because of government suppression. There are no specifically gay organisations, no openly gay clubs or bars, and other former meeting places such as public baths have been shut down.

'Egypt is carrying out a crackdown,' Human Rights Watch reported in 2004. 'The professed motive is cultural authenticity coupled with moral hygiene. The means include entrapment, police harassment, and torture. The agents range from government ministers to phalanxes of police informers fanning out across Cairo.' The report continued:

> Since early 2001, a growing number of men have been arrested, prosecuted, and convicted for having sexual relations with other men. Human Rights Watch knows the names of 179 men whose cases under the law against 'debauchery' were brought before prosecutors since the beginning of 2001; in all probability that is only a minuscule percentage of the true total. Hundreds of others have been harassed, arrested, often tortured, but not charged.[13]

The most publicised of these cases was the trial of fifty-two men following a police raid on the Queen Boat, a floating night club on the Nile that was popular with gay men. The trial, described by Human Rights Watch as 'an extravaganza rather than a judicial process', was accompanied by lurid tales in the press alleging everything from prostitution to a gay wedding to devil worship. Egypt's prosecutor-general, Maher Abdel-Wahid, accused the defendants of 'exploiting Islam through false interpretation of verses from the Muslim holy book, the Qur'an, in order to propagate extremist ideas'. They were also charged with 'performing immoral acts; the use of perverted sexual practices as part of their rituals; contempt and despite

of heavenly religions, and fomenting strife'.[14] To highlight
the supposed danger to the nation, the case was sent to the
state security court, specially set up under an emergency law
established in 1981 to deal with suspected terrorists. A Cairo
newspaper reinforced this view with its front-page headline:
'Perverts declare war on Egypt.'[15]

'You are allowing homosexuality abroad,' Nabil Osman, the
Egyptian government's chief spokesman, told the *New York
Times* in 2003. 'It is not accepted here, and everybody should
accept that what is good for America or for Europe may not be
good for another place.'[16]

The exact reasons for the crackdown are still debated, and
probably several factors were involved. Hossam Bahgat, of the
Egyptian Initiative for Personal Rights, saw it as an effort to
deflate growing Islamist opposition by portraying the state as
the guardian of public virtue:

To counter this ascending [Islamist] power, the state resorts
to sensational prosecutions, in which the regime steps in
to protect Islam from evil apostates ... The regime seems to
have realised that suppression and persecution of Islamists
will not uproot the Islamist threat unless it is combined with
actions that bolster the state's religious legitimacy.[17]

He also noted the regime's practice of using sensational trials to
divert public attention from the worsening state of the economy
and similar issues. The Queen Boat case was one of three big
sex stories that helped to squeeze bad news out of the papers
around the same time. One involved a businessman said to have
married seventeen women and another was the leaking (possibly

by state security) of a video that showed a former Coptic priest having sex with women who visited his monastery in search of healing.

One of the immediate effects of the crackdown was that half-a-dozen Egyptian gay websites disappeared, leaving only gayegypt. com (registered in London and using a server in California) which posted a warning on its home page that visitors to the site could be monitored by the Egyptian authorities. Gay emailing lists, in turn, were deluged with 'unsubscribe' messages: one dropped from 300 subscribers to nine (of whom only six were Egyptians). Three years on, Billy, a political science student in Cairo, says:

> It's very lonely. There used to be a cruising area in Heliopolis, coffee shops, and night clubs, but they have all gone now. Most of the people I knew have either left the country or created a very close-knit underground community. They no longer use the Internet as a way of making contact. Others have turned into fundamentalists.[18]

There has been no comparable crackdown against lesbians in Egypt, but Laila, in her twenties, also feels lonely. 'We cannot find a specific way to meet and talk, not just to have sex,' she said. 'There are no lesbian organisations, either for discussion or support. Heterosexuals and gay men have their pick-up points, but we don't.'[19] One popular meeting place used to be a public bath where women would go for hair removal by a traditional method known as *halawa*, though it's now closed, apparently on health grounds.

As a result, younger women use the Internet extensively to

make contact. There is a lot of deception, however. The 'lesbians' purportedly seeking lovers often turn out to be men or married couples. Laila has learned to be careful when arranging meetings: she arrives early and stays some distance from the meeting place, keeping an eye on it to see who turns up.

The general pattern of same-sex contacts among Arab women seems very similar to that among men: large numbers of women, including many who are married, have sexual contact with members of their own sex and this is seen as neither unusual nor particularly remarkable. A much smaller number regard themselves as lesbian. In contrast to male homosexuality, lesbianism attracts virtually no attention from the public or the authorities. Iman al-Ghafari observes:

> Erotic relations among women are devalued as a temporary substitute for the love of men, and are considered of no real threat to the dominant heterosexual system as long as they remain undercover, or in the closet.[20]

For married women, lesbian activity – whether occasional or regular – is a relatively safe way of adding spice to their sex life. A husband's primary concern is to guard his wife from the attentions of other men, and so the possibility that his wife might be having a lesbian affair is unlikely to occur to him. The wife, in turn, has no need to account to her husband for time spent with other women: he will be satisfied merely to know she is not spending the time with men. According to Laila, based on her experience of Internet contacts, a surprisingly large number of married couples in Egypt also fantasise about having threesomes with a lesbian.

Lesbian invisibility does have some advantages. In the big cities of Egypt, two women living together as 'flatmates' would not arouse much curiosity, Laila said – though that would depend to some extent on their choice of district. Neighbours would first of all want to establish whether they were prostitutes and would probably quiz the *bawwab*, the doorman who watches all comings and goings in Egyptian blocks of flats. If satisfied on that count, they might then imagine other explanations for the girls' presence – quarrels with parents, etc. 'They would think of anything else but lesbianism,' Laila said. She recalled how much one lesbian couple had been adored by their landlady. 'I wish all my tenants were like you,' the landlady told them, suspecting nothing.

Employment is a much bigger problem for Egyptian lesbians, Laila said. Young women who are not engaged or married invariably receive sexual advances from male bosses, and giving them the brush-off can be difficult. Declaring a preference for other women is not normally an option and can lead to discrimination – 'We don't employ lesbians here,' Laila was informed by one boss shortly before she walked out of her job. She had left several other office jobs for similar reasons.

\* \* \*

IN SAUDI ARABIA, sexuality of any kind is something to be kept out of view. Everyone is required to be 'decently' dressed; women should not be seen in public unless chaperoned by a male relative and, in the case of married couples, wives walk modestly behind their husband – by tradition keeping a distance of four paces. As in much of the Middle East, however, it is socially acceptable for men to walk hand in hand and greet each other with kisses on the cheek: since members of the opposite sex are not involved, everyone presumes there is no sexual chemistry in that:

> Walking around any shopping centre, you'd see dozens of teenage boys holding hands and dressed in tight flared pants and tight Ts [T-shirts]. Here, this is considered normal. You just assume that they're trying to be stylish … Of course you would see the actual gays. I mean the people who were so incredibly obvious, how could you not know? The guys that would stare you up and down, lick their lips at you, wink. The kind of behaviour that makes you feel somewhat dirty. Sometimes they even drive by you, and offer you money for your services. But this is the gay life that's on the surface.[21]

The writer here is an unnamed contributor to a gay website, describing his initiation to the scene in Saudi Arabia. He started cautiously, as many do, by chatting anonymously on the Internet and it was some time before he plucked up the courage to meet anyone. But after that first meeting a whole new world appeared:

> It was absolutely astonishing to me. There was this whole underground sort of thing going on here, and for the most part it was very discreet. Parties every weekend, where you could feel completely free to do anything you've always fantasised about doing in public. Dancing with people of the

same sex, kissing, hugging, flirting, and looking at people you're attracted to without having to worry if someone is watching you in disgust.

Most importantly these parties are secure, in private homes, with the music not too loud as to disturb the neighbours. Sometimes you even run into people that you know from school or from work, or people that you notice in the mall. The people that you would never expect to harbour the same sexual tendencies as you.[22]

Other accounts confirm this picture. A writer for *OutUK*, arranging to meet 'Haitham' at a hotel lobby in Riyadh for an interview, was assured that despite the near-ubiquitous dress code of white *thobe* and head-dress, there would be no problem recognising him. 'I'll be wearing a red T-shirt,' the man said:

I enter the lobby at the designated time, on the lookout for the signature coloured garment. I spot Haitham immediately ... he's wearing red sneakers and tight jeans, and his hugging red shirt shows off a muscular body that is obviously a regular at the gym ... The short, thick black curls on the top of his head are kept stiff with mousse.

Later, after we go to my room, the only place Haitham and the other men feel safe speaking openly, he tells me that his dress code is one sure sign to other gay men of his sexuality. But more importantly, it's a symbol of just how much the country has opened up for gay men in the past decade. These days, he says, gay men can be 'out' in the way they dress. 'If I wear a tight or flashy T-shirt, straight men just think I am trying to show off,' he says, smiling. 'But other gay men know.'[23]

Shopping malls are an obvious cruising ground. Apart from the opportunities to hang around pretending to look in shop windows, they provide one of the few public spaces where people in Saudi Arabia and the Gulf states can stroll comfortably (because of the air-conditioning) during the heat of summer. For those less inclined to walk, several streets in Riyadh have a reputation for late-night cruising in cars. Many Saudis, both male and female, have their first homosexual experience while still at school – a practice that the segregated educational system tends to encourage.[24]

According to Haitham's account, there are three gay cafés in Riyadh and private parties form an important part of the social life – at least one each weekend, attended by twenty to fifty men.[25] Another account, this time from the Red Sea city of Jeddah, talked of shopping malls as cruising areas and 'gay-friendly' coffee shops, adding: 'A big gay disco takes place at a private villa in the north of the city once a week.'[26]

The writer for *OutUK* persuaded a Saudi to take him to one of the gay cafés in Riyadh on the strict understanding that he would not disclose its whereabouts. They arrived around 10pm on a Wednesday night and found it packed, though the writer was surprised to see most of the customers in traditional Saudi dress rather than the tight T-shirts he had been expecting:

At first, I wonder how gay this café really is. But within minutes, I feel the heavy gazes of men cruising a newcomer, and all doubts melt.

Inside, the walls are painted a bright peach, and colourful strands of neon light overhead liven up the place. The waiters are mostly Filipino, and rush back and forth from the kitchen with trays of hot sandwiches, cappuccinos and French deserts.

Fahed, a tall, slim twenty-five-year-old who drives his father's Mercedes, is a little nervous about being at the coffee house. He's been before, but not for a several months. The last time he visited, he found a note from an anonymous admirer on the car windshield. It freaked him out that a secret suitor knew what car he drove.[27]

* * *

TOGETHER, Saudi Arabia, Lebanon and Egypt reflect a range of contrasting experiences: Egypt, where there is no law against same-sex acts and yet people are prosecuted and persecuted; Lebanon, where there is a law but also the beginnings of openness; Saudi Arabia, where in theory the death penalty applies but gay men cruise and party undeterred. These differences, perhaps, reflect differing levels of denial by the authorities. Denial is the first line of defence against a problem and also the easiest, since it requires no action. In Saudi Arabia, denial is almost an institution: the authorities' refusal to accept that most of the September 11 hijackers were Saudis and their denial, for some time before and after that, that the kingdom was under attack internally from terrorists are just two examples. Similarly, it suits the authorities to deny that homosexual activity exists in the kingdom to any significant extent, and it suits gay Saudis (who well understand how the rules work) to assist that denial by keeping a low profile. If it reaches a stage where denial is no longer possible, however, the authorities are obliged to respond. The choice then is between tolerance and repression, though in practice, especially if the authorities are unsure how to handle it, they may opt for a combination of both. Egypt, over the last few years, has leaned mainly towards repression while the Lebanese authorities lean slightly but not exclusively towards tolerance.

The use of private parties for gay social contact in Saudi Arabia carries minimal risk because it fits the established norms. Strict segregation of the sexes means that a few dozen men visiting a private house attract little attention so long as they avoid disturbing the neighbours, and rotating the location of parties so that they do not occur too frequently at any particular house helps to deflect suspicion. The partying also makes use of an important distinction between the public and private spheres, and what may happen in each. The kingdom's Basic Law (in effect, the constitution) states:

> The home is sacrosanct and shall not be entered without the permission of the owner or be searched except in cases specified by statutes.[28]

The inclusion of this clause is significant because it reflects an attitude towards domestic privacy that is particularly strong in traditional Arab societies. The clause is as much a social statement as a legal one. It stems partly from the assumption that every household contains a number of secluded women whose privacy must not be violated, but also from a concept of the household as an autonomous, self-governing unit in which the state does not interfere.[29] In Saudi Arabia this principle also includes, to a great extent, the territory enclosed by housing compounds – privately-guarded walled villages with roads, shops and recreational facilities that are inhabited by the better-off foreign workers and, increasingly, by young Saudis who value their personal freedom.

In some ways, clear separation of the public and private spheres is useful and helps the authorities. Enforcing strict behavioural codes in public becomes easier if there are protected private spaces where different rules apply. Followed to extremes, however, it can turn into a living lie where pretence and hypocrisy take over. This social dualism, and the personal conflicts it can cause for individuals in Saudi Arabia, is well explored in Turki al-Hamad's banned novel, *Adama*.[30] Essentially a coming-of-age/loss-of-innocence story, it provides a rare insight into the less visible side of Saudi life: illicit political activity, illicit sex, illicit alcohol, and more.

Although much justifiable anger is directed by Western gay organisations at the Saudi law prescribing execution for sodomy, gay men in the kingdom seem to view execution as an extremely remote possibility. Two multiple executions have been reported in recent years but these may have been exceptional.[31] Four gay Saudis interviewed by *OutUK* all 'rolled their eyes and laughed' when asked about executions. One said:

> Oh come on, please, that is so exaggerated. Americans love those kind of dramatic stories, but they are mostly lore. I mean, it's well known there are several members of the royal family who are gay. No one's chopping their heads off.[32]

A twenty-three-year-old man, interviewed with gay friends at a coffee shop in Jeddah, insisted:

I don't feel oppressed at all ... We have more freedom here than straight couples. After all, they can't kiss in public like we can, or stroll down the street holding one another's hand.[33]

Another, in a posting on a gay website, wrote:

As for the threat of being caught by the government or the *mutawa* [the religious police] ... I feel that people are sufficiently causcious [*sic*]. They know how far they can push it, and what they can and can't do in public. And as far as I know, you can not get into any kind of trouble just because someone thinks you are gay. They have to catch you in the act of sexual contact with the gender, and in this case it is punishable by death. Actually I learned that from a friend of mine ... they taught it to him in school.[34]

Fear of the law seems less immediately relevant than fear of the 'shame' that would be heaped upon a gay man's family if his sexuality became known. 'If I would come out,' one told *OutUK*, 'I wouldn't just ruin my life. I'd ruin four other lives too' (a reference to his mother, father, brother and sister). His father, a highly placed Saudi government official, would lose his job, and the family would be totally disgraced, he said.[35]

In February 2004, police in the holy city of Medina raided what was initially described as a gay wedding party. The raid, in which about fifty people were arrested, had been instigated by the religious police and came at a time when the issue of same-sex marriages in the US was arousing worldwide attention – which may possibly have had some bearing on the matter. Unlike most gay parties in the kingdom, the event was held at a small hotel rather than a private house and the alleged marriage partners were two African men from Chad.

One of the Chadians later told the police the gathering was a rehearsal for his real wedding (to a woman), and in this he was supported by his Saudi sponsor who also said he had provided money to meet the marriage expenses. However, according to the daily *Arab News*, investigators said that invitations to the party 'indicated it was a gay function' and thought it suspicious that many of the guests had fled at the sight of the police and left their cars behind. More than thirty abandoned cars were impounded.[36]

What was really going on is still uncertain and it is not known if anyone was prosecuted. However, just over a year later security forces in the port city of Jeddah arrested more than 100 men at another party which, again, was initially described as a gay wedding. *Al-Wifaq*, an online newspaper with good connections at the interior ministry, said the authorities had raided a wedding-hall following a tip-off and found the men – all Saudis – dancing and 'behaving like women'.[37] Enquiries by Human Rights Watch established that thirty-one of the men were sentenced to between six months and a year in prison, with 200 lashes each. The exact nature of the charges was unknown; a court had heard the case in closed session, with defence lawyers excluded. Four other men were jailed for two years, with 2,000 lashes. A further seventy men, who had been released shortly after their arrest, were later summoned to a police station and informed that they too had been sentenced to a year in jail.[38]

The Egyptian police, meanwhile, not content with merely

raiding gay parties, have been known to collaborate in organising them. In September 2001, a man identified by the nickname Mishmisha ('Apricot') invited seven other men to what he said was his birthday party, at a flat in Giza, a western suburb of Cairo. When the guests arrived, Mishmisha announced that he was going out to buy drinks and left the flat, locking the door behind him. That was the last they saw of him. A little while later, a key turned in the lock, the door opened and a dozen uniformed police officers burst in. The partygoers, who said they had all been fully dressed at the time, sitting and standing around normally, were arrested, charged with 'habitual practice of debauchery', beaten up and kept in detention for six weeks. They then went into hiding but were tried in their absence and sentenced to six months' imprisonment each. Mishmisha, the party host, turned out to be a police informant who had set up the men for arrest. In August 2002, he arranged another party where twelve men were arrested by the same police squad and later sentenced to three years in jail.[39]

In Saudi Arabia the Internet is the most popular way for making gay contacts. 'The government blocks a lot of sites,' Haitham told *OutUK*, 'but if you know how to navigate the Net, you can get around it.'[40] All Internet traffic from the kingdom's service providers is routed through a huge and complex system at King Abdulaziz City of Science and Technology in Riyadh, which is designed to block culturally or politically 'undesirable' web pages.

In June 2003, the Saudi authorities blocked access to Gay Middle East (GME),[41] a German-based website which carries gay news and information about the region but no pornographic material. Internet users inside the kingdom who tried to access the site were greeted by a message saying: 'Access to the requested URL is not allowed.' GME complained that this was a violation of free speech and the Universal Declaration of Human Rights. Other activists complained too, the affair attracted some publicity, and a couple of weeks later the banned site was suddenly unblocked. This change of heart, GME suggested, may have been prompted by a desire to avoid bad publicity at a time when Saudi Arabia was spending millions of dollars on an advertising campaign aimed at improving its image in the United States. Access to GME continued for a while, but in March 2004 it was again blocked, along with several other websites: gay.com, gaydar.com, and 365_gay.com.[42]

These Saudi antics are a minor tribulation, though. For sheer cruelty, it is difficult to match the efforts of Egypt's Internet Crimes Unit. With Internet use in Egypt mainly confined to the law-abiding middle classes, this newly-established department of the interior ministry found little real work to do but badly needed some successes to justify its existence. At that point it began to take an interest in international dating sites where Egyptian men were seeking to meet other men ...

Amgad (not his real name) was a young professional in his twenties, living with his parents in Upper Egypt, secretive about his sexuality and very, very lonely. Towards the end of 2002, he placed a personal ad on one of the sites and got a reply from raoul75@hotmail.com. Raoul struck Amgad as a 'good romantic nice guy' – though in reality he was an undercover policeman. They chatted on the Internet and exchanged emails, and Amgad sent Raoul a photo of himself looking smart in a suit and tie.

Before long, Amgad was pouring his heart out to Raoul. 'I've never told someone the things I told you yesterday,' he wrote. 'I always keep my feelings concealed in my heart, but I couldn't hide them from you.'

Raoul's replies convinced Amgad that he had at last found love and, in one of his final emails, he sent Raoul a little poem in English:

> I was rewarded
> for being good
> for having good intentions
> and a faithful soul
>
> I was rewarded
> and YOU are my reward ...
>
> I waited
> waited for someone
> someone exactly like you
>
> Oh God is so merciful to send you to me.[43]

He then set out for Cairo to meet his new-found friend at an agreed spot in Tahrir Square. Raoul was not there but the Vice Squad were waiting and they arrested Amgad – a fate that he shared with at least forty-five other Egyptian men known to have been entrapped through the Internet since 2001.[44]

# THREE

# Images and Realities

IN *The Yacoubian Building*, Alaa al-Aswani's novel of Cairo life, Hatim Rasheed is the successful editor of a daily newspaper. Everyone among the seventy staff knows he is gay and yet, despite their feelings of revulsion, no one ever mentions it directly in the office, and only fools allude to it in his presence. On one of the latter occasions, a journalist who is on the point of being sacked tries to embarrass his boss at an editorial meeting by proposing an investigation into 'the phenomenon of homosexuality in Egypt'.

Amid a shocked silence the reporter says: 'There has been a major increase in the number of homosexuals and some of them now occupy leadership positions in the country, and scientific studies show that the homosexual is psychologically unfit to lead the work of any institution.'

Hatim, without a flicker of acknowledgment that the reporter is referring to him, hits back: 'Your outmoded style of thinking is one of the reasons for your failure as a journalist.' But the reporter persists: 'Has homosexuality now become a progressive behaviour?'

'Neither that nor is it the national issue in our country,' Hatim replies. 'Egypt has not fallen behind because of homosexuality but because of corruption, dictatorship, and social injustice. Likewise snooping into people's private lives is a vulgar way of behaving that is inappropriate for a long-established newspaper ... The discussion is closed.'

Regardless of their own sexuality, most Arab editors, most of the time, would probably agree with Hatim that this is not a suitable topic for discussion in respectable newspapers. But while silence may be the preferred option, homosexuality can be difficult to ignore entirely. As a compromise between reticence and speaking out, one common solution in the Arab news media is to treat it as a foreign phenomenon.[1] A search for the words 'gay', 'homosexual' and/or 'lesbian' on al-Jazeera's English-language website, for instance, retrieved twenty news items, of which all but two dealt with homosexuality in a non-Arab context – mostly stories about same-sex marriage or gay (Christian) clergy.[2]

Depicting homosexuality as 'something that foreigners do' is a familiar practice in cultures where it is considered morally or socially unacceptable. The idea of a licentious West that many Arabs hold today closely mirrors the view that Europeans had of the Middle East a couple of centuries or more ago. In 1800, a European traveller to Egypt wrote:

The inconceivable inclination which has dishonoured the Greeks and Persians of antiquity constitutes the delight, or, more properly speaking the infamy of the Egyptians ... the contagion has seized the poor as well as the rich.[3]

The 'contagion' in question was spelled out more bluntly in the early seventeenth century by Thomas Sherley, describing the Turks:

> For their Sodommerye they use it soe publiquely and impudentlye as an honest Christian woulde shame to companye his wyffe as they do with their buggeringe boys.[4]

A seventeenth century French visitor to the Middle East went so far as to claim that Muslims were bisexual by nature, and numerous male writers gave descriptions of 'licentiousness' (i.e. lesbianism) among women in harems and bath houses that they could never have been permitted to witness.[5] In one of the earliest comparative studies of sexuality, Sir Richard Burton, the nineteenth-century British diplomat, explorer, translator and orientalist, described the 'Sotadic Zone'[6] – a region between the northern latitudes of $30^\circ$N and $43^\circ$N where same-sex activity was thought to be especially prevalent:

> In old Mauritania, now Morocco, the Moors proper [in contrast to the Berbers] are notable sodomites; Moslems, even of saintly houses, are permitted openly to keep catamites, nor do their disciples think worse of their sanctity for such licence ...
>
> As in Morocco, so the Vice prevails throughout the old regencies of Algiers, Tunis and Tripoli and all the cities of the South Mediterranean seaboard, whilst it is unknown to the Nubians, the Berbers and the wilder tribes dwelling inland. Proceeding Eastward we reach Egypt, that classical region of all abominations which, marvellous to relate, flourished in

closest contact with men leading the purest of lives, models of moderation and morality, of religion and virtue. Amongst the ancient Copts the Vice was part and portion of the Ritual and was represented by two male partridges copulating ...

Syria has not forgotten her old 'praxis'. At Damascus I found some noteworthy cases among the religious of the great Amawi mosque. As for the Druzes we have Burckhardt's authority 'unnatural propensities are very common amongst them'.

The Sotadic Zone covers the whole of Asia Minor and Mesopotamia, now occupied by the 'unspeakable Turk', a race of born pederasts ... The Kurd population is of Iranian origin, which means that the evil is deeply rooted ...[7]

Burton's purpose in writing this is still debated.[8] Stephen Murray points out that while it can be read as a condescending account of wayward orientals, aimed at bolstering Christian readers' sense of their own superiority, it might instead be a covert attempt, using the 'rhetoric of disparagement', to raise questions about differing attitudes to male-male sexuality. Since it would have been unthinkable in 1886 to publish an open defence of homosexuality, Murray suggests the latter is likely: Burton was more respectful of other cultures than many of his contemporaries, he says, and would not have gone to the trouble of writing at such length merely to reinforce British smugness and xenophobia.[9]

Today the tables have been turned and in popular Arab mythology it is the West that has become a 'Sotadic' zone. As with Burton's writings, it is conceivable that some reports in Arab newspapers (covering Western debates about same-sex marriage, for example) focus on the behaviour of foreigners in order to broach a subject that is difficult to mention in a local context. On the whole, though, Arab portrayals of homosexuality as a foreign phenomenon can be attributed more plausibly to a reversal of old-fashioned Western orientalism. Western orientalism, as analysed by Edward Said in his influential book,[10] highlights the 'otherness' of oriental culture in order (Said argued) to control it more effectively. Reverse orientalism – a comparatively new development in the Arab world – taps into the same themes but also highlights the 'otherness' of the West in order to resist modernisation and reform. Homosexuality is one aspect of Western 'otherness' that can be readily exploited to whip up popular sentiment.

In modern Arabic literature same-sex intercourse with foreigners, even in the hands of otherwise progressive authors, often becomes a political metaphor depicting, in the words of Frédéric Lagrange, conflict between the Arab world and the West as 'a sexual encounter and a fight for domination'.[11]

> Literature often displaces the shock of the encounter with the West into the arena of sexuality ... Domination and submission are symbolised through sexuality, and the effect is described in its pathological dimensions. The Arab man is symbolically or physically abused by the West ... [12]

Where symbolism of this kind applies, the sexual act must necessarily be described in terms that maximise the reader's disgust: there is no scope for portrayals of homosexuality that are anything but negative.

Sun'allah Ibrahim's 1997 novel, *Sharaf* (*Honour*) opens

with a twenty-year-old Egyptian strolling in downtown Cairo looking at the Western goods on display in the shops – Swatch, Nike, Adidas, etc. While debating with himself whether to buy a packet of Marlboro or watch a Schwarzenegger movie, he is approached by an American who invites him home for a drink. When the American makes sexual advances, the Egyptian resists and kills him while trying to escape. The Egyptian then ends up in jail – unjustly, the book implies. This heavily symbolic episode, Lagrange suggests, is utterly improbable: what twenty-year-old Egyptian would be innocent enough to misinterpret the foreigner's invitation?[13]

In a short story entitled *This is What Happened to the Boy who Worked in a Hotel* ('*Hadha ma gara lil-shabb al-ladhi asbaha funduqiyyan*') by Gamal al-Ghitani, a young Egyptian graduate, unable to get the government job he longed for, finds work in a five-star hotel. The manager, noticing his extreme good looks, assigns him to a highly visible position escorting guests to their table in the restaurant. The downside of this easy but well-paid job is that he is expected to satisfy every desire of the guests. He does so for a Dutch woman and an American woman but when a Saudi man tries to seduce him (this time, the Gulf states are exploiting Egypt too), he refuses and quits his job – only to be falsely accused of theft and reported by the manager to the police.[14]

The most graphically explicit of these 'foreign encounters' appears in Mohamed Choukri's fictionalised autobiography, *For Bread Alone*, in which the impoverished young Moroccan narrator has oral sex in a car with an elderly Spaniard for payment of fifty pesetas. The scene is described in extremely crude terms obviously calculated to disgust.[15]

* * *

XENOPHOBIC views of homosexuality also appear in the Arab press. 'Golda Meir was a lesbian,' the Egyptian paper *Sabah al-Kheir* announced in a headline marking the thirtieth anniversary of the October War with Israel.[16] Israel and homosexuality were linked again during the Queen Boat trial in Egypt when *al-Musawwar* magazine printed a three-page feature on 'Lot's people' with a doctored photograph of Sherif Farhat, the main defendant in the case, wearing an Israeli army helmet and sitting at a desk with an Israeli flag.[17]

When local instances of homosexuality come to light, blaming foreign influences implies such things could not occur naturally in an Arab-Islamic society. 'Confessions of the 'satanists' … we imported the perverse ideas from a European group,' a headline in *al-Masa'* said, again referring to the Queen Boat defendants.[18] Other coverage of the case in the popular media depicted homosexuality as a disease that Egyptians sometimes caught from foreigners. Having caught it they might, in the words of one newspaper, 'infect others', thus threatening the Egyptian way of life.[19] Later, when a group of American legislators condemned the Queen Boat trial, the semi-official *al-Ahram al-Arabi* magazine headlined a spread of articles, 'Be a pervert and Uncle Sam will approve.' It continued: 'Washington uses the aid card, and Europe offers a grape leaf: the homosexual sodomy-revolution.'[20]

Europe's 'sodomy revolution' also interested the English-language *al-Ahram Weekly* following the election of a Labour government in Britain in 1997. 'Not all British MPs are homosexual,' the paper informed its readers, 'but are we seeing the emergence of a new and gay establishment? Is Britain now in the hands of a "gay mafia"?'[21] The basis for all this was that three members of the new government were openly gay.

News items about same-sex marriage and gay clergy in the West tend to be reported factually and straightforwardly by the Arab media, often with quotes from opposing sides. Besides the stories dealing specifically with these topics there were many others during the American presidential campaign of 2004 that mentioned gay rights as an election issue. The relatively calm tone of these reports in comparison with the more hysterical stories about local homosexuality may be partly explained by their reliance on Western news agencies. As with the nineteenth-century writings of Richard Burton, however, they can be read in different ways by different readers. They can be interpreted either as confirming Arab perceptions of Western decadence or as familiarising readers with alternative views of sexual behaviour. The problem, though, is that the dearth of coverage about Arab homosexuality encourages the idea that it is almost entirely a foreign phenomenon.

Considering the amount of attention devoted to gay Christian clergy and same-sex marriages in the West, Arab journalists might reasonably ask whether there are any gay Muslim clerics, or whether any Arab couples of the same sex live together in a state of unofficial marriage, but nobody is eager to ask such questions. This is partly due to social taboos but also to a general lack of independent-minded inquiry in the Arab media. Articles that probe into social issues risk being viewed as divisive or subversive.[22] One highly unusual exception to this occurred in Saudi Arabia, where *Okaz*, a leading daily newspaper, published an unprecedented two-page investigation into 'endemic' lesbianism among schoolgirls. The article told of lesbian sex in school lavatories, girls stigmatised after refusing the advances of fellow students, and teachers complaining that the girls were unwilling to change their behaviour. To justify publishing its report, the paper quoted a saying attributed to the Prophet's wife, Aisha, that 'there should be no shyness in religion'.[23] In Yemen, on the other hand, the editor of *al-'Usbua* and two of his reporters were given suspended jail sentences and temporarily banned from their profession for violating 'Yemeni morals and customs' in an article about homosexuality. According to conflicting reports, the article mentioned sexual acts practised by schoolgirls and/or included interviews with men jailed for same-sex activity.[24]

Crime reports in the Arab media generally adopt the authorities' line and leave no doubt about the guilt of those involved, even before trial. 'Major network of perverts arrested in Beheira: social security employee turned his home into a lair of perversion,' the Egyptian newspaper, *al-Wafd,* announced. Police investigators had stormed an apartment and caught eight defendants in debauched positions during a party for group perversions, the report said. They were wearing nightgowns and make-up at the time, it added.[25] This was followed, a few days later, by the text of the 'ringleader's confession' in *al-Osboa* newspaper which added that the case had 'caused much popular anger in Beheira; some people tried to kill the suspects while they were being arrested'. A colleague of the alleged ringleader was quoted as saying: 'It is a crime for this civil servant to be a civil servant. He is mentally ill. Society should be purged of him and his like.'[26] In fact, the entire tale was a police invention. No orgy had been raided. The defendants in the case were arrested separately but the police, with the aid of torture, concocted a joint case against them. The men were later acquitted by an appeal court judge who complained about the behaviour of police and prosecutors, and ruled: 'There is no crime or offence that could be pressed against the defendants.'[27]

Conspicuously lacking in this media coverage is anything that portrays the human face of homosexuality[28] – though it is a simple enough exercise for a journalist to interview a few gay people about their lives. In 1999, Lilian Liang wrote an article for the Cairo-based *Middle East Times* which began:

> Many girls at Alexandria University have fallen for the charms of twenty-two-year-old Michael, an Egyptian art student with delicate features and green almond-shaped eyes. But he has lost count of the number of times he has refused to go out on dates – and not because he likes playing hard to get. He is just more interested in spending time with his French boyfriend ...

The writer interviewed several other gay people, together with an anthropologist and a doctor specialising in HIV/AIDS. The tone of the article was generally sympathetic but it never appeared in the paper because of the Egyptian censor. Instead, it appeared in a special section of the *Middle East Times* website reserved for the articles it was not allowed to print.[29]

A couple of years later the *Middle East Times* tried to print a Reuters report about a Muslim man who took part in San Francisco's gay pride parade. It quoted Faisal Alam, founder of al-Fatiha, the organisation that provides support for Muslims who are seeking to reconcile their faith with their sexual identity. 'For a long time nobody knew that there could be such a thing as a gay Muslim. Well, here we are,' Mr Alam was quoted as saying – but the Egyptian censor had other ideas about that.[30]

In the absence of proper information about homosexuality in the Arab media, not only the public but journalists themselves remain seriously ill-informed. One effect of this is that on the rare occasions when the subject crops up journalists are in no position to make sensible judgements and may allow ludicrous statements to pass unchallenged, thus perpetuating the cycle of misinformation. In 2001, for instance, *al-Ahram al-Arabi* – which has close links to the Egyptian government – quoted Dr Ahmed Shafiq about ways of 'curing sexual perversion'. Dr Shafiq, described as a 'professor of surgical medicine', informed the magazine (and its readers) that the most successful method 'has been cauterising the anus, which, by narrowing the anus, makes it more painful for the passive homosexual to be penetrated, which makes the active homosexual also unable to penetrate, and causes the sexual encounter to fail'.[31]

Although homosexuality rarely surfaces in the media with a human face attached, the picture at street level is rather different. There are plenty of people in Arab countries – some of them prominent, others not – who are considered (rightly or wrongly) to be gay, and reactions are much as described by Alaa al Aswani in the case of his fictional newspaper editor: people gossip about their sexuality in private with a mixture of distaste and fascination but generally avoid raising the matter in public. As with the gay stereotypes historically found in the West, allowances are made for people in certain types of occupation (the arts, entertainment, fashion, etc) where a degree of nonconformity is more readily accepted. In these areas of society homosexuality can be an open secret – very open indeed, so long as it is not formally declared. Lebanon has male belly dancers whose performances are appreciated and applauded by seemingly heterosexual audiences of both sexes. In Morocco, men in drag can be found working at funfairs.[32]

Alongside these limited nod-and-a-wink areas of acceptance is the idea that homosexuality does not mix with more serious types of work – hence the remark by the disaffected reporter in Aswani's novel that 'the homosexual is psychologically unfit to lead the work of any institution.' This is very similar to the objections put forward by conservatives in Kuwait to prevent women from being allowed to vote or stand for parliament: women are emotionally unstable, they said, menstruation can cloud their judgement, and so on. As in the entertainment field, there are a number of political figures whose sexuality is the subject of much private comment and this, in the eyes of many Arabs, calls into question their fitness for office far more than any complaints about corruption or the suppression of dissent. It is an issue rarely discussed in print, but an article by Mark Katz (Professor of Government and Politics at George Mason University, Virginia), assessing the political stability of Oman in an academic journal, provides one example:

Sultan Qaboos [the ruler of Oman] has been reported by several sources to be a homosexual, which would not be judged favorably by his subjects if they were to believe this claim, whether or not it was true. What Omanis think about this issue is hard to determine. Although I have been following

Omani affairs for over two decades, only three Omanis have discussed this subject with me openly. Although such a tiny number may not be representative of an entire society's opinion, their statements on this matter indicate that it has wider political implications:

All three agreed that the sultan is generally believed to be homosexual by Omanis;

All three agreed that Omanis only discuss this subject with trusted relatives and friends since more open discussion of it could result in negative consequences (including imprisonment);

All three agreed that all Omanis whom they have discussed this subject with believe that the sultan's alleged homosexuality raises serious doubts as to his legitimacy as a ruler.

One of the three – a young Western-educated male related to one of those arrested in 1994 – stated vehemently that Qaboos's alleged homosexuality is utterly shameful, that it reflects badly on Oman as a whole, and that it completely undermines Qaboos's legitimacy as sultan. The second – a young Western-educated female – saw the sultan's alleged homosexuality as causing Omanis both to see him as ridiculous and to discount or disregard much of what he has done that has benefited the country. The third – an older Middle Eastern-educated male – indicated that the sultan is widely believed to spend an inordinate amount of Oman's scarce resources on his reputedly numerous paramours and on projects favoured by them.

If these views are at all representative, then the sultan's

alleged homosexuality could become an important political factor in the event of a regime crisis, or in aggravating events that might lead to a regime crisis.[33]

In the wider Islamic world, allegations of sodomy were used by the Malaysian prime minister, Mahathir Mohamad, to sack and imprison his former deputy, Anwar Ibrahim, in 1998. It was essentially a political quarrel in which Mahathir invoked homosexuality for the purposes of character assassination. 'Mahathir used that to humiliate Anwar, to make his respect bad, to bring him down so people would not feel sorry for him,' one gay Malaysian explained in an interview for a website. 'The big problem was Anwar's bad policy decisions without asking Dr Mahathir, so he had to remove him. It was a political situation but Mahathir used the sex scandal to ruin Anwar's character.'[34] The ensuing trial was a particularly sordid affair in which a mattress allegedly stained with semen was carried into court. In 2004, a few months after Prime Minister Mahathir left office, Malaysia's highest court overturned Anwar's sodomy conviction and he was released from jail.[35]

Tales of homosexuality in high places were a significant factor in the Iranian revolution of 1979 and may help to explain the tough approach taken by the Islamic regime that replaced the Shah:

There is ... a long tradition in nationalist movements of consolidating power through narratives that affirm patriarchy and compulsory heterosexuality, attributing sexual abnormality and immorality to a corrupt ruling élite that is about to be overthrown and/or is complicit with foreign imperialism. Not all the accusations levelled against the Pahlavi family [the Shah's family] and their wealthy supporters stemmed from political and economic grievances. A significant portion of the public anger was aimed at their 'immoral' lifestyle. There were rumours that a gay lifestyle was rampant at the court. Prime Minister Amir Abbas Hoveyda was said to have been a homosexual. The satirical press routinely lampooned him for his meticulous attire, the purple orchid in his lapel, and his supposed marriage of convenience. The Shah himself was rumoured to be bisexual. There were reports that a close male friend of the Shah from Switzerland, a man who knew him from their student days in that country, routinely visited him.

But the greatest public outrage was aimed at two young, élite men with ties to the court who held a mock wedding ceremony. Especially to the highly religious, this was public confirmation that the Pahlavi house was corrupted with the worst kinds of sexual transgressions, that the Shah was no longer master of his own house. These rumours contributed to public anger, to a sense of shame and outrage, and ultimately were used by the Islamists in their calls for a revolution. Soon after coming to power in 1979, Ayatollah Khomeini established the death penalty for homosexuality. In February and March 1979 there were sixteen executions for crimes related to sexual violations ...[36]

\* \* \*

ALTHOUGH homosexuality and homoeroticism abound in classical Arabic literature,[37] they are generally avoided in modern fiction. 'Among the modern Arab novelists,' Frédéric Lagrange writes, 'there is no Proust, Wilde or Gide whose works can be read in a "gay" light, let alone a Gore Vidal or David Leavitt whose works include openly gay content. Homosexual characters are scarce, although not necessarily depicted in derogatory terms. AIDS is unheard of ...'[38] This reluctance to deal with same-sex relationships is puzzling, Lagrange suggests, because the Arabic novel emerged as a realist genre: it is as if the realists have chosen to ignore a whole aspect of reality. Despite the outward puritanism of Arab societies, it is difficult not to notice the eroticism that lies just below the surface:

> Perhaps because sexual desire, whether heterosexual, homosexual or undefined and unwilling to be defined, has to be so thoroughly concealed in Arab societies, it paradoxically cannot be restrained to special places or situations. As a result, desire is disseminated everywhere and at any time, even on the most unlikely occasions. There is a strong, almost palpable erotic and homoerotic tension obvious in such formal events as *mawlids,* as well as in daily life, on buses and other forms of public transport, in cinemas, even in the streets where gauging glances are exchanged.
>
> In the homosexual field, the non-existence (and impossibility) of a gay ghetto means that homosexual desire is to be found throughout the anonymous metropolises like Cairo and Beirut. But much of this atmosphere is suppressed, unseen or ignored in modern literature, although one can hardly imagine writers to be so blind as to miss it.

The universal figure of the 'queen' is not alluded to, even humorously, in written works.[39]

The prevalence of homoeroticism in the classical period is partly explained by a belief that the *adib* (man of letters) was entitled to read and write about 'lower' subjects in order to rest his mind. This could be sexually explicit, so long as the language used was suitably literary. Thus, a famous treatise on erotology by Ahmad al-Tifashi, who died in 1253, is 'ripe with piquant and often hilarious anecdotes on the underworld of active and passive homosexuals, their slang, their classifications of the male organ according to shape and size, and their witty (often blasphemous) replies when scorned by heterosexuals or men of religion.'[40] Lagrange adds: 'Whether homoeroticism is to be found in its chaste and often symbolic versions, or on the contrary in its coarsest expression ... it is in classical literature a pervasive phenomenon, whether connected to love or to condemnable ribaldry. If a tragic tone is to be found, it is because unrewarded love is tragic, never because of its homosexual nature.'[41]

Another difference noted by Lagrange is that male beauty – which historically has been widely acknowledged in Arab-Islamic culture – is rarely mentioned in modern literature:

'One seldom finds any sensuality in the portrayal of a male character.'[42] Furthermore, 'while homosexual intercourse is referred to in modern literature, homosexual passion is almost totally absent.'

Historical factors undoubtedly play a part in these differences between modern and classical literature. Classical literature reflects a period of self-confidence and Arab-Islamic empire. More recent times have brought colonialism and foreign domination followed, in the second half of the twentieth century, by humiliating wars with Israel which had a lasting effect on the Arab psyche. 'Modern literature,' Lagrange says, 'is often an expression of self-doubt, sometimes of self-hatred, and the Arab male's certainty of being at the centre of the universe has vanished. Politically, economically and culturally challenged, his power, thus his virility, cannot be exerted as it was in the age of certainties. The view of homosexuality could not remain unaffected by this major shift.'

As a way of asserting Arab-Islamic identity, there has also been a retreat into imagined 'customs and traditions'. The puritanical moral values that accompany them are similar to those once favoured in the West though, as Lagrange notes, the West itself began to question them profoundly from the 1960s onwards. In such a climate, homosexuality provides Arab writers with a convenient symbol for decay, decadence and various types of power relationship that will strike a chord with readers – and this, almost automatically, rules out descriptions of same-sex relationships based on mutual respect, tenderness, sensuality, love, etc.

* * *

UNLIKE male homosexuality, lesbian relationships cannot readily be turned into metaphors for degradation or foreign domination. Instead, if they figure at all in contemporary Arab literature, they tend to be treated as logical – even natural – behaviour for women who have no male partner or those whose husbands fail to satisfy their needs. *Presence of the Absent Man*[43] is a short story by Iraqi-born Alia Mamdouh. It tells of a widow in her forties, living alone except for her cat. While shopping in a crowded market she accidentally collides with another woman:

> When the other opened her arms and clasped her, fearful she would fall, the two of them looked at each other. The two pairs of eyes were pierced by the light from a match that had just been struck, and the two bodies released a blaze of high tension, while between their fingers crept cold, damp sweat.

A snatch of conversation follows that is brief and polite, though there is no mistaking its sexual undertones:

> 'Every Thursday I come here – and you?' ...
> 'I'm on a visit.'
> 'Anyone with you?'
> 'My husband and children are waiting for me at the entrance to the market.'

With this signal that she is not available at the moment, the woman vanishes into the crowd but both know they will return to look for each other another day. And so the widow's Thursday visits to the market become a weekly ritual of anticipation: tidying the house, washing herself and her clothes ... and fantasising as she goes about her chores:

> She will begin from her toes. She will tickle them first, so

as to see her smile. Maybe she will cry out with joy ... She leans against the bathroom wall and sings an old folk song. She places her dirty clothes in an ancient washbowl, scouring them with her hand while continuing to sing ... And she will seat her in front of her and at first she will look into her eyes ...

For six Thursdays there is no sign of the other woman, but on the seventh they finally meet. 'The very evening I met you my husband left me,' the other woman says. He has abandoned her because she is pregnant and he dislikes the look of pregnant women. They leave the market hand in hand and catch a bus to the widow's home:

> The other woman takes hold of her *abaya*, drawing it out from under her, and sits comfortably. The rustling of her dress sighs with this naked joy. She radiates beams of light. She murmurs between her teeth, 'How close you are to me: your arm is like his, your muscles strong like his ...'

But the sublime moment they have both awaited so long is rudely interrupted by the dramatic entrance of the widow's jealous cat.

*Menstruation*, a novel by the Syrian dissident, Ammar Abdulhamid, entwines several characters through their sexual liaisons. Highly controversial by Syrian standards, it was written in English and has never been translated into Arabic. It is a story in which sex becomes a form of rebellion against religious and social constraints. One of the characters is a veiled young woman called Batul:

Despite having been married for the last three years and having a two-year-old son, Batul was rumoured to be a lesbian. There had always been talk in the local conservative women's circles to that effect, and many women accused Batul – not to her face of course – of having approached them, at one time or another, in a suggestive way. They all claimed to have turned her down, of course ... [44]

Batul's reputation, it turns out, is undeserved until the day she meets Wisam, a former schoolfriend who is unhappily married, and they gossip about a neighbour who is asking her husband for a divorce. 'According to my sources,' Batul says, 'he wasn't able to perform. Isn't that something? I mean, at least our husbands can perform. True, not to our satisfaction, but they do perform, don't they?' At this, Batul and Wisam exchange knowing looks and giggles, making clear that they are both having problems in the bedroom department too:

> As both women laughed and threw themselves at each other, Wisam suddenly found herself with her head thrust into Batul's bosom, her mouth, lips and tongue roaming all over Batul's breasts and nipples ... After a few minutes of this, Batul gently pulled Wisam's head away from her shirt, held it in her hand, and gazed deeply into Wisam's eyes ... Soon afterwards, Wisam had her first real orgasm, and Batul had started her first lesbian affair.[45]

Their relationship continues, but it is not long before Batul has had a succession of casual liaisons with other women. The real target of her affections, though, is Hasan, the good-looking son of a local imam. (Hasan, it transpires, has experimented sexually with a male friend before turning his attention exclusively to women.) One day, as Batul lies with her head on Wisam's thighs, she talks of the many women she has met:

> Some of the married women have wonderful husbands, by their own admission, I mean, husbands who perfectly satisfy them sexually, still they go for me, they turn to putty in my hands ... I asked them why ...
>
> It's because they need a change, you see. Many of their men had the chance to fool around before marriage. But these women have only had the opportunity to do so after marriage ... Since men usually brag about their affairs, the women decide it's much safer to fool around with other women. Because even if women talk, and that doesn't happen a lot in this sort of case, but even if they do, men don't usually get the opportunity to listen in on such conversations.[46]

While lesbianism as a temporary substitute for heterosexual relations is a theme sometimes tapped by Arab feminist writers, lesbianism as a sexual identity in its own right remains almost totally unexplored. Iman al-Ghafari, of Tishreen University in Syria, blames this partly on feminist ideas which tend to focus on lesbianism as a political reaction to male dominance, at the expense of 'inborn' lesbians. 'Amid feminist discussions around sex as power, there emerged an assertion of lesbianism as a political choice, a means of escaping relationships as decided and controlled by men,' she writes. 'In fact, the feminist discourse that turns lesbianism into a political choice is not liberating. Instead, it puts ['inborn'] lesbians in a troublesome position where they have to play a major role in fulfilling the desires and fantasies of some heterosexual feminists at the expense of their true lesbian desires.'[47]

*Misk al-Ghazal* (*Women of Sand and Myrrh*),[48] by the Lebanese feminist writer, Hanan al-Shaykh, tells of four women in an unnamed Arab country who struggle in different ways against a patriarchal order. They include Suha, a graduate of the American University of Beirut, who misses the freedom she enjoyed in Lebanon and embarks on a relationship with another woman. Nevertheless, she insists that her natural attraction is towards men and that despite the pleasure of her lesbian experience it is only a temporary outlet. Ghafari comments: 'If feminism wins its battle against men in such a manner, lesbianism will surely lose its legitimacy, in the sense that there is no reason for its existence from a heterosexual perspective.'[49]

Viewed in that light, the only book that might be regarded as a truly lesbian novel in Arabic is Elham Mansour's *Ana Hiya Anti* (*I Am You*) which centres on the problems of a lesbian woman trying to assert her identity in a heterosexual society.[50] 'The importance of Elham Mansour's novel,' Ghafari writes, 'is that it brings to light the difference between lesbian desire that stems from the body and the one that stems from feminist politics. The former is seen as authentic, natural and forthright ...'

* * *

CENSORSHIP and self-censorship are probably one cause

of Arab novelists' reluctance to write about homosexuality,
though the actual effect of state censorship is difficult to judge:
there are long-established ways of circumventing it and banned
novels often sell well as a result of being banned. Condemnation
or threats from offended Islamists may be a more serious
deterrent, however. The inclusion of homosexuality in *Midaq
Alley* by Naguib Mahfouz, the nobel-winning Egyptian author,
caused an outcry when the book was published in 1947. Seyyed
Qutb, one of the pillars of the Muslim Brotherhood, objected
to 'so much perversion in the alley' while Adeeb Muruwwah,
a Lebanese critic, found it 'offensive to good manners'.[51] Those
reactions were comparatively mild by current standards and
Mahfouz was determined to resist them, though other writers
may see little point in inviting trouble.

Another reason for increased self-censorship is that writers
of the classical period were not addressing their work to a
mass audience, as most writers are today. As Mahfouz once
explained:

Classical Arabic *adab* was a literature of pleasant conversations
at night with friends, and was restricted to private salons.
There was no publisher nor media. Abu Nuwas, al-Husayn
bin al-Dahhak and their boon companions would sit
together and recite verses. In [twentieth-century Egypt]
we've had al-Awadi al-Wakil and his circle composing even
'hotter' verses, but those are not published. These things did
not disappear, but remained in private literary circles. All
the [neo-]classical poets have verses in this genre, even Hafiz
Ibrahim ... but when poets collect their *diwan,* they suppress
such verses ... The modern diffusion of works provokes self-

censorship ... Publishers want the authors to respect public opinion and religious values.[52]

Increased literacy today means that writers are no longer thought to be addressing a cultured élite who can be trusted with such material. The unspoken and fearful supposition nowadays is that whatever gets printed could fall into the hands of the masses and lead them astray.

This generally dismal picture of the way homosexuality is portrayed (or rather, ignored) in Arabic novels today is just one reflection of a literary scene that in many other ways, and with relatively few exceptions, has become somewhat stale. If processes of reform and regeneration are to take hold in society at large, they will need writers who can question and explore the Arab condition, including sexuality in all its aspects. There are a few signs that this may be happening, though it is far too early to describe them as the start of a trend.

Among authors of North African origin, there is a growing body of 'gay writing' in French – from Rachid O and Abdallah Taia, for instance. Taia's short story, *Moroccan Slave,*[53] taps the familiar theme of Arab-Western relations but it is not the usual tale of sexual exploitation. Its narrator, a young Moroccan man who has moved to Paris, is totally infatuated with an older American called Marlon. 'I always thought of myself as a child,' he says. 'I am Marlon's child. I like to repeat this to convince myself that it's true. The repetition keeps me feeling secure. Marlon loves me and protects me.' It is a beautiful, loving relationship, but an unequal one. The Moroccan is utterly dependent on Marlon, though he does not wish it to be otherwise. Marlon tries to reciprocate: he enjoys the Moroccan food that his lover prepares for him and wants to learn how to make mint tea. The story ends with a twist that suggests their idyllic life cannot last, when Marlon asks his lover to teach him Arabic. 'A great proof of his love!' the narrator says. 'I accepted, I will be his professor. We start today, September 11.'

Probably the most daring recent book by an Arab author is Rabih Alameddine's *Koolaids*, published in 1998, which cross-cuts between the Lebanese civil war and the AIDS epidemic in the United States in order, as one reviewer put it, to explore the meaning of death and the meaninglessness of life. Stitched together from apparently random snippets, and with a good deal of sex and black humour, it might be classified as the first 'gay novel' by an Arab. Although Alameddine is from a Lebanese family, he has lived in the United States for a long time and writes in English.

Less flamboyantly, though more significantly for Arab readers, two recent novels in Arabic have broken new ground. *The Stone of Laughter* (*Hajar al-Dahik*, 1990) by Hoda Barakat, and *The Yacoubian Building* (*'Imarat Ya'qubyan*, 2002) by Alaa al-Aswani were both well-received by critics and aroused little or no public hostility.

Aswani's book, reputedly the best-selling Arabic novel for years, tackles several potentially sensitive themes – power, corruption, sex, exploitation, poverty and extremism – through a series of parallel stories about the inhabitants of a once-grand (and non-fictional) apartment block in central Cairo. As often in Arabic fiction, each character represents some aspect of Egyptian society: a rags-to-riches businessman who deals in drugs and turns into a corrupt politician; a devout youth who tries to become a policeman but ends up a terrorist, etc.

Among these is Hatim Rasheed, the cultured, Westernised gay newspaper editor. In common with several other purportedly fictional characters in the book, Hatim is said to resemble a prominent real-life Egyptian.

In the story, Hatim's father is a famous jurist educated in Paris during the 1940s, married to a French woman and with a thoroughly un-Egyptian lifestyle. At one level, Hatim's family background reflects popular Arab notions about the causes of homosexuality: Western influence, a remote father preoccupied by work, and childhood sexual experiences with a male servant. Daringly though, Aswani does not portray Hatim's introduction to homosexuality as a typically malevolent case of child abuse; it is described with a good deal of tenderness. Hatim is a lonely, only child and, in the absence of his ever-busy parents, spends much time in the company of Idris, a handsome servant from upper Egypt who tells him stories and sings beautiful Nubian songs. Idris appears equally lonely, having been sent away from his village to work in Cairo:

Hatim loved Idris and their relationship grew till they were spending many hours together every day and when Idris started kissing Hatim on his face and neck and whispering, 'You're beautiful. I love you,' Hatim felt no revulsion or fear. On the contrary, the burning sensation that his friend's breath left on his body excited him.

They continued to exchange kisses until one day Idris asked him to take off his clothes. Hatim was nine at the time and felt embarrassed and confused but in the end he gave in to the insistence of his friend. The latter was so aroused by the sight of his smooth, white body that during the encounter he sobbed with pleasure and whispered incomprehensible Nubian words. Idris, despite his lust and vigour, entered Hatim's body gently and carefully and asked him to tell him if he felt the slightest pain ...

When Idris was finished, he turned Hatim to face him and kissed him ardently on the lips, then looked into his eyes and said, 'I did that because I love you. If you love me, don't tell anyone what happened.'

... Hatim's relationship with Idris lasted years, until Dr Rasheed [Hatim's father] suddenly died of a brain haemorrhage caused by overwork and his widow was obliged to get rid of many of the servants because of the expense.[54]

As an adult, Hatim is not a stereotypical queen – 'in appearance and behaviour he always chooses a skilful compromise between elegance and femininity' – nor is he particularly content with his sexuality as he struggles to reconcile it with his dignity and his public persona:

His secret, homosexual, life ... is a kind of locked box full of forbidden, sinful, but pleasurable, toys that he opens every evening to play with, then locks again and tries to forget ... He tells himself that most men in the world have some special pastime that they use to relieve life's pressures. He has known men in the most elevated positions – doctors, councillors, and university professors – who were devoted to alcohol or hashish or women or gambling and this never lessened their success or their self-respect. He convinces himself that homosexuality is the same sort of thing – just a different kind of pastime. This idea appeals to him greatly because it brings him relief, balance, and respect.[55]

It is a credible, realistic picture, though by no means an affirmative one.[56] In many ways Hatim is a sad and unlikeable figure but, given the nature of the book, he could scarcely be otherwise. One of Aswani's main themes is that Egypt's ills are the fault of no one in particular and everyone in general: he portrays a cruel society in which the book's main characters are both villains and victims, exploiting of others and exploited themselves.

As an adult, Hatim strikes up a relationship with Abduh, a young army conscript from upper Egypt who reminds him strongly of the servant Idris. Hatim is genuinely in love with Abduh – there is no doubt of that – and their affair becomes one of sensuous (though discreetly told) passion. But Hatim is also highly manipulative: since Abduh is married with a baby son, the journalist embarks on what is obviously a well-practised routine to ensnare him. Hatim showers the younger man with generosity and dresses him in new clothes – 'tight pants that showed off the strength of his muscles, shirts and undershirts in light colours to illuminate his dark face, and collars that were always open to reveal the muscles of his neck and the thick hair on his chest'. Abduh seems to be enjoying the affair but then, as the couple lie in bed after a night out celebrating his birthday, Abduh becomes serious: 'I'm afraid,' he says. 'All my life I've been God-fearing. In the village they used to call me 'Sheikh Abduh'. I always prayed the proper prayers at the proper time in the mosque and I fasted in Ramadan and all the other times I'm supposed to ... till I met you and I changed ... How can I pray when every night I drink alcohol and sleep with you? I feel as though Our Lord is angry with me and will punish me ... Our Lord has forbidden us that kind of love. It's a very big sin. In the village there was a prayer leader called Sheikh Darawi, God have mercy on his soul, who was a righteous, holy man, and he used to say to us in the Friday sermon, "Beware sodomy for it is a great sin and makes the throne of heaven shake in anger."'[57]

When Abduh's baby son becomes ill, Hatim unhesitatingly pays for the best medical treatment, but the baby suddenly dies. Abduh, convinced that this is God's punishment, decides to end the relationship. Hatim, undaunted, offers him a large cheque to spend one last night together. They make love as never before, but when Abduh attempts to leave, Hatim says the deal they agreed was that he would stay the whole night. A row ensues in which Abduh, realising he can never escape from Hatim's snare, beats him to death.

This dramatic ending can be interpreted (by those who wish to do so) as a just retribution for Hatim's sinfulness. But the real reason for Hatim's death, as described in the book, is not sexual; it is his abuse of power – his use of wealth and influence to manipulate, dominate and ultimately seek total control over a poor and uneducated young man from the Egyptian countryside.

In a subsequent interview about his book, Aswani said: 'I tried to present the homosexual as a person. It is not something to make fun of or to look at with disgust, and not all evil is concentrated in him as a person. He is a human being who has a different lifestyle. He may be happy with it or he may not ... Literature should examine the areas that people don't talk about, to show us things we could be feeling but not seeing. Its function is to teach us we are different, that we should be forgiving, and that we should not look at human traits as being either wrong or right. The issue is more complex.'[58] While researching the book, Aswani – who is twice married and has three children – visited several gay-frequented bars in Cairo. During one such visit, police raided the bar. After identifying himself and explaining his reason for being there, he was advised by an officer: 'You should go to the Meridien [hotel] to drink a beer. You shouldn't come here. These places are full of thieves.' He eventually reached an understanding with the police that he would be left alone if any more bars were raided while he was there.

The book's success prompted Egyptian director Marwan Hamed to begin work on a film version, scheduled for release in 2006, though it was unclear how closely this would follow Aswani's original text. Initially the director had problems finding anyone to play the part of Hatim (coyly described in one report as a 'bizarre' journalist). Several prominent actors were said to have turned down the role 'due to the sensitivity of it and fear of expected criticism.'[59]

Whereas Aswani has included a gay man as one of several characters in his book, *The Stone of Laughter* appears to be the only modern novel in Arabic with a gay man as its central character and – interestingly – its author, Hoda Barakat, is a woman. Set in Beirut during the Lebanese civil war, it tells the story of Khalil, a lonely, isolated figure who keeps the war at bay by cleaning and dusting his room, cooking, listening to radio phone-ins and day-dreaming about the men he secretly admires. There is no pop-psychologising here, no theorising about the causes of Khalil's gayness, no agonising about sinfulness. This is simply the way Khalil is. And it is a tender, affectionate portrait:

how could anyone condemn him or wish him harm?

Describing Khalil as he dozes alone on a bed, Barakat writes:

> When one looks at his narrow shoulders, no wider than the little pillow where he lays his head, one is led to question the wisdom of Mother Nature when, sometimes, she stops a stage short and fails to send on hidden desires to their appointed ends ...
>
> The eye only has to fall upon him in this light sleep of his for the heart to be moved, for you to imagine yourself to be Khalil's father, filled with regret for the excessive violence with which you punished him for some foolish mistake ... All you wish to do now is put his little head in your lap and stroke his hair ... a wish that lifts you out from the pit of guilt and sets him gently back in the blithe garden of childhood where, as he should, he gallops around among his companions.[60]

Khalil's problem is that in war-torn Beirut there are only two kinds of masculinity, and he does not fit either of them:

> The first group ... is made up of youths ... who have broken down the door of conventional masculinity and entered manhood by the wide door of history. Day by day they busy themselves shaping the destiny of an area of patent importance on the world map, concerned with people's public and private lives, even with water, with bread, with dreams, with emigration. The second group ... is made up of men ... who have got a grip on the important things in life, and who, holding the tools of understanding, awareness and

close attention to theory have laid down plans to fasten their hold on the upper echelons ... in politics, in leadership, in the press ...

But the doors of both kinds of manhood were closed to Khalil and so he remained, alone in his narrow passing place, in a stagnant, feminine state of submission to a purely vegetable life, just within reach of two very attractive versions of masculinity, that force which makes the volcano of life explode.[61]

During infrequent visits from his friend Naji, who lives on the other side of the Green Line that divides Muslim and Christian Beirut, Khalil searches for any excuse to prolong his stay by just a few more minutes, plying him with offers of tea. Not that Khalil pays much attention to what his friend is talking about: his eyes are transfixed by glimpses of Naji's hairy legs between the bottom of his trousers and the top of his socks. Walking in the street, he is unable to keep pace with Naji, but following a step or two behind gives him a chance to gaze pleasurably at Naji's strong shoulders.

When Naji is killed, Khalil transfers his unspoken affections to Youssef, a cousin whose family have moved to Beirut to escape Israeli bombing in the south. When he arrives, Youssef is still a boy – 'so beautiful he made the Renaissance sculptors seem like fools' – but he grows up, starts hanging around with the local militia, and soon embodies the kind of masculinity that nature has denied to Khalil – filling the room with his confident presence, sitting with his legs wide apart, laughing and joking with his mates, and no longer talking to Khalil except for 'exchanging greetings in the manner of men who know how to fill the time that they have'. Youssef, of course, has no sexual interest in Khalil and is unreachable. Khalil, nevertheless infatuated, muses on his unrequited love:

> What do I want from Youssef? Khalil asked himself. What do you want from Youssef, Khalil? Give yourself one clear answer and you'll feel better. But no one answer was clear, no one clear answer was convincing and no one clear convincing answer made him feel better.[62]

Barakat's choice of the name 'Youssef' is no accident: it alludes to the prophet Youssef (Joseph in the Bible) who was noted for his beauty and was lusted after by Potifar's wife. In his thoughts, Khalil recalls the story in the Qur'an where Potifar's wife makes advances to a reluctant Youssef and, in her pursuit of him, tears his robe from behind:[63]

> Whenever I touch the hem of his robe I tear it from behind. I've torn it thousands of times from behind but he did not see me nor did he turn around nor has any robe of his been torn.
>
> I tore *my* robe ... Look what Youssef is doing to me ... I tore my heart and screamed, look, and no one looked, no one heard. Even Youssef did not look and did not hear ... I am a wife of the wrong sex as if, in my stupidity, I wait for Youssef to come one day to ask for my hand. To knock at the door in his most splendid raiment and ask me ... while I blush, shyly, hesitating a little before nodding my head in agreement.[64]

Citing the Qur'an to express same-sex love has the potential to inflame religious sensibilities but Barakat seems to have got away with it. *The Stone of Laughter* won the prestigious al-Naqid Prize for First Novels and was favourably reviewed in the Arab press – though according to Barakat the reviewers managed to avoid mentioning Khalil's sexuality. 'I haven't seen any attacks on me as a Christian writing gay stories and using images from the Qur'an,' she said. 'All the game is how you write. I take the reader slowly. There is a gay man ... but it's not shocking because he narrates a real sentiment of love. He is someone you cannot reject because he suffers and he's really in love and when I describe how much he is in love and how much he suffers and the beauty of the other [man] I take a passage from the Qur'an. I took it step by step, from the feeling, not in a sexy or a shocking way. People accept it and they feel what I feel, really.'[65]

At one level, Khalil reflects the experiences and uncertainties of many young Arab men struggling to come to terms with sexuality and masculinity, but in the context of the civil war he is trapped in a sexual and political no-man's land – neither one thing nor the other. He is not part of the war but neither is he able to remain isolated from the conflict that rages around him. Unnoticed by Khalil, a powerful and sinister man known simply as 'The Brother' has been eyeing him and offers him a position in return for sexual favours. Whether Khalil obliges is not spelled out but at the end of the book he returns, swaggering and brutalised, to his old neighbourhood and rapes a woman. This extraordinary transformation does not mean that he has suddenly become heterosexual, however. 'Khalil is a homosexual character in the denial phase because of society's definition of manhood,' Barakat explained.[66] 'The social pressure made him search for his manhood by raping a neighbour.' His transformation, and his acceptance of the violence of war, is thus a sign of his moral collapse and failure. Rather than become a victim, he has chosen to join the oppressors. The war has finally claimed Khalil, along with everyone else.

\* \* \*

WHEN the Beirut-based rights organisation, Hurriyat Khassa, launched a campaign in 2004 to abolish Lebanon's sodomy law, it began with a public showing of *Victim*, a film made in 1961 which is widely credited with having paved the way for legalisation of homosexuality in Britain.[67] *Victim* is the story of a lawyer (played by Dirk Bogarde[68]) who risks his career and his marriage to do battle with a blackmailer who has photographs of him engaging in sexual contact with a man. The lawyer soon discovers that he is not alone in this. Others are also facing extortion from the same blackmailer because of their sexuality: a star of the London theatre, a Rolls-Royce salesman and an elderly barber. They all know they can stop the racket by calling the blackmailer's bluff, but nobody is willing to go to the police. Reluctantly, the lawyer decides to take the extortionist on, even though his wife may leave him and his professional reputation may be destroyed – and is helped by an enlightened police inspector who regards anti-sodomy laws as nothing less than a blackmailers' charter. At the time, the vast majority of extortion cases in Britain involved homosexuality and the film's main point was that laws against sodomy encouraged such crimes: fear of exposure and the possibility of a long jail sentence for same-sex acts created a ready supply of victims for the extortioners.[69]

Although British made, *Victim* has a relevant message for all countries where laws against homosexuality persist, but the choice of a forty-three-year-old foreign film to launch the Lebanese activists' campaign is also revealing, because Arab cinema, in its long history, has produced nothing remotely comparable.

Arab interest in the cinema developed early. The first imported films, made by the Lumière brothers, arrived in Egypt in 1896 – only a few months after they were shown in Europe.[70] Full-length feature films produced by Arabs began appearing in the 1920s but it was not until the 1930s, with the arrival of sound and the opening of Studio Misr in Egypt, that Arab film production really took off. Egypt soon dominated the industry, partly because it had the largest domestic audience in the Arab world, partly because of the existence of local entrepreneurs – such as Tal'at Harb of Bank Misr – who viewed cinema as an investment opportunity, and also because Egypt's flourishing cultural and artistic life had not been suppressed by colonialism[71] as in some countries nor (yet) by religious puritanism. As the industry expanded so did its repertoire, and the original musical/comedy genres were supplemented by farces and melodramas, with tales of 'seduction, implied rape, adultery, murder and suicide'.[72]

In an essay on homosexuality in Arab films, Garay Menicucci suggests that from the 1930s onwards, 'cinematic references to gays and lesbians abound, if often in heavily coded forms. The most ubiquitous coding for gay and lesbian cinematic imaging has been cross-dressing.'[73] How much of this cross-dressing was actually intended to refer to homosexuality, and how much was simply a convenient theatrical device, is debatable. Disguising men as women, and vice-versa, creates situations that can be easily exploited for comic effect and can also be used for more serious purposes such as highlighting social inequalities between the sexes. It is doubtful how many of the homosexual characters that appear are included for anything other than colourful decorative effect, however. Yousri Nasrallah, one of the younger generation of Egyptian directors, observes:

> Many popular films – mostly comedies – show homosexuals. Most often, effeminate characters, transvestites. This image of the homosexual is tolerated perfectly. It makes the public laugh and, in a way, confirms the ideas they have about virility. On the other hand, they are much more reticent when it's about a 'normal' homo – loving and successful.[74]

Whether homosexual characters are deemed suitable for inclusion in films depends largely on the message they convey. This is well-illustrated by the 1963 film version of Naguib Mahfouz's novel, *Midaq Alley,* where Kirsha – the bisexual café owner who is one of the book's central characters – almost disappears from the film script while a brothel *khawal*[75] is retained as a symbol of moral degradation. Kirsha is a more problematic figure from a film-maker's viewpoint because in the book he is morally more ambivalent and seeks to justify his behaviour.[76]

Homosexuality is by no means the only area where Arab film-makers have had to tread carefully, however. The following summary of the Egyptian censorship law issued in 1976 sets out the general requirement for films that reflect 'proper' moral values:

'Heavenly' religions [Islam, Christianity, and Judaism] should not be criticised. Heresy and magic should not be positively portrayed. Immoral actions and vices are not to be justified and must be punished. Images of naked human bodies or the inordinate emphasis on individual erotic parts, the representation of sexually arousing scenes, and scenes of alcohol consumption and drug use are not allowed. Also prohibited is the use of obscene and indecent speech. The sanctity of marriage, family values, and one's parents must be respected. Beside the prohibition on the excessive use of horror and violence, or inciting their imitation, it is forbidden to represent social problems as hopeless, to upset the mind, or to divide religions, classes, and national unity.[77]

Viola Shafik, in her book on Arab cinema, comments:

In general, criticism of Islam is not allowed, this being the official state religion in most Arab countries. By extension, a positive representation of atheism is not appropriate. Even the overtly secular Algerian cinema attacks only maraboutism and practices of popular Islam, steering clear of orthodox Muslim conviction. National unity is maintained not through a just representation of different native religions but through the exclusive representation of Muslim conditions of life and convictions. Although there are many Christian directors working in Egypt – including Youssef Chahine, Samir Seif, Khairy Beshara, Daoud Abd el-Sayyed, and Yousri Nasrallah – Christian characters hardly ever appear on the screen, and then mostly in minor roles. The representation of Jews is also frowned upon.[78]

Public bath-houses – a normal feature of Cairo life until most of them were closed for reasons of health and/or morality – provide a suitable excuse for homoerotic scenes in several Egyptian films. In *The Malatili Bath* (*Hamam al-Malatili*, 1973), a homeless young man takes shelter in a bath house and meets a gay artist who (for once) is not an exploitative foreigner. The artist takes him back to his apartment and plies him with wine and cigarettes while James Brown's 'Like a Sex Machine' plays in the background. After some frenzied gyration, both men – by now bare-chested – collapse with exhaustion next to each other. 'This particular scene,' Menicucci says, 'is the closest that Arab cinema has come to portraying gay sexuality.'

Directed by Salah Abu Saif, *The Malatili Bath* proved highly controversial at the time it was made. Through the character of the artist it makes a plea for sexual tolerance which does not entirely succeed. The artist tells the youth there was unrestricted freedom in the past whereas nowadays there is none. As he imagines what a tolerant society would be like the camera cuts to a fantasy scene where the artist, wearing a long wig and unmanly clothing, struts along a street in downtown Cairo attracting shocked looks from passers-by (as well he might). Menicucci comments:

> In an unfortunate case of pop psychologising, Abu Saif explains the artist's homosexuality as stemming from a love/hate relationship with his overbearing mother which causes the artist to abhor the idea of sexual involvement with women and, at the same time, to desire to become a woman in his outward appearance. Thus, homosexuality is associated with women's supposed emasculation of men,

transvestism, perversion and the social ills accompanying rapid urbanisation. Nonetheless, the overall message is 'live and let live' and that every person has the right to human affection no matter what form it takes.

Several films by Youssef Chahine, who is widely regarded as Egypt's greatest director, depict homosexuality in a positive, matter-of-fact way. In *The Nile and its People* (*al-Nass wal Nil*, 1972), a joint Egyptian-Soviet epic about the construction of the Aswan High Dam, a male Soviet technician and a male Egyptian worker strike up a close friendship which can be interpreted, by those who prefer not to look too deeply at its sexual implications, as symbolising international socialist solidarity.[79] In *An Egyptian Fairy Tale* (*Hadduta Misriyya*, 1982) Yehia, a film-maker, goes to London for an operation (as Chahine himself had done) and has a brief affair with a taxi driver.[80] Like *An Egyptian Fairy Tale*, the films in Chahine's 'Alexandria' series are partly autobiographical. In *Alexandria, Why?* (*Iskindiriyya Leeh?*, 1978), one of the characters from Chahine's family is an uncle who plots to assassinate drunken British soldiers during the Second World War but instead takes one of them home and sleeps with him. 'The telling scene has the British soldier waking up in the uncle's bed in his underwear not knowing what has happened. The uncle goes on to act as a role model and mentor for the adolescent Yahya who represents Youssef Chahine.'[81] *Alexandria Once Again* (*Iskindiriyya Kaman wi Kaman*, 1989), is an autobiographical film-within-a-film fantasy where Chahine plays himself as a director. He is infatuated with a young male actor who he has chosen for the lead role in an epic about Alexander the Great, and although the sexual undertones are not explicit they are hard to miss. One scene has Chahine and the actor doing a Ginger Rogers-Fred Astaire dance number together after being nominated for a prize at the Cannes Film Festival. In the story (though not in real life) Chahine has a jealous wife competing with the actor for his affections.

Although Arab film makers potentially face severe restrictions on what they can show on screen, there are creative ways of stretching the rules, and the degree of latitude they are allowed can vary from time to time and from country to country. A lot also depends on the amount of effort individual film makers are prepared to invest in negotiating with the authorities. Chahine's stature within the film industry probably helps, as does the involvement of foreign backers. In the early 1970s, Chahine formed his own production company which survives with mainly Western financial support.[82]

Foreign involvement may also help to explain why the Tunisian cinema has acquired a reputation for tackling controversial sexual topics: most Tunisian films are produced with French financing for simultaneous European distribution. This, however, has led to complaints that their content is designed to appeal to a European audience and distorts the reality of Arab social life.

Two films by Tunisian director Nouri Bouzid have attracted the attention of gay audiences in the West: *Man of Ashes* (*Rih al-Sadd*, 1986) and *Bezness* (1992). *Bezness* (a mis-pronunciation of 'business' which in Tunisia refers to young men earning a living by their wits) is another sex-with-foreigners tale – in this case gigolos who sell their bodies to tourists of either gender. It is not the usual story of exploitation, nor is it really a film about homosexuality; its basic theme is cultural schizophrenia among young Arabs torn between East and West, between tradition and modernity. *Man of Ashes* is a sensitive and ground-breaking portrait of young men grappling with doubts about their masculinity, but the film is spoiled by blaming their identity crisis on a carpenter who sexually abused them as children.

In Egypt, Yousri Nasrallah has adopted Chahine's practice of including homosexuality in his films – often in a more forthright way than his mentor. *Mercedes* (1993), which has been shown at gay film festivals, features a protagonist who has a gay brother with a lover, and also a drug-addicted lesbian aunt. '*Mercedes* is not really a gay film in the militant sense of the word,' Nasrallah said in an interview with a French newspaper. 'What mattered to me most at the time when I shot it was to applaud difference in all its senses – religious, sexual, political, racial … This film is above all against dictatorship by the majority and majority attitudes.'

Asked how it had been received at the time, he replied: 'Rather well, but many people were shocked. Someone even said that this film represented everything that was most "non-Egyptian". The hero is Christian (like a large part of the Egyptian population), communist (Egypt has an official communist party); there are doubts about his parentage (an Arab proverb says that to know who someone's father is you should ask the mother!) and he has a queer brother (the recent trial[83] shows that not only are there queers in Egypt but they threaten the security of the state!). People said that the duty of a responsible film-maker is to conform to the dominant moral standards. In short: it was much discussed.'[84]

# FOUR

# Rights and Wrongs

THE UNIVERSAL Declaration of Human Rights is probably the most important document ever issued by the United Nations. Approved by the General Assembly in 1948, it spells out in clear and uncompromising language 'the equal and inalienable rights of all members of the human family'. The word 'universal' in the title is not to be taken lightly. It means exactly what it says: human rights should apply equally to everyone, everywhere, at all times. Article Two of the declaration states:

> Everyone is entitled to all the rights and freedoms set forth in this declaration, without distinction of any kind, such as race, colour, sex, language, religion, political or other opinion, national or social origin, property, birth or other status.[1]

While this does not mention sexual orientation specifically, it has no need to do so. The phrase 'without distinction of any kind' is absolutely clear, and sexual orientation cannot be excluded from any sensible interpretation of its meaning. 'Lesbian and gay rights,' Amnesty International says, 'belong on the human rights agenda because if we tolerate the denial of rights to any minority, we undermine the whole protective framework of human rights by taking away its central plank – the equal rights and dignity of all human beings. When governments ignore their responsibility towards one sector of society, then no one's human rights are safe ... Perhaps most centrally of all, lesbian and gay rights belong on the human rights agenda because sexual orientation, like, for example, gender or race, relates to fundamental aspects of human identity.'[2]

The essential principle here is equality, and there is no room for selectively excluding some human beings on the pretext of local circumstances or cultural norms. Either the equality principle is accepted in whole or it is not: there are no half measures. The equal rights established by the declaration include an equal right to life, equal freedom from arbitrary arrest, equal freedom from torture and ill-treatment, equal freedom of expression and association, and equality before the law.

Despite this, and despite ample evidence of abuses in various parts of the world, the United Nations has been slow to grapple with what, for a large number of its members, is a highly sensitive issue. It was only in 2003 that the UN Commission on Human Rights got around to discussing homosexuality for the first time when Brazil put forward a resolution expressing 'deep concern at the occurrence of violations of human rights in the world against persons on the grounds of their sexual orientation'.[3] Speaking in support of the proposal, a Canadian representative said it set out important goals and principles for all states to follow. Discrimination on the grounds of sexual orientation was a serious problem throughout the world, and Canada itself had treated same-sex practices between consenting adults as a crime until 1969. In that year, the representative continued, Canada had rightly concluded that 'the state has no business in the bedroom of the nation.'[4]

On its own, approval of the Brazilian resolution would not have stopped the abuses but it would have provided an explicit statement that sexual orientation is a human rights issue and sent an important signal that discrimination is unacceptable. In the event, it was blocked by opposition from five Muslim countries – Saudi Arabia, Egypt, Libya, Malaysia and Pakistan. Muslim nations could not accept the proposal, the Pakistani ambassador, Shaukat Umer, said. In any case, he suggested, the correct term was not 'sexual orientation' but 'sexual disorientation'. He continued: 'This is a question that concerns the fundamental values of our society ... It's an attempt to impose one set of values on to people who have another ... We say: we respect your value systems, but please handle those within your own countries.'[5]

Acting on behalf of the Islamic Conference Organisation[6] which represents fifty-six Muslim countries, Pakistan proposed a motion of 'no action' on the resolution – in effect to abandon it. The draft resolution aimed to create 'new rights' that were in discord with the religious and cultural values of several states and was 'not a proper subject' for discussion, Pakistan argued. It would create discord at best, and huge divisions within the commission at worst.[7] The Pakistani move was narrowly defeated by twenty-four votes to twenty-two,[8] but next day the five Islamic allies launched a filibuster, with a series of amendments and procedural manoeuvres that resulted in the commission halting further debate.

Regardless of the topic, such antics are by no means unusual at the UN Commission on Human Rights, where member governments are often less concerned with principles than with shaping the human rights agenda to meet their own domestic policy requirements. This particular episode, however, not only broached a topic that the leaders of some countries are reluctant to discuss but also brought into focus a gaping philosophical divide about the function of government. On one side were those who believe governments should police the morals of their citizens and, on the other side, those who say that what consenting adults do in private is not a matter for the authorities – that 'the state has no business in the bedroom of the nation,' as the Canadian representative had put it.

The worldwide trend, over several decades, has been towards the latter view and away from the former. Throughout the European Union, for example, following a ruling by the Court of Human Rights, any laws that criminalise private consensual sex between adults of the same gender are now invalid. Legalisation of same-sex activity has also been accompanied, in many countries, by measures to protect against discrimination on the basis of sexual orientation. South Africa was the first to do this, in 1996, and it has been followed by others such as Canada, France, Ireland, Israel, Slovenia and Spain.

Muslim and Arab countries are a notable exception to the trend. Among the eighty-one countries identified by the International Lesbian and Gay Association as outlawing same-sex acts, thirty-six belong to the Arab League and/or the Islamic Conference Organisation. Furthermore, the few countries that retain the death penalty for same-sex offences all justify it on the grounds of Islamic law.[9] While it would be easy to cite this as one more reason for severe criticism of Islam, the reality is less black-and-white than it might seem. For a start, there is no uniform 'Islamic position' regarding homosexuality and the law: twenty-one of the fifty-six countries belonging to the Islamic Conference Organisation and six of the twenty members of the Arab League are *not* listed by the ILGA as clearly outlawing same-sex acts.[10] Among the others punishments vary quite widely and, even where the death penalty theoretically applies, the only Muslim countries known to have carried out executions for sodomy during the last decade or so are Afghanistan, Iran and Saudi Arabia.[11] This suggests that while Islamic teaching often provides a rationale for anti-homosexual laws, the law in practice is shaped mainly by the prevailing attitudes in each country, and particularly by the extent to which government seeks to police personal morality.[12]

\* \* \*

ALTHOUGH gay rights campaigners have good reason to focus on the situation in Arab and Muslim countries, they often oversimplify the problem, attributing it to immutable features of religion and culture. In doing so, they inadvertently endorse the case of Arab and Muslim traditionalists who invoke heritage to defend all manner of unsavoury practices that cannot be justified by rational means and who demand the right to continue punishing homosexuality out of respect for their religion and culture. Treating Islam, rather than social attitudes, as the main obstacle minimises the hope for reform and gives fuel to those on both sides of the divide who favour a clash-of-civilisations approach. A different and perhaps more profitable way of addressing the problem is to pay less attention to the 'otherness' of Arab-Islamic culture and more attention to its sameness. The arguments against homosexuality voiced in Arab and Muslim countries today – that it will result in the collapse of civilisation, social decay, and so forth – are essentially no different from those that once held sway (and are sometimes still heard) in Western and Christian countries; the harmful effects of laws against homosexuality in the Arab world – entrapment, blackmail, forced emigration, etc – are also much the same as they were elsewhere and so, too, are the arguments for abolishing them.

It is also important to note that acceptance of homosexuality in other parts of the world is a fairly recent development. The attitudes found in Arab countries now were commonplace in many parts of the world fifty years ago, but while other countries have moved on and tried to overcome their hang-ups the Arab world has not. It is worth recalling that Britain, over several centuries, waged a war against homosexuality – in the name of religion, social order, decency, etc – that certainly equalled, and in its scale probably outstripped, anything that happens in Arab countries today.

In 1533, when King Henry VIII incorporated contemporary Christian teaching into the English legal system, the 'detestable and abominable vice of buggery' became a capital offence. The Buggery Act, as it was known, was twice repealed and twice reinstated during the sixteenth century but the penalty of death by hanging remained in place continuously from 1563 for almost three centuries. The legal definition of buggery was also extremely wide and, until 1817, included oral sex. It was only in 1861 that the death penalty for buggery was formally abolished.

Homosexual acts between males remained a criminal offence in Britain, however, and it was not until the 1950s that the law began to be seriously questioned following the appointment of a particularly stern home secretary (interior minister), Sir David Maxwell-Fyfe. A year after his appointment, the number of prosecutions for homosexuality in England soared to 5,443 – more than four times the rate in 1939.[13] This was achieved partly through dubious or illegal methods, such as entrapment by *agents provocateurs*. In the process, a number of prominent people were arrested, including the newly-knighted actor, Sir John Gielgud, Lord Montagu of Beaulieu (an old Etonian and former officer in the Grenadier Guards), Montagu's second cousin, Michael Pitt-Rivers (grandson of a famous archaeologist), and a Daily Mail journalist, Peter Wildeblood.[14]

'Homosexuals in general are exhibitionists and proselytisers and are a danger to others, especially the young,' Maxwell-Fyfe told the British parliament in 1953. 'So long as I hold the office of Home Secretary, I shall give no countenance to the view that they should not be prevented from being such a danger.'[15] But Maxwell-Fyfe's crackdown, hysterically supported by the popular press, did little to deter same-sex activity and merely highlighted the inconsistency of the courts when passing sentence: penalties could range from a small fine to life imprisonment. Those convicted were often forced to accept medical treatment, including aversion 'therapy' (electric shocks) or hormone injections as a condition of parole or probation.

High-profile prosecutions and the obviously chaotic state of the law led in 1954 to the appointment of a committee headed by John Wolfenden, vice-chancellor of Reading University, to investigate. Its task was to review the law relating to homosexuality and also prostitution, but in line with the sensibilities of the times, the committee felt unable to use either term in its internal deliberations for fear of offending secretarial staff. Adopting a practice that seems comical today, it used the word 'Huntley' in place of 'homosexual' and 'Palmer' in place of 'prostitute' (Huntley & Palmer was one of Britain's largest biscuit manufacturers; unfortunately, its views on this use of its name are not recorded).[16] The committee deliberated for three years, interviewing a large number of witnesses who included religious leaders, policemen, judges, probation officers, psychiatrists, social workers, and 'Huntleys'. Its report, published in 1957, caused a furore by recommending that homosexual acts should be legalised if they took place in private between consenting adults aged at least twenty-one.[17] The Home Secretary rejected these findings, saying that 'sodomistic societies and buggery clubs' fostered 'lying, cruelty and indecency',[18] and it was a further ten years before the British parliament finally voted to implement the report's proposals.

The Wolfenden committee's views were not particularly liberal. They regarded homosexuality as immoral and destructive to individuals but concluded that private morality or immorality should not be a matter for the law. The function of the law, the committee wrote, 'is to preserve public order and decency, to protect the citizen from what is offensive or injurious, and to provide sufficient safeguards against exploitation and corruption of others, particularly those who are specially vulnerable ... It is not, in our view, the function of the law to intervene in the private life of citizens, or to seek to enforce any particular pattern of behaviour, further than is necessary to carry out the purposes we have outlined.'[19] This argument, though challenged by some high-ranking jurists at the time, has since been accepted in many parts of the world though not, as yet, in the Arab countries.

\* \* \*

FOLLOWING the birth of Islam, the rapid expansion of empire under the first four caliphs prompted efforts to develop a comprehensive Islamic legal system. The Qur'an, the ultimate religious authority for Muslims, gives limited guidance on legal matters: it specifies penalties for a very small number of crimes (known as the *hadd* crimes) but does not provide anything approaching a systematic legal code. Guidance found in the Qur'an therefore had to be supplemented in other ways. The most important of these were the *hadith* – the reported words and deeds of the Prophet Muhammad. Where the *hadith* did not suffice, legal issues could be resolved by a process of reasoning or analogy (*qiyas*) and, failing that, through *ijmaa* – the consensus of believers, as determined by Muslim scholars.[20]

This, as might be expected, became a complex business with plenty of scope for differences of interpretation and did not produce a single, unified body of Islamic law. In the Sunni branch of Islam (to which most Muslims belong), it resulted in four main 'schools' of law – Hanafi, Maliki, Shafi and Hanbali – whose relative influence varies from country to country. The main school among Shi'a Muslims,[21] meanwhile, is the Jafari. One major difference between these schools is in the reliance they place on the *hadith*, since there are often questions regarding the authenticity of words and deeds attributed to the Prophet. While some *hadith* may be genuine, others are plainly later inventions. Assessing their credibility, therefore, is a matter for critical scholarship in which the chain of transmission – the way they were handed down from the time of the Prophet – often plays an important part.

The Hanafi school tends to be more wary of the *hadith* than the other schools, with the result that its judgements are often more flexible. The Maliki school is also somewhat critical of the *hadith*. On the other hand, the Shafii, Hanbali and Jafari schools – which generally produce the most conservative legal judgements – all rely heavily on the *hadith* and, in the words of the Oxford History of Islam:

> ... can be criticised for reifying and idealising tradition to such a degree that the corpus of *hadith* is not subjected to rational analysis or content criticism. Individual *ahadith* [plural of *hadith*] are accepted as true by these schools even if only one transmitter links these traditions to either the Prophet or an imam and regardless of whether they agree or disagree with an apparent ruling in the Qur'an.[22]

In the light of these differences, and contrary to popular opinion in the West, it cannot be said that any universally-agreed 'Islamic punishment' for homosexual acts exists. Sodomy is not among the *hadd* crimes specified in the Qur'an, and so the penalties assigned for it by the various schools of Islamic law are the result of human (and therefore fallible) processes of deduction.

In the most radical challenge to traditionalist views published so far, Scott Siraj al-Haqq Kugle asserts that the issue of homosexuality is not explicitly addressed anywhere in the Qur'an and, furthermore, that there is no reliable evidence of the Prophet ever having punished people for same-sex acts:

> At a certain point in history, *hadith* attributed to the Prophet Muhammad began to circulate which addressed the issue of punishing men for having anal sex. This is just one specific case of a very general problem for Muslims ever since: the existence of reports, on a whole range of subjects, that circulate in the name of the Prophet without being reliably or verifiably known to represent the Prophet's actual actions and teachings ... It is probable that such *hadith* came into being long after the Prophet had died, and were attributed to him in order to give them the force of association with the Prophet's respected and revered personality.
>
> ... It is very difficult to establish the authenticity of most reports that circulate in the name of the Prophet Muhammad. But clearly, many reports were projected retrospectively back upon the Prophet without being reliably attributed to him. Muslims are confronted with *hadith* in which the Prophet reportedly speaks about issues that did not exist in his lifetime: such as the Shi'a-Sunni schism, various theological 'heresies', and even the systematic collection of *hadith*. Reassessment of the authenticity of *hadith* reports is the key to legal and social reform among Muslims.[23]

The radical part of Kugle's argument is that he takes these widely-acknowledged criticisms of the *hadith* and applies them in a new way to question conventional Islamic views of homosexuality. Most statements in which the Prophet apparently condemns same-sex acts are not included in the most authoritative collections of *hadith*, he says. They have weak chains of transmission and in some cases were explicitly debunked by medieval scholars as forgeries.[24] A further reason for suspicion is that '*hadith* that address the issue of punishing men for having anal sex are not linked to any specific case or event in the Prophet's life. This is in marked contrast to the *hadith* that address the issue of adultery between a man and woman, which are linked to very detailed cases that preserve the names of the men and women involved'. Kugle adds in a footnote:

> Forged *hadith* reports condemning same-sex sexual relations began to circulate in earnest during the Abbasid period (750–1258 AD), when it became aristocratic and courtly fashion to own young male slaves, employ handsome wine-bearers, and flaunt same-sex romances. Many *hadiths* were circulated in the name of the Prophet to address these practices, as part of the traditionalist cultural war on the cosmopolitan élite of Abbasid-era cities.[25]

The view that the Prophet prescribed no penalties for same-sex acts, and that relevant statements in the *hadith* are later fabrications, is further reinforced by the disagreements among classical jurists as to the appropriate punishment for such acts. Al-Qurtubi, a Maliki jurist who died in 1273, argued that anal sex between men should be treated as a *hadd* crime because it was legally equivalent to *zina* (adultery or sexual penetration between a man and a woman who are not joined by a contractual relationship or marriage).[26] In classical Islamic law, the *hadd* punishment for *zina* is flogging in the case of an unmarried person, or stoning to death for someone who is already married. Shafii and Hanbali jurists reached a similar conclusion about punishing homosexual acts, though the Hanbali argument is based on Qur'anic interpretation and *hadith* rather than analogy with *zina*. Some jurists have also based their arguments for stoning to death on God's punishment of 'the people of Lut' [the Biblical Lot, of Sodom and Gomorrah fame] when stones rained down upon them from heaven. This, Kugle notes, is an argument by rhetorical association, not legal reasoning. Hanafi jurists, meanwhile, say that anal sex between men cannot be considered a *hadd* crime. *Hadd* crimes, by definition, are those specified in the Qur'an and it is not permissible to add to the list by making analogies. The Hanafi view, therefore, is that any punishment of same-sex acts is a matter for governments, not religious scholars, to decide.

The key point here – and it cannot be emphasised too strongly – is the lack of unanimity and the weakness of many of the arguments. To say that 'Islam' prescribes 'death for homosexuals' is simplistic and misleading, even though religious conservatives and Western gay rights campaigners (each for their own reasons) like to claim that it does. One British activist, Peter Tatchell, writes:

> The form of punishment is specified in Islamic law, the *Shari'a*. This is the clerical interpretation of the Koran and the Hadith. It demands the death penalty for both lesbian and gay sex.[27]

This sort of propagandising is particularly unhelpful to those gay and lesbian Muslims who are struggling to reconcile their sexuality with their religion. The implication is that anyone who rejects the supposedly 'Islamic' penalties must reject Islam as a whole – which is not necessarily so.

* * *

IN PRACTICE, the legal systems of Arab states are less dependent on the various schools of Islamic law (shari'a) than might be imagined. In some countries the constitution describes shari'a as 'the main source' of law, while in others it is merely 'a source'. The only Arab country that claims to follow Islamic law totally is Saudi Arabia, where the ultra-conservative Hanbali school prevails. Arab legal systems have also been shaped by British, French and Italian colonial influences, however. The penal code that Britain introduced for India in 1861 was also applied to some other parts of the empire, including Aden (southern Yemen), Bahrain, Kuwait, Oman, Qatar, Sudan and the area now known as the United Arab Emirates. Article 377 of the code punished sodomy by deportation for twenty years, imprisonment for up to ten years, or by a fine. In 1956 this was replaced in the British-controlled areas of the Gulf with a new code which punished sodomy by up to ten years' jail with the possibility of corporal punishment too. The French Napoleonic code, on the other hand, made no legal distinction between same-sex and opposite-sex intercourse.[28]

According to the website sodomylaws.org, sodomy is punishable by death in five Arab countries: Mauritania, Saudi

Arabia, Sudan, Yemen and possibly the United Arab Emirates (the wording of the UAE's penal code is ambiguous and can be interpreted as applying to sodomy in general or to male rape only[29]). Iran, a non-Arab country in the Middle East, also has the death penalty. Elsewhere in the region, the maximum penalty for sodomy in Bahrain is ten years' imprisonment; seven years in Kuwait; five years in Libya and possibly Qatar; three years in Algeria, Oman, Morocco, Somalia, Tunisia; and one year in Lebanon and Syria.[30] The legal position in Iraq since the overthrow of Saddam Hussein is difficult to determine.[31] An absence of specific anti-sodomy laws in other countries does not necessarily mean an absence of prosecutions, though: Egypt, which has recently been the most active of the Arab countries in persecuting gay men, makes use of laws against prostitution, immoral advertising and incitement to debauchery. There are also a few parts of the Arab world where government control is minimal and communities take it upon themselves to impose discipline. In rural areas of Yemen, for example, the application of non-governmental 'tribal justice' is quite common, though rarely reported. One such case was the execution, in 1999, of an eighteen-year-old man accused of raping a four-year-old boy: 'Following local tradition, elders from Asfal Gargar, in Abyan province, east of Aden, decided to have the man executed. He was shot at dawn on Wednesday to the approval of villagers ...'[32]

The only Arab country where official executions for same-sex acts have been reported in recent years is Saudi Arabia,[33] which applies the death penalty to a wide range of offences besides sodomy, including murder, adultery, highway robbery, drug smuggling, sabotage, witchcraft, apostasy (renunciation of Islam) and 'corruption on earth' – an extremely vague charge that was

whether the same police officers were involved in both cases.

The mention of extortion in the reports is intriguing, but there is no indication of who the men demanded money from – presumably not from the boys who had allegedly been drugged, raped and photographed. A plausible scenario is that the accused had provided boys for other men who did not figure in the trial, secretly photographed them in the act and then blackmailed them. There are at least two other possibilities, however. One is that the accused were just ordinary gay men and that the charges against them were embellished to make their behaviour look worse and supported by confessions extracted through torture – a not uncommon occurrence in the kingdom. Alternatively, it is conceivable that their real offence was something entirely different and the sex charges were simply a way of discrediting them. Such is the nature of Saudi 'justice' that it is impossible to know for sure.

In Iran, the *sharia*-based crime of *lavat* (equivalent to *liwat* in Arabic) covers both penetrative and non-penetrative sexual acts between men. For penetrative acts the death penalty applies. Non-penetrative acts are punished by flogging for the first three offences, with execution for a fourth offence. Sexual acts between women are defined differently under the law but punished in the same way as non-penetrative acts between men.[37]

As in Egypt, Iranian police have made use of the Internet for entrapment. In June 2004 undercover agents in Shiraz arranged meetings with men through chatrooms and then arrested them. One of those arrested, a 21-year-old man called Amir, was held in detention for a week, repeatedly tortured and later sentenced him to 175 lashes, according to Human Rights Watch. After his release he was kept under regular surveillance and subjected to periodic arrests before eventually fleeing the country. Police in Shiraz also raided a private – apparently gay – house party in September 2003 and arrested a group of men. Five were later fined, reportedly after being tortured into confessing to 'participation in a corrupt gathering'.[38] It seems likely that this type of harassment will increase following the establishment of the Special Protection Division, a new body set up by the judiciary in 2004 which empowers volunteers to police moral crimes in their local neighbourhoods.

As in other countries where homosexual acts are illegal, the Iranian law of *lavat* creates opportunities for blackmail and evidence of this has surfaced in some recent court cases. One man executed in the city of Bojnurd in April 2005 was said to have made videos of sexual acts with his male partners in order to blackmail them. The man, who had a string of previous convictions for other crimes, appears to have been executed for rape rather than *lavat*, on the grounds that blackmail removed any element of consent from his sexual acts.[39] In another case, reported by Etemaad newspaper, Tehran criminal court sentenced two men to death after a video was found showing them engaging in homosexual acts. According to the paper, one of the men told the authorities he had made the video as a precaution in case his partner withdrew the financial support he had been providing in return for sex.[40]

It is difficult to be sure how many people have been put to death for *lavat* in Iran, and newspaper accounts are often sketchy, but executions appear to be not uncommon. On 13 November 2005, the semi-official Tehran daily, *Kayhan*, reported the public hanging of two men, identified as Mokhtar N (aged 24) and Ali A (aged 25), in the northern town of Gorgan.[41]

Four months earlier, two male teenagers, Mahmoud Asgari and Ayaz Marhoni – believed to be aged 18 and 19 – were publicly executed in the city of Mashhad. A press release issued by the London-based OutRage group (citing a report from the Iranian Students News Agency) initially said they had been put to death for 'homosexuality', though other reports said their offence was raping a thirteen-year-old boy. OutRage suggested the allegation of sexual assault 'may either be a trumped up charge to undermine public sympathy for the youths ... or it may be that the thirteen-year-old was a willing participant.' It added that the youths had claimed in their defence 'that most young boys had sex with each other and that they were not aware that homosexuality was punishable by death'.[42] Human Rights Watch (HRW), on the other hand, said there was no substantial evidence that the teenagers had been punished for consensual sodomy and focused instead on the fact that at least one of them had been a minor at the time of the alleged offence – in which case his execution was a breach of international law.[43] According to Scott Long, director of HRW's Lesbian, Gay, Bisexual and Transgender Rights Project, a report in an Iranian newspaper on the morning of the executions described the case in some detail. 'It is clearly identified there as a rape case, with a lengthy interview with the father of the thirteen-year-old apparent victim,' Long told a gay website. 'The account there is that the case dates back two years, that the boy in question was seized outside a shopping area by the two boys ultimately convicted, who took him to a deserted area where five other boys were also waiting ... He was gang-raped at knifepoint, according to his father's account, which is supported by three passers-by who interrupted the act. Passers-by were attacked with knives and had their cars vandalised.'[44] It is unclear what happened to the other members of the reported gang.

Meanwhile, the British Ahwazi Friendship Society suggested there might be an ethnic dimension to the case. It noted Iranian press reports saying the executed teenagers originally came from the province of Khuzestan, which is home to Iran's Ahwazi Arab minority. Similar executions had taken place a couple of months earlier, the society said, 'when three indigenous Ahwazi Arab men were executed in Susangerd, Khuzestan, for the alleged rape and murder of a six-year-old. In each case, the men's names were continually repeated in the Iranian press, to highlight their Arab identity.' It continued:

> By targeting Arabs, the Iranian regime is clearly using the social taboo of homosexuality and the heinous crime of child rape to justify the social marginalisation of the Ahwazi Arab population. Racial discrimination against Arabs and the summary nature of the Iranian justice system mean that Arabs rarely receive a fair trial. Criminal charges are often trumped up to achieve political ends, in this case the portrayal of Arabs as morally degenerate. In the past, the government used a moral purge on pornography to raid shops that sell Arabic language literature and seize satellite dishes capable of receiving foreign transmissions. The regime is keen to highlight problems of alcoholism and heroin addiction in Khuzestan – problems that are also prevalent in many other impoverished areas of Iran – to underline its portrayal of Arabs as lawless, backward and immoral.[45]

Jonathan Raban, in *Arabia Through the Looking Glass*, suggests that crime and punishment in the Middle East sometimes acquire metaphorical qualities. During his visit to North Yemen in the 1970s, rumours of an attempted coup were swiftly followed by a series of public executions, including one in which three men variously described as soldiers or army officers were shot. Enquiring about the men and their crime, Raban was given a number of conflicting accounts but noted that one 'fact' was common to every version of the story: they had raped and killed a thirteen-year-old boy.

> The age of the boy never varied, nor did the details of his killing; he had been clubbed to death after an orgy of buggery. In this contradictory tangle of information, one statement alone seemed totally suspect to me – the story about the boy. Its exactitude had the ring of untruth about it. It is possible that it really happened, but I doubt it. It's much more likely that it was a metaphor. One cannot publicly punish people for crimes which one cannot publicly announce: Hamdi [the assassinated former president] had been killed for 'keeping prostitutes in his house' – a neat enough analogy for his dalliance with the communist south. 'Raping and killing a thirteen-year-old boy' seemed to me like another convenient figure of speech.[46]

Metaphorical crime was also a feature of the Egyptian 'Queen Boat' case in 2001 when attempts were made to link homosexuality to 'contempt of religion' by portraying the main defendant as head of a deviant religious cult to which he had tried to recruit other gay men. State Security officers claimed to have found a booklet in his home entitled *Agency of God on Earth: our Religion is the Religion of Lot's People, our Prophet and Guide is Abu Nawas*.[47] The document, which was never produced in court, allegedly contained such subversive statements as 'Sex can make people love each other more than anything' and 'Homosexuality is a human right, and not an offence that angers God, because it does not leave any harm.'[48]

Crime stories in Saudi newspapers often read like parables aimed at inculcating sound moral values into their readers. In October 2003, the Saudi newspaper, *Okaz*, reported that a twenty-year-old man from a village near Jeddah had been sentenced to death for twice raping a twelve-year-old boy, then 'strangling him, hitting his head with a rock and pushing him off a cliff'. The man, identified only by his first name, Ali, was said to have been assisted by his sixteen-year-old cousin, Sultan, who was sentenced to five years in jail and 400 lashes. *Okaz*, a paper with close links to the interior ministry, apparently secured an interview with the cousin, who gave the following account:

Ali asked Sultan to lure twelve-year-old Ibrahim to Sultan's house so they could sodomise him while his family was away. 'I asked Ibrahim to come and have lunch and play video games with me,' he said.

Ali, who had been drinking, joined the two and began beating the boy. Both Ali and Sultan then sexually assaulted the boy.

'When I had a feeling that my family were about to come back, I asked Ali and Ibrahim to leave. I quickly tidied up the room so my family wouldn't suspect anything,' Sultan said.

He said Ali then took Ibrahim away. 'In the evening I

went out looking for them. I found Ali on a nearby hill and the body of Ibrahim lay dead in the valley in his bloodstained clothes.' Ali and Sultan then fled the village. During his trial, Ali acknowledged his guilt but said he acted 'under the influence of liquor.'[49]

The motive for the murder – if that is really what it was – remains unexplained, but the point of the story becomes clear in the last sentence. It is a lesson about the perils of drink: alcohol leads to sodomy and sodomy leads to murder.

Another Saudi case that leaves much to be explained occurred in April 2000 when nine young men were sentenced to jail and flogging for 'deviant sexual behaviour'. Citing an unnamed police officer, the Associated Press news agency said that a court in Qunfuda (on the Red Sea coast) had sentenced five of the men to six years in prison and 2,600 lashes (fifty sessions of fifty-two lashes at fortnightly intervals), and the others to five years with 2,400 lashes (fifty sessions of forty-eight lashes). According to the officer, police started tailing the men after reports that they were acting strangely. He said police found that 'they were dressing in women's clothes and engaging in deviant sexual behaviour with each other'. All nine reportedly confessed to the charges.[50] Although all the previously-mentioned caveats apply to this case too, it does perhaps indicate that where sexual 'deviance' is not complicated by additional charges of rape, paedophilia, extortion, etc, the penalty in Saudi Arabia is likely to be a stiff jail term with severe corporal punishment rather than execution.

* * *

UNLIKE Saudi Arabia, Egypt has no specific law against
sodomy though it uses several other means to bring prosecutions
for same-sex activity. The most important of these is a law
originally introduced to combat prostitution which has the
effect of criminalising almost any sort of casual or promiscuous
sex, regardless of the gender of the people involved.

Prostitution has a long history in Egypt. In pre-colonial times
it generally thrived and, despite occasional crackdowns, provided
a source of income for the government through taxation.[51]
Towards the end of the nineteenth century, under the rule of
Khedive Tawfiq, the state began to regulate prostitution for
health reasons and in 1905 the British authorities introduced a
system of licensed brothels in certain parts of Egypt, with weekly
medical checks for their workers. The popularity of these brothels
among the British troops, together with legal arrangements
that favoured non-Egyptian prostitutes, soon turned them
into a symbol of foreign domination around which nationalist
and religious sentiment could be mobilised. Nevertheless, the
licensing system, which included male prostitutes as well as
females, remained in place for more than a quarter-century after
Egyptian independence. In 1949, with the country under martial
law as a result of the war with Israel, a military decree abolished
all brothels and outlawed prostitution – a move intended to
alleviate pressure on the government from both nationalists and
the Muslim Brotherhood. A parliamentary committee then set
about drafting a permanent anti-prostitution law.

The normal Arabic term for 'prostitution' is *di'ara*, but the committee studying the draft law recommended inserting the word *fujur* (debauchery) as well. Consequently, the law as it stands today talks about 'debauchery or prostitution'.[52] One practical reason for including 'debauchery' might have been to make it easier for the police to arrest prostitutes without evidence of money changing hands, but this was not the reason given by the committee. Instead, it argued that *di'ara* referred only to female prostitution and that in order to cover male prostitution too, the word *fujur* was needed.[53] Although the committee said there were 'judicial precedents' using *di'ara* to refer to female prostitution and *fujur* to refer to male prostitution,[54] Human Rights Watch has since questioned the existence of any precedents that make such a distinction.[55] In terms of ordinary language, Human Rights Watch says, *di'ara* is normally understood to mean commercial sex, regardless of the gender of those involved, while *fujur* is much broader and conveys 'immorality in general, with a sexual tinge but no inherent commercial implications'.[56]

Though commercial sex was plainly the law's original target, the government seems to have been in no position at the time to resist this vague drafting that vastly extended its scope. 'The law was brought forward under conditions not friendly to fine distinctions,' Human Rights Watch says. 'With the country in turmoil, the state needed to vindicate both its religious rigour, against the burgeoning Muslim Brotherhood, and its nationalist credentials.'[57] The inclusion of *fujur*, and the consequent removal of any need to prove a monetary element allowed the law to be treated as criminalising the habitual 'practice of vice with others with no distinction'[58] and 'acts that could satisfy the lust of others directly with no distinction'[59] – an interpretation that amounts to outlawing not just prostitution but promiscuous and casual sex in general, with a jail sentence of up to three years as punishment. For a prosecution to succeed, these acts and practices are supposed to be 'habitual',[60] which has been interpreted by the courts as meaning acts committed more than once, with more than one person, within a three-year period. 'In practice,' Human Rights Watch notes, 'both habituality and the want of "distinction" are almost impossible to prove – a fact which does not stand in the way of prosecutions and convictions.'

Another part of the anti-prostitution law prescribes up to three years in jail for anyone who publishes 'an invitation which includes inducement to debauchery or prostitution'.[61] This – as well as sections of the Egyptian Criminal Code that prohibit advertisements 'violating public morals'[62] and the commission of 'scandalous' acts in public[63] – has been used to entrap men seeking to meet other men over the Internet. Typically, one or more of these charges would be deployed in combination with the core charge of habitual debauchery. Usefully for the police, the Criminal Code also states:

Whoever is found on a public road or a travelled and frequented place inciting the passers-by with signals or words to commit indecency shall be punished with imprisonment for a period not exceeding one month.[64]

This can be brought into play when a man who has been targeted on the Internet is lured by an undercover detective to a meeting and then arrested in the street. The police reports of such arrests follow a standard (and almost certainly fictitious) formula:

by the law for 'intercourse' is *mujaama'a* which, according to lawyer Nizar Saghieh of the Hurriyat Khassa (Private Rights) organisation, refers to acts of copulation.[67] Article 534, he says, is therefore intended to deal with anal intercourse, or sodomy, but its application has been extended by judges to include non-copulative acts such as fellatio, masturbation and even sex between lesbians. There have since been calls from some quarters to bring the law into line with the practice of the courts by changing *mujaama'a* to *'alaaqa jinsiyya* (sexual relations) – an even wider and more ambiguous term which would certainly include lesbians and conceivably same-sex kissing as well. Saghieh believes Article 534 might be rendered inoperative or at least severely limited in its scope by a successful challenge in court – 'We could claim that it's not unnatural and question the definition of copulation' – but so far there has not been a suitable test case. 'In general, cases are very rare and the law is not applied unless there are special circumstances, such as murder, theft, prostitution, drugs,' he said. 'It is difficult to campaign if murder, etc, is involved. We haven't had an exemplary case.'

The practice of invoking Article 534 against gay and lesbian people suspected of unrelated crimes is illustrated by a case in 2002 when police raided the home of a lesbian whose mother had filed a complaint accusing her of stealing the mother's jewellery – and found her with another woman.

According to judicial sources, the women, who were caught *in flagrante delicto*, confessed to having relations for several years and said they wished to be united in matrimony. The sources said the two also sought to have a test-tube baby together, and affirmed to Mount Lebanon assistant public prosecutor Shawki Hajjar that they would join each other once released from jail.[68]

To prevent any further sexual activity while in custody, prosecutor Hajjar gave special orders that each woman be held in a separate cell.

Although much is quietly tolerated in Lebanon, according to Saghieh such prosecutions are brought as a reminder that homosexuality is forbidden in law and 'to keep some taboo on it'. Using Article 534 selectively and in combination with other criminal charges encourages the idea that gay and lesbian people are generally dissolute. The Lebanese police seem less inclined than their Egyptian counterparts to go looking for gay people who might be prosecuted, but others sometimes do that job for them. In May 2003, Hizbullah, the militant Shi'a organisation, kidnapped five suspected gay men and handed them over to the police who duly arrested them,[69] and private homes have reportedly been raided following tip-offs from disapproving neighbours or vindictive acquaintances.[70] A senior vice squad officer stated in a magazine interview that the police also keep records of individuals who are believed to be gay or lesbian.[71]

As in Egypt, the Lebanese authorities have taken an interest in gay use of the Internet, though to far less effect. In April 2000, two plainclothes officers from the vice squad visited the offices of Destination, a Lebanese Internet service provider, inquiring about a website called gaylebanon.com. According to reports, the officers behaved in a high-handed manner, harassing staff and forbidding them to make any phone calls. The officers appeared confused about the workings of the Internet, initially believing that Destination had produced the website when in fact it was only hosting it. They then demanded the name of the site's owner and, after Destination refused, allegedly threatened to have the company closed down if the information was not provided within forty-eight hours. At the time of the police visit, gaylebanon.com appears to have been a new website, still under construction and with no actual content.

Shortly after this, Mirsad,[72] a Lebanese human rights organisation, sent out an email alert informing its members of the incident. Nothing much happened for almost a year, but then the director of Mirsad, Kamal Batal, and the owner of Destination, Ziad Mughraby, were summoned before a military tribunal, charged with 'tarnishing the reputation of the vice squad by distributing a printed flyer'. Their forty-minute trial was taken up mostly by lectures from Brigadier-General Maher Safieddine, head of the tribunal, to Mughraby on the evils of homosexuality, and to Batal on the shortcomings of human rights organisations. Although the 'printed flyer' at the centre of the case was not produced in evidence, Brigadier-General Safieddine found them both guilty and sentenced them to three months in jail. After some further deliberation, he reduced the sentences to one month and finally, after yet more deliberation, to a fine of 300,000 Lebanese pounds each (about $200).

The pair were astonished at their conviction, and though Mughraby was simply relieved at not having been sent to prison, Batal decided to appeal. It was only at this stage that the 'printed flyer' allegedly distributed by Batal and Mughraby finally surfaced in court and was found to be a computer print-out, made by one of the vice squad officers, of the email alert that Mirsad had circulated to its members. Following lengthy legal debate about what constituted 'distribution' and what could be considered a 'flyer', Batal's conviction was overturned. In the meantime, the original cause of all the fuss – the police investigation into gaylebanon.com – seems to have been forgotten.[73]

\* \* \*

THE NUMBER of people prosecuted or arrested for same-sex offences in the Arab world is almost impossible to determine. One of the few published figures relates to Lebanon in 1993 when, according to the police, sixty-eight people were arrested under Article 534, of whom twenty were minors.[74] It is not known how many of them were brought before the courts or convicted. This may seem a low figure (and the Lebanese authorities have a reputation for being relatively tolerant) but if Lebanon's small population is taken into account, the equivalent annual figure would be more than 1,300 for a country the size of Egypt and almost 5,400 for the United States. In Egypt, researchers for Human Rights Watch identified 179 men who were prosecuted for 'debauchery' during a period of slightly more than two years, between 2001 and 2003, but the organisation commented: 'In all probability that is only a minuscule percentage of the true total,' adding that hundreds of others had been harrassed, arrested and often tortured, but not charged.[75]

Nevertheless, anecdotal evidence from across the region suggests that on the whole, and with the exception of Egypt, prosecution rates are fairly low – at least in comparison with the 5,443 prosecutions that were recorded in England in the last year before the Wolfenden committee was set up. Even the

Egyptian witch-hunt at its peak does not appear to have come anywhere close to that figure. Though the lack of reliable statistics cautions against reaching firm conclusions, logic suggests that keeping prosecutions at a moderate level would suit Arab authorities best: enough to appease moral outrage and make an example of a few people, but not so many as to cast doubt on the public fiction that there is little or no homosexuality in the country. Large numbers of prosecutions, or prosecutions involving foreigners, also risk attracting international attention – something that Arab governments are clearly aware of and try to avoid. Several foreigners were present on the Queen Boat in Egypt when it was raided in 2001, but the police took no interest in them. In general, foreigners whose sexuality comes to the authorities' attention are more likely to be sent home than prosecuted. Bahrain and Qatar, for example, have both expelled large numbers of guest workers from the Philippines (where same-sex acts are legal). A news report in 1997, citing the Filipino embassy in Doha, mentioned thirty-seven expulsions from Qatar, while in 2002 some 2,000 Filipinos were reportedly forced to leave Bahrain following a crackdown on allegedly gay beauty salons, massage parlours, flower shops and clothes shops.[76]

To some extent, this comparatively restrained use of the laws against homosexuality makes it harder to campaign for their abolition. The more prosecutions there are (unfortunate as they may be for those prosecuted), the more the defects in the law become apparent. It was the zeal of a government minister who tried to stamp out homosexuality in the 1950s that brought matters to a head in Britain and inadvertently began the long process towards legalisation. In Britain, the issue was further highlighted by prosecutions of prominent people, but in Arab countries the likelihood of that is almost nil: should anyone important accidentally get arrested, the system of *wasta* – a quiet word in the right ear or a bribe to the right official – would normally ensure that the matter never came to court.

Regardless of how much laws against homosexuality are actually used, the case for abolishing them is simple and clear. They are a striking example of the general malaise that afflicts Arab legal systems. Legislating on personal behaviour just because many consider it sinful or repugnant is an archaic use of the law and, in the long run, is unworkable. For a host of practical reasons, such laws can never be effectively enforced. Unenforceable laws bring the legal system as a whole into disrepute and have no appreciable deterrent effect; for deterrence to work, there has to be a reasonably high chance of being caught. In Britain at the time of the Wolfenden report it was estimated, based on surveys of sexual behaviour, that for every homosexual act that came to the notice of the authorities about 30,000 others went undetected[77] – and there is no reason to suppose that the detection rate in Arab countries is any higher. In Britain it was also very doubtful whether those who had been fined or imprisoned changed their behaviour as a result – except, perhaps, by taking extra precautions against getting caught. Another practical difficulty is that homosexual acts, since they tend to be private and consensual, are almost impossible to prove in court on the basis of normal evidence. This has a corrupting effect on the police, who are then tempted to resort to other methods such as enforced confessions or entrapment (where no crime would have been committed if the police had not created the right conditions for it to happen).

Sometimes, as has been reported in Egypt and Palestine, the police do not prosecute but use the threat of prosecution to turn their suspects into informers.

Ill-conceived and unworkable though they are, laws that criminalise same-sex acts between consenting adults play an even more damaging role in setting the tone for society as a whole, providing a framework of legitimacy for acts of harassment or discrimination by individuals and institutions. There is thus no way that any country can meet the standards of tolerance and equality envisaged by the Universal Declaration of Human Rights while they remain on the statute books.

# FIVE

# 'Should I Kill Myself?'

'DEAR IMAM,' the letter begins, 'I fear Allah, and believe in him so strongly that I cry when I pray ... my problem is homosexuality.' The writer is seeking guidance as to whether he should kill himself. His letter, posted on the IslamiCity website,[1] continues:

> I pray to Allah that I am dead for having these uncontrollable feelings, I do not want to be gay, I try to change, but all this seem to be bryond [sic] my capability. For many years I've prayed to Allah to correct me, I really prayed very Sincerely with a clean heart, but I am only the same since I was a young boy ... If i ever commit an act with another man, should not I be killed? I must admit, i have, and I wish I am dead. In such a situation, (and since we do not live in a Muslim state where islamic law should be upheld) should I not kill myself and therefore [be] upholding the law and MAY BE getting forgiveness from Allah.. I know suicide is not allowed, but in a case like mine, and being well aware

of some islamic laws, shouldn't we have an exception and allow suicide?[2]

On the question of suicide at least, the advice from IslamiCity's imam is very clear. 'Two wrongs don't make one right,' he says. 'While homosexuality is wrong, it doesn't justify suicide under any conditions or circumstances.' But the imam has little to offer by way of help beyond urging repentance:

> What you should do is to truly repent to Allah, the Merciful, the Gracious, and pledge to Him never to get involved in any homosexual acts anymore. If medical or psychological counselling helps, then get it, but know that Allah is the Curer, and the Qur'an is your best companion. Give charity, pray, make *dua'*, and Allah will not leave you alone. You have got to believe in the infinite amount of Mercy Allah provides to His servants, and you should also realise that He forgives, if He wishes, all types of sins, except the sin of disbelieving in Him. Therefore, don't lose hope in Him and write us anytime you want ...

In reply to other questions, the imam says that homosexual feelings are not in themselves sinful. 'What is sinful in homosexuality is the actual sexual act between the couple of a similar sex.'[3] A person who feels attracted to someone of the same sex should keep quiet about it and also take the following action:

1. Ask God to help him/her to get rid of the feeling and overcome the problem,

2. Be patient and never get physically involved with a person other than his own wife (if he is a man) or her own husband (if it is a woman),

3. Seek medical advice to first diagnose the problem (whether physiological or psychological) and then correct it through appropriate means,

4. Seek religious help from a trusted and qualified imam if deemed necessary.[4]

This, broadly speaking, is as much support as a gay Muslim is likely to get from a mainstream Islamic scholar. IslamiCity's imam may be unrealistic in expecting that 'the problem' can be overcome with help from God and 'corrected' by medical intervention but his tone is calm and not unsympathetic. There are many others who take a much harder line, denouncing gay people as 'paedophiles and AIDS carriers' and likening homosexuality to alcoholism, drug addiction or a 'cancer tumour' that must be eradicated in order to preserve society.[5]

In contrast to IslamiCity, IslamOnline[6] describes homosexuality as 'the most heinous'[7] sin in Islam and 'one of the most abominable';[8] a sin so 'enormous in intensity and gravity' that it must be punished both in this life and the next.[9] These are not casually-aired views; they come with a stamp of religious authority. IslamOnline is one of the largest Muslim websites and to ensure that none of its content 'violates the fixed principles of Islamic law',[10] everything is vetted by a scholarly committee. The head of the committee is Yusuf al-Qaradawi, a popular and highly influential religious figure in the Arab world whose fame has been spread by regular appearances on al-Jazeera television. Born in 1926 in Egypt, where he was involved in the Muslim

Brotherhood, Qaradawi later became dean of the College of Shari'a and Islamic Studies at Qatar University. Among his numerous other roles, he is chairman of the European Council for Fatwa and Research, and an adviser on Islamic affairs for the Algerian government. Many of his *fatwas* (religious rulings) are published by IslamOnline.

In the West, Qaradawi is often described as an extremist. He has been banned from the United States since 1999 on the grounds that he advocates violence, and more recently has been accused of supporting suicide bombers.[11] A visit to Britain in 2004, when he was welcomed by the mayor of London, aroused much controversy, partly because of his opinions about homosexuality.[12] In the Arab world, however, he is regarded as relatively moderate. He condemned the September 11 attacks on the United States and urged all Muslims to donate blood to help the injured. During the Bahrain election in 2002 he issued a *fatwa* supporting the principle of female candidates – a ruling that was promptly declared un-Islamic by a Saudi scholar. In 2001 he opposed the destruction of Buddha statues by the Taliban regime in Afghanistan and was duly condemned for supporting 'idol worship'.[13] He also opposes discrimination between men and women in the payment of blood money (compensation when someone is killed). The usual practice is to treat the value of a woman's life as half that of a man, but he argues there is no basis in Islamic law for paying different amounts.[14]

Qaradawi's pronouncements are addressed primarily to a Middle Eastern audience and, contrary to perceptions in the West, are often aimed at tempering the most extreme forms of behaviour. One example is a *fatwa* which permits wife-beating, but only in moderation – thus discouraging the brutal domestic violence[15] that occurs in many Muslim countries:

> If the husband senses that feelings of disobedience and rebelliousness are rising against him in his wife, he should try his best to rectify her attitude by kind words, gentle persuasion and reasoning with her. If this is not helpful, he should sleep apart from her, trying to awaken her agreeable feminine nature so that serenity may be restored, and she may respond to him in a harmonious fashion. If this approach fails, it is permissible for him to beat her lightly with his hands, avoiding her face and other sensitive parts. In no case should he resort to using a stick or any other instrument that might cause pain and injury.[16]

Though Qaradawi favours a 'kind words' approach to dealing with disobedient wives, the same cannot be said of his attitude to homosexuality. 'This perverted act is a reversal of the natural order, a corruption of man's sexuality, and a crime against the rights of females,' he says in a *fatwa* for IslamOnline. 'The spread of this depraved practice in a society disrupts its natural life pattern and makes those who practise it slaves to their lusts, depriving them of decent taste, decent morals, and a decent manner of living.'[17]

In comparison with other Muslim websites, IslamOnline – under Qaradawi's supervision – talks about homosexuality rather a lot. It acknowledges that in doing so it is breaking a tradition of silence and explains why:

> Discussing the issue of homosexuality has been taboo in

most societies for ages. Being considered an act of sin by most cultures and religions, there had not seemed to be much that required discussion. In recent years, however, gay lobbies have cropped up in the West, and talk of 'coming out of the closet' has become commonplace. The pressure formed by these lobbies on political and legal institutions, the media, and society in general has resulted in a different definition and concept of homosexuality in the mindset of the common Westerner ... Groups of gay Muslims have also become more vocal and have been organising in an effort to convince themselves and others that there is no contradiction between being a Muslim and being a proclaimed homosexual.[18]

Noting that 'sometimes evil is spread through discussion', one of the website's muftis initially sounds uneasy about bringing the subject into the open. When people hear a sinful act mentioned repeatedly, he says, 'they get used to it and then slowly it loses its gravity in their minds and souls.' But on balance he concludes that silence is increasingly impractical. 'Nowadays this act has become a phenomenon. There are agencies and lobby groups that are working hard to propagate it and to make it an acceptable and legitimate lifestyle. For this reason it is important that we should speak against it.'[19]

In deciding to talk about homosexuality, then, IslamOnline is not merely offering moral guidance but campaigning against a supposed threat from Western liberal values and from subversive fifth-columnists who call themselves gay Muslims. The result is what might be described as a neo-Islamic view in which the usual religious distinction between forbidden deeds and permitted feelings becomes blurred: as described by IslamOnline, homosexuality is both a 'perverted act' and a 'devilish lifestyle'. Qaradawi spells this out clearly when he writes: 'Almighty Allah has prohibited illegal sexual intercourse and homosexuality and *all means that lead to either of them*' [my italics] – a phrase that dramatically extends the boundaries of forbidden territory.[20] Thus, in the words of IslamOnline, homosexuality is not just 'a prohibited act' but 'an assault on the humanity of a person, destruction of the family, and a clash with the aims of the Divine Legislator, one of which is the establishment of sexual instincts between males and females so as to encourage the institution of marriage and procreation.'[21] Muslims who experience same-sex attractions therefore have no alternative but to try to acquire the right instincts and become heterosexual: 'It is their responsibility to know how they can orient this craving.'[22]

Furthermore, people who experience same-sex attractions are blamed not only for what they do, or might do, but also for what they don't do in terms of fulfilling their duty to help populate the world. Since marriage 'is a means for the survival of humankind',[23] homosexuality is 'a fierce attack on progeny and pregnancy, which increases the human race'.[24] It is also described as a 'crime' against the rights of women (presumably by depriving them of the opportunity to become pregnant). 'The same applies equally to the case of lesbianism,' Qaradawi says.[25] For good measure, IslamOnline adds that homosexuality destroys the morality of the younger generation, destroys the lives of women 'whose husbands leave them in pursuit of this perversion' and causes dangerous diseases that are 'unavoidable and fatal'.[26]

In the light of this, it is natural that readers of IslamOnline should wonder how to react in the event that they meet someone of a homosexual disposition. One questioner is advised:

> Those who insist on this lifestyle, consider it legitimate and feel 'gay pride', we should not associate with them and should not take them as friends. We should certainly avoid those people.[27]

A further reply, to a question about gay and lesbian Muslim organisations, says:

> The Muslim needs to take precautions against these deviants and not to give them any opportunity to mix with and corrupt their children. Furthermore, they are neither fit to establish *masajid* [mosques] and frequent them, nor are they fit to lead those who frequent the *masjid* whomever they may be. More importantly for them is to seek a cure for themselves from their own illness ... [28]

To support the argument that homosexuality and 'all means' that lead to it are sinful, IslamOnline claims that sexual orientation is a choice – and therefore something that can be corrected. For a man who 'was sexually abused in his childhood and now ... only likes sex with males', it recommends the following simple treatment:

> If he is a Muslim, he is left with no choice but to change ... Let him convince himself that the pleasure that he derives from such an abominable behaviour is in reality nothing but pain and suffering in the long term. So instead of associating this behaviour with pleasure, let him learn to associate and

link it with pain; so every time he is tempted to do it, let him picture the pain and suffering of hell-fire. By repeatedly going through this exercise, he will eventually come to abhor and shun this behaviour altogether.[29]

In the absence of grateful testimonials on the effectiveness of this remedy, IslamOnline turns for additional support to the National Association for Research and Therapy of Homosexuality (Narth), a fringe psychiatric organisation in the United States which promotes 'sexual reorientation therapy'.[30] Although Narth's approach has some backing from Christian and Jewish conservatives in the US, it is rejected by all the main professional bodies,[31] including the American Psychological Association (150,000 members) and the American Psychiatric Association (35,000 members) – both of which removed homosexuality from their lists of recognised mental disorders in the 1970s and now regard efforts to 'cure' it as liable to do more harm than good. The American Psychological Association states:

> Human beings cannot choose to be either gay or straight. Sexual orientation emerges for most people in early adolescence without any prior sexual experience. Although we can choose whether to act on our feelings, psychologists do not consider sexual orientation to be a conscious choice that can be voluntarily changed ...
>
> Even though most homosexuals live successful, happy lives, some homosexual or bisexual people may seek to change their sexual orientation through therapy, sometimes pressured by the influence of family members or religious groups to try and do so. The reality is that homosexuality

is not an illness. It does not require treatment and is not changeable ...

Some therapists who undertake so-called conversion therapy report that they have been able to change their clients' sexual orientation from homosexual to heterosexual. Close scrutiny of these reports however show[s] several factors that cast doubt on their claims. For example, many of the claims come from organisations with an ideological perspective which condemns homosexuality. Furthermore, their claims are poorly documented. For example, treatment outcome is not followed and reported over time as would be the standard to test the validity of any mental health intervention. The American Psychological Association is concerned about such therapies and their potential harm to patients.[32]

Conveniently for IslamOnline, the theories and therapies favoured by Narth meet its ideological needs. In a series of articles under the heading 'Homosexuality in a Changing World: Are We Being Misinformed?', the website's health and science editor, Dr Nadia el-Awady, looks at the development of sexual orientation, research into homosexuality, therapy, etc, in what is described as 'an Islamic and a scientific light'.[33] Adopting 'the fact' that homosexuality is a matter of choice as their premise,[34] the articles rely almost exclusively on material from Narth and its supporters. There are no fewer than twenty-six links from Dr Awady's articles to Narth's website, and just one each to the websites of the American Psychological Association and the American Psychiatric Association. A news item subsequently posted on Narth's website reciprocates; it notes the 'rather comprehensive' psychological and scientific studies quoted by IslamOnline and welcomes its 'very useful contribution to the on-going dialogue'.[35] Readers of Dr Awady's articles, if they are unfamiliar with the debate in the United States, might easily form the impression that Narth reflects the scientific consensus while the mainstream professional bodies are mere dissenters, but Dr Awady brushes their views aside by regurgitating Narth's claim that they have simply caved in to pressure from gay activists.[36]

* * *

HOMOSEXUALITY is not the only facet of human nature that troubles Islamic scholars. Another is left-handedness, which some regard as an evil habit that is contrary to 'the laws of Islam'. Like homosexuality, left-handedness affects a minority of the population – around ten percent on average – and nobody knows the cause, but it occurs naturally in some people and is not a matter of choice. Needless to say (for reasons that will be discussed in the next chapter), scholarly reactions to left-handedness often echo the reactions to homosexuality. Replying to the concerned relative of a child who shows signs of being left-handed, Sheikh Muhammad Salih al-Munajid[37] begins:

Doing good is a habit and doing evil is a habit ... When a person gets used to doing something, he becomes very fond of it and loves it, and dislikes anything else. Then he thinks that the thing he is not used to is not possible, but this way of thinking is not right and it goes against both the laws of Islam and the facts of reality.[38]

Sheikh Munajid (a government-employed cleric in Saudi Arabia who was trained by the kingdom's late grand mufti, Abd al-Aziz bin Baaz) continues in a familiar vein, citing various *ahadith*. Satan eats and drinks with his left hand, the sheikh says, and people who don't eat and drink with their right hand are therefore emulating Satan. Sheikh Munajid also recounts the tale of a man who was ordered by the Prophet to eat with his right hand. The man said: 'I cannot' – to which the Prophet replied: 'May you never be able to!' Munajid continues: 'Nothing was stopping him but his stubborn arrogance, and he never raised his right hand to his mouth after that ... This man suffered paralysis because of the *du'aa'* of the Prophet (peace and blessings of Allaah be upon him).'

Sheikh Munajid then provides the left-handed child's relative with the standard advice that Islamic scholars give for curing homosexuality, masturbation and a host of other personal 'problems'. Make the boy change his ways or seek medical help:

> Try to get him used to eating with his right hand and keep on advising him and reminding him to do so. You could seek the help of psychiatrists, because some of them may have some useful ideas. We ask Allaah to give you strength.

This is undoubtedly bad advice. Trying to 'cure' left-handedness in children is potentially harmful, with a risk of causing psychological and emotional problems. Experts nowadays urge parents and teachers not to fight left-handedness but to help children overcome any difficulties that result from it.[39]

Beliefs that left is bad and right is good are extremely old. They can be found in numerous religions and cultures, and certainly pre-date Islam. Many languages have negative words associated with the left and positive words associated with the right; the English word 'sinister', for example, is derived from the Latin for 'left'. Similar associations can be found in the Bible – 'The right hand of the Lord is exalted: the right hand of the Lord doeth valiantly,'[40] etc. On the Day of Judgement the good will be placed on the right-hand side and the bad on the left:

> Then shall he say also unto them on the left hand, Depart from me, ye cursed, into everlasting fire, prepared for the devil and his angels.[41]

By tradition, Christian artists of the Middle Ages depicted Satan as left-handed, and left-handed people were often suspected of sorcery or witchcraft. Well into the last century, Roman Catholic schools punished children who attempted to write with their left hands.[42] Early Muslims adopted the ancient beliefs about left and right and turned them to practical use: the right hand was for 'honourable' purposes, such as eating, while the left was reserved for non-'honourable' purposes, such as wiping private parts of the body after excretion. In an age when effective washing was often impossible, the rule helped to improve levels of hygiene.[43] Today, with higher standards of cleanliness in many parts of the world, the left-right distinction is less important than it was in the time of the Prophet. Today we also have a better understanding of left-handedness and the hazards of trying to 'correct' it. While some Muslims cling rigidly to the old ways, others are more flexible. IslamiCity's website, for example, offers reassurance to a twelve-year-old who has been told he will go to hell for eating and writing with his left hand:

> Let me tell you straight away that no one will go to hell for using his left hand for eating, drinking, writing or indeed for any other purpose. Any one who suggests otherwise does not know and ... betrays a degree of ignorance of God, His compassion and fairness ... A left-handed person does not choose to make his right hand the weaker hand. This is something that he is created with and cannot change, just like the colour of his eyes or his hair ...
>
> If you find it too difficult [to use your right hand], then you should not bother about what people may say. You just explain that this is a natural difficulty and that it is God who created you so.[44]

Here, for once, is a compassionate face of Islam – a face that is rarely seen among the grim strictures and warnings on Muslim websites. IslamiCity does not make the obvious connection, but with a little adaptation it is easy to see how the imam's advice might be applied in other circumstances:

> Let me tell you straight away that no one will go to hell for being gay. Any one who suggests otherwise does not know and ... betrays a degree of ignorance of God, His compassion and fairness ... A gay person does not choose to be attracted to people of his own sex. This is something that he is created with and cannot change, just like the colour of his eyes or his hair ...

If you find it too difficult [to be straight], then you should not bother about what people may say. You just explain that this is a natural difficulty and that it is God who created you so.

\* \* \*

IN THEIR condemnations of homosexuality, IslamOnline, Yusuf al-Qaradawi and others clearly tap into a populist vein, harnessing existing prejudices for a supposedly Islamic cause. Whether they have given serious thought to the implications of their attitude, or how it squares with Islamic teaching on other matters, is doubtful. IslamOnline's views on homosexuality contrast sharply with its more temperate approach to adultery, for example. In answer to a man who is thinking of divorcing his wife on grounds of adultery, IslamOnline cautions against precipitate action. A better solution, it says, is for the wife to repent and for the husband to forgive her: 'To forgive is better.'[45] Although Islamic scholars usually equate sodomy with adultery,[46] there is no suggestion here that an adulterous wife is depraved, corrupted by Western deviants or likely to spread fatal diseases.

Aside from the purely religious issues, IslamOnline's factual assertions about the nature of sexual orientation are problematic. In order to claim that sexual orientation is a choice it allies itself with some highly questionable scientific theories. Its moral arguments therefore rest on the hope that these theories will not, at some point in the future, be conclusively disproved. Paradoxically, despite its generalised disapproval of 'the West',

IslamOnline shows no hesitation in basing a crucial element of its case against homosexuality on the views of conservative American Christians.

Claiming that sexual orientation is a choice – and a choice that can be reversed – removes any need for tolerance or compassion towards people who are homosexual: it's simply their fault. Those who insist on pursuing 'this lifestyle' should be avoided, IslamOnline says. In addition, 'the Muslim needs to take precautions against these deviants and not to give them any opportunity to mix with and corrupt their children.' That is a clear invitation to discriminate in employment and education – for example, by refusing to have Muslim children taught by a gay or lesbian teacher. Besides conflicting with a key principle of the Universal Declaration of Human Rights, in some countries it could also bring Muslims into direct conflict with anti-discrimination laws.

One Muslim organisation that takes issue with this approach is the Straightway Foundation.[47] 'Condemning and insulting these people will not help,' Straightway's chairman, Mujahid Mustaqim, writes in a critique of IslamOnline's articles about homosexuality.[48] He continues: 'We know that Allah does not punish people on the basis of their temptations or simply due to the way they are. Rather, He judges mankind based on what they do ... Even many of the most learned people seem to have missed the point somewhat, which is why their answers to questions about homosexuality often seem to be harsh or unfeeling.'

Straightway also rejects IslamOnline's claim that people can choose their sexuality:

... surely it cannot be described as a choice. People are free, of course, to choose whether or not to perform various actions. We must acknowledge that the vast majority of people who feel same-sex attractions do not do so out of any choice. If anything, most of them would much prefer *not* to feel that way.[49]

Straightway, as its name suggests, shares IslamOnline's belief that same-sex acts are sinful and should be avoided, but it differs from IslamOnline in rejecting the term 'homosexuality', on the grounds that it is un-Islamic. Instead, it insists on maintaining the traditional Islamic distinction between acts and what it refers to as 'same-sex attractions', or SSAs. 'Muslims who have SSAs should understand that Satan is working on them, and inviting them to sin,' it says. 'They should reject his call and turn to Allah. Surely He is the best guide.' Straightway's emphasis, therefore, is on helping Muslims with SSAs to avoid sinful acts rather than passing judgement. Some Muslims who describe themselves as gay agree with this argument; they accept that they can never express their feelings sexually without sin, and regard it as a test of their faith. Others disagree and ask what harm is done if two people come together in private for mutual pleasure and affection. One letter sent to Straightway and posted on its website says:

I am muslim and I am gay ... and I have no desire to change either ... I challenge you to show me why you believe someone who is gay should try to be straight ... whose benefit does it serve? sex is a natural outlet as is masturbation ... as long as its consensual an not forced as in rape then for me its whats in the heart that matters ... and the love in my heart is not brought from something evil but from something good ...[50]

Straightway's answer is that consenting adults need God's consent, too. There is good reasoning behind every divine command or prohibition, it says, though 'we do not necessarily know what the reasoning is.' This, of course, assumes that the religious rules themselves are clear and universally agreed – which, in many cases, they are not. They are the result of scholarly interpretations that often vary in their application of *shari'a* principles and are inevitably coloured to some extent by perceptions of what the *umma* (the community of believers) regards as acceptable conduct.

Muslim discussion of homosexuality often refers vaguely to 'sinful acts'. In the minds of most people, this means anal intercourse. For a fuller picture, however, it is necessary to examine what contemporary scholars say about a variety of practices that may be relevant to same-sex behaviour. The brief survey that follows is not an attempt to provide definitive *shari'a* answers but merely to reflect commonly-held views and explain some of the reasoning behind them. In most cases scholars are concerned with the sinfulness or otherwise of the acts themselves, regardless of whether they occur in a heterosexual or homosexual context. Underlying the quotations from the Qur'an and the *hadith,* two general principles guide much of the discussion. One is the importance attached to the procreative function of sex: acts that cannot lead to pregnancy meet with suspicion or outright disapproval. The other principle is that sexual activity should take place within a formalised framework. Nowadays that means marriage, though historically sex has also been permitted within certain other contractual relationships, for example between a man and his female slaves.

*Kissing:* Although kissing between unrelated members of the opposite sex is generally forbidden, same-sex kissing is allowed so long as it is done without 'lust' and has no sexual significance. It is 'reprehensible' to kiss someone on the mouth, even without lust; the preferred places are the hand or forehead. Scholars sometimes refer to a *hadith* in which the Prophet is said to have greeted a man, Ja'far ibn Abi Talib, by kissing him between the eyes. IslamOnline cites a ruling by Sheikh Atiyyah Saqr, former head of al-Azhar Fatwa Committee in Egypt:

> There is nothing wrong with kissing between the members of the same sex, like men with men and women with women, on two conditions:
>
> 1. There is no chance for any temptation.
> 2. It is not done for an invalid purpose like kissing the hands of the wicked people with the purpose of showing respect to them.[51]

*Masturbation:* Masturbation is an indecent practice that has 'crept into the youngsters of today', the Inter-Islam website says. It blames the prevalence of masturbation on a tendency to marry later (contrary to the advice of the Prophet), with the result that young people feel a need 'to fulfil their carnal desires but... cannot do so in the normal way, i.e. sexual intercourse'.[52] Numerous Muslim websites assert that masturbation is forbidden. 'Islam strictly forbids the waste of seminal fluid through masturbation,' one says. 'This evil practice removes the normal bright look of a man's face, and he looks melancholy and dejected. He loses his health and quite frequently his vitality and sexual stamina through this disgusting practice.'[53] Islamic Voice describes it as an 'abominable and wicked act' which is forbidden in Islam. 'Its harms are great and it has disastrous consequences as established by doctors.'[54]

Many of these websites state that masturbation causes medical problems; those most frequently mentioned are damage to eyesight and the sexual organs. Several give identical lists of 'proven' medical effects which include disruption of the digestive system, inflammation of the testicles, damage to the spine ('the place from which sperm originates'), and 'trembling and instability in some parts of the body like the feet'. In addition, they say, there is a weakening of the 'cerebral glands' leading to decreased intellect and even 'mental disorders and insanity'. Furthermore, 'due to constant ejaculation, the sperm no more remains thick and dense as it normally occurs in males.'[55] This results in sperm which is not 'mighty enough' to make a woman pregnant or produces children who are 'more prone to disease and illness'. The source of all this medical information, according to Islamic Voice, is Abd al-Aziz bin Baz, the late Grand Mufti of Saudi Arabia.[56]

The grounds usually cited for prohibiting masturbation in Islamic law derive from a passage in the Qur'an which describes believers as those:

> ... who guard their modesty – save from their wives or the [slaves] that their right hands possess, for then they are not blameworthy. But who so craveth beyond that, such are transgressors.[57]

Opinions of scholars differ as to what the phrase 'who so craveth beyond that' means. Some think it refers to extra-marital sex (i.e. adultery) and some interpret it more broadly to include masturbation. Between those two viewpoints, others argue that masturbation is basically forbidden but may be permissible if the person is unmarried or masturbates in order to avoid a more serious sin such as adultery, or if the masturbation is to release 'sexual tension' rather than to fulfil 'sexual desire'. In a *fatwa* for IslamOnline, Sheikh Mustafa al-Zarqa says:

> I conclude that the general principles of *shari'a* go against this habit, because it is not the normal way of fulfilling sexual desire; however it is a deviation – and that is enough to condemn it, even though this act does not fall under the category of absolute prohibition.[58]

IslamOnline's 'cure' for masturbation is remarkably similar to its 'cure' for homosexuality. In reply to a new Muslim convert who asks for help with an addiction to pornography and masturbation, it tells him to seek counselling and therapy and suggests a few self-help remedies too:

> Visualize and meditate on the ugliness of this heinous sin and conjure up images of hell fire as painted in the Qur'an and the Sunnah as many times as possible until such time that whenever you are tempted to ... read such magazines, the scenes of hell fire will be playing in your mind. Thus, even as you have associated this addiction with pleasure, you will come to associate it with pure pain and suffering.
>
> Imagine how terrible a loss you will be facing were you to die while being addicted to this most heinous sin.

Schedule your time in such a way that you are never left with any time to think of such matters ...

Always hang around with good Muslims who are busy doing good works; join a *halaqah* (study circle) where spiritual training is imparted together with the study of Islam.

Once you have been weaned of these pernicious habits, you should seriously consider marriage; marriage is the protection against temptations.[59]

*Oral sex:* Asked to give a ruling on oral sex, Yusuf al-Qaradawi begins by describing it as a disgusting Western practice, resulting from Westerners' habit of 'stripping naked during sexual intercourse' but he continues:

Muslim jurists are of the opinion that it is lawful for the husband to perform cunnilingus on his wife, or a wife to perform the similar act for her husband (fellatio) and there is no wrong in doing so. But if sucking leads to releasing semen, then it is *makruh* (blameworthy), but there is no decisive evidence (to forbid it) ... especially if the wife agrees with it or achieves orgasm by practising it.[60]

This relatively permissive view is contradicted by several other scholars on the Internet. One states plainly that oral sex is forbidden, adding that 'this hideous practice will draw the anger of Allah.'[61] Another, asked if oral sex is permitted, replies: 'I don't know what oral sex is, please define it.'[62]

*Anal sex:* According to Grand Ayatollah Ali Sistani, the highest-ranking Shi'a cleric in Iraq, anal sex between a husband and wife is permissible if the wife agrees, but it is 'strongly undesirable'.[63] The idea that it is a matter for mutual consent seems to be quite widespread, though many Sunni clerics insist that consent is irrelevant. 'Anal sex is a grave sin and is completely forbidden, regardless of whether the wife agrees to it or not,' one says. 'The futile excuse of it being better than a contraceptive doesn't carry any weight. If you are justified in using a contraceptive, then there are many different options on the market which could be adopted, instead of this hideous practice.'[64]

Although there are several *ahadith* in which the Prophet is reported to have forbidden anal sex within marriage, there is no indisputably clear prohibition in the Qur'an itself. Scholars often quote an obscure – and much debated – verse which says:

Your women are a tilth for you (to cultivate) so go to your tilth as ye will, and send (good deeds) before you for your souls, and fear Allah, and know that ye will (one day) meet Him. Give glad tidings to believers, (O Muhammad).[65]

IslamOnline says the word 'tilth' (arable land; *harth* in Arabic) indicates that 'only vaginal sex is permissible in Islam, because it is from this place that children are produced. The semen lodged in the womb from which offspring comes is likened to the seeds that are planted in the ground, bringing vegetation.'[66] IslamOnline adds that 'it is allowed to caress the wife and stimulate her around the anus, without having sex in this area'. Some go further and suggest that only insertion of the penis is forbidden – which would allow fingers, for example, to be inserted. IslamOnline continues:

If one does have anal sex with his wife, he has committed a grave sin, which requires repentance. He should regret and feel contrite for committing such a sin. Allah Almighty destroyed a whole nation who were accustomed to this evil habit.

But, the wife is not considered divorced as many people think, because there is no evidence to support this view. However, scholars maintain that if a man habitually does this or insists on having anal sex with his wife, she has the right to ask for a divorce, because he is considered an evil-doer who is causing harm by his action, and also because the purpose of marriage cannot be achieved through this action.[67]

Although several websites refer to the anus as an unclean part of the body, the main religious objection to anal intercourse is that it is a non-procreative act. It cannot lead to the birth of children and, if performed repeatedly as an alternative to vaginal intercourse, frustrates what is viewed as the main purpose of marriage.

*Cross-dressing:* In a much-quoted *hadith*, the Prophet is said to have cursed men who imitate women and women who imitate men. 'Aspects of such imitation include the manner of speaking, walking, dressing, moving, and so on,' according to IslamOnline. This not only appears to rule out cross-dressing but also camp mannerisms by gay men and butch mannerisms by lesbians. Islamic scholars often extend the rule further to include male use of 'feminine' adornments such as neck-chains, bracelets and earrings.[68] Segregation of the sexes, as practised to varying degrees in Muslim societies, is one way of preventing illicit sexual contacts, and the prohibition of cross-dressing should perhaps be viewed in that context: a man who disguises as a woman, or vice versa, is presumed to be up to mischief.

*Gender reassignment:* Transgender issues have not received much attention from Islamic scholars, though obviously the rulings on cross-dressing are relevant.[69] Traditionalist ideas about segregating the sexes result in a bizarre situation in the case of a *khuntha* (a hermaphrodite, or person of indeterminate gender) where, according to a former Grand Sheikh of al-Azhar, such people must not mingle with either sex:

> Among the religious rulings pertaining to the hermaphrodite is the one stating that a hermaphrodite is not allowed to mix with women, due to the fact that the gender has not been determined yet. The same thing explains the reason why it is not allowed for a hermaphrodite to mix with men. In case a hermaphrodite is in one place with women, he [*sic*] should be placed in front of them while when with men, he is to sit behind them.[70]

The ruling goes on to suggest that this should be a temporary measure 'until after medication, carried out by a Muslim and competent doctor, which will determine his/her sex'.

There are differing scholarly opinions about gender reassignment ('sex change') operations, and debate hinges mainly on whether they amount to 'changing' the way a person was created by God or carrying out a 'correction'. The absence of a clear religious consensus on this seems to allow some flexibility. In 2004, *Arab News* reported that five Saudi sisters were undergoing operations to become men at King Abdul Aziz University Hospital in Jeddah. Three of the operations had already been completed when the story became public. According to *Arab News,* the surgeon in charge insisted on describing the procedure as 'gender correction'. 'We are taking the person back to his or her original sex according to the intensive tests that are done, but we will not operate on people ... to change them to the opposite sex just because they want to,' he said.[71] In Arab countries children are sometimes wrongly registered as male or female. The doctor explained that this can happen if the external organs are not fully developed and unqualified midwives assisting at home births 'misinterpret' a baby's gender.

Another reported case involved Hiba, a thirty-three-year-old Syrian woman who had been raised as a male. 'I discovered at eighteen that I was incapable of any male sexual behaviour and I was deeply embarrassed by the girls who looked at me with pity and preferred to stay away,' she said. 'I took poison several times and tried to drown myself.' When her father threw her out of the house in 1997, Imad (the male name by which she was known at the time) tried to start a new life in a Gulf Arab country but was jailed for homosexual activity. Later, on the advice of an Iraqi cleric, she had medical tests which confirmed that she was predominantly female and an operation was performed. 'I now live in peace with myself,' she said, though only her mother had accepted the transformation. The rest of the family had rejected her.[72]

In predominantly Shi'a Iran, although gender reassignment/correction operations were frowned upon in the early years of the Islamic revolution, they are not at all uncommon nowadays. A BBC television programme in 2005 reported that the leading surgeon in the field, Bahram Mirjalali, had done 320 operations in Iran during the previous twelve years.[73] A philanthropic organisation known as the Imam Khomeini Charity Foundation also reportedly provides loans equivalent to about $1,200 to help pay for surgery.[74] The comparatively liberal attitude of the Iranian clergy is mainly due to a ruling by the late Ayatollah Khomeini, the spiritual leader of the 1979 revolution, that transgender issues should not be confused with homosexuality and that operations were permissible. One of the few religious experts on transsexuality is Hojatulislam Muhammad Kariminia, who wrote his doctoral thesis on the implications of sex-change operations for Islamic law – with full approval from the clerics at his seminary in Qom. The legal questions he has addressed include whether married people need permission from their spouse before a sex change operation, whether a marriage is automatically annulled afterwards and what should happen to the wife's dowry money or inheritance rights if she becomes a man. 'I want to suggest that the right of transsexuals to change their gender is a human right,' Kariminia told the BBC.[75] In most Muslim countries, though, an operation is often only the first of many hurdles: insults, rejection by relatives, and problems obtaining legal recognition of the change of gender may follow.[76]

PROMINENT Islamic scholars who go out of their way to urge tolerance of sexual diversity are extremely rare. In 2000, Zaki

Badawi, head of the Muslim College in London, took the radical step of agreeing to be interviewed by *Gay Times*. 'Homosexuality has always existed and continues to exist in all Islamic countries,' he told the magazine. 'Many high-ranking leaders in the Islamic world are gay.'[77] Recalling the film, *My Beautiful Laundrette*,[78] which portrays a love affair between a British-Asian Muslim and his white boyfriend, he described it as 'a useful reminder to the Muslim community that they cannot simply sweep gays and lesbians under the carpet'.

Badawi's comments reflected a more liberal attitude sometimes found among Muslims living in the diaspora. Critics accuse them of succumbing to Western influence, but the reality is that they have more of a vested interest in tolerance than their brethren in the traditional Arab-Islamic heartland. In countries where Islam is dominant, there is less need to grapple with the challenges of diversity that diaspora Muslims face, so the focus is on maintaining religious 'purity', often by enforcing compliance with whatever 'correct' interpretation of Islam prevails locally. This tends to breed intolerance – of other Islamic interpretations, of other religions, and of non-conformism in general. A textbook for six-year-olds, introduced by the Saudi education ministry in 2003 as part of its newly 'reformed' curriculum stated: 'All religions other than Islam are false,' and a note for teachers added that they should 'ensure to explain' this point.[79] An earlier textbook for teenagers had instructed children not to befriend Christians or Jews: 'Emulation of the infidels leads to loving them, glorifying them and raising their status in the eyes of the Muslim, and that is forbidden.'

For Muslims in the diaspora – or at least the more astute members of their communities – such views are not only offensive but hopelessly unrealistic. Unless diaspora Muslims want to cut themselves off from the life that goes on around them, they have to come to terms with other religions and other ways of thinking. In countries where Muslims form a minority, liberal values such as tolerance, diversity, pluralism, freedom of expression, freedom of worship, etc, are not threats to their Islamic identity but a means for preserving it. In the diaspora, of course, Muslims are one minority among many (including sexual minorities) and tolerance for one requires tolerance for all. In his *Gay Times* interview, Badawi criticised several British Muslim organisations that had campaigned against homosexuality. 'In Britain,' he said, 'we Muslims are in a minority, and it should not be our task to encourage intolerance towards other minorities.'[80]

Some Muslims, meanwhile, prefer to join forces with intolerant Westerners in pursuit of common goals. IslamOnline quotes a ruling by Sheikh Faysal Mawlawi, deputy chairman of the European Council for Fatwa and Research, that Muslims in the diaspora can collaborate with non-Muslims on issues that are consistent with Islamic law, such as 'banning' homosexuality:

A Muslim living in the West can call for anything that benefits the whole society such as banning abortion, homosexuality and lesbianism or the like since such matters are prohibited in Islam and there are people among Westerners themselves calling for banning such matters.[81]

Another of IslamOnline's scholars, Sheikh Ahmad Kutty,[82] goes further and says that working with non-Muslims to make the streets 'free' from homosexuality is a religious duty:

It is important for us Muslims to join with our fellow citizens in all laudable and beneficial projects that are intended for the betterment of the country and people. To do so is not only our duty as citizens but a religious duty since, as Muslims, we must always serve as instruments of goodness, mercy and compassion to all people and to all of Allah's creation. Among such noble and laudable projects we can include the following: working to eradicate poverty and homelessness; to save the children; to make our streets free of drugs, alcoholism, prostitution and homosexuality ... We must never have any hesitation or reservation about cooperating with our non-Muslim neighbours for such causes.[83]

This is more than just rhetoric. The power of Muslim countries to block progressive social measures at an international level was amply demonstrated by their filibuster at the UN Commission on Human Rights in 2003 [see Chapter 4], and Christian conservatives, especially in the United States, have been quick to spot the value of Muslim support. The idea of forging an international Christian-Muslim alliance to oppose liberal social policies began to develop in 1996 when an event known to conservative activists as the Istanbul Miracle occurred. It happened at a UN conference in Turkey called Habitat Two. Richard Wilkins (now head of the Mormons' World Family Policy Center) was there and, according to his own account, helped to initiate the miracle:

The Istanbul conference was convened in large measure by a worldwide, well-organised and well-funded coalition of governments, politicians, academicians and non-governmental organisations that were eager to redefine marriage and family life. Natural marriage, based on the union of a man and a woman, was described by professors, politicians and pundits as an institution that oppressed and demeaned women. The constant claim was that 'various forms of the family exist', and all these 'various forms' were entitled to 'legal support'. The 'form' most often discussed by those in charge of the conference was a relationship between two individuals of the same gender.[84]

Wilkins challenged all this with a four-minute speech on traditional family values which also castigated sex education in schools. He was hissed by some of the delegates as he returned to his seat but afterwards, he recalled, 'I was approached by the ambassador from Saudi Arabia who embraced me warmly.' Wilkins gave the Saudi ambassador a list of suggested changes to the draft Habitat agenda, and the Istanbul Miracle was born. 'Thirty-six hours later, the heads of the Arab delegations in Istanbul issued a joint statement, announcing ... that its members would not sign the Habitat agenda unless (and until) certain important changes were made,' Wilkins wrote. As a result, the draft was altered to define marriage as a relationship between husband and wife, and references to 'abortion' were changed to 'reproductive health'.[85]

International arguments about 'the family' have raged ever since. The UN has said several times that 'in different cultural, political and social systems, various forms of family exist'. This is a statement of fact as much as anything, but it is anathema to religious conservatives who dislike the idea of unmarried couples living together, and especially those of the same gender.

The UN points out that ideas of what a family is have changed over the last fifty years. Worldwide, there has been a shift from extended families to nuclear families as well as an increase in the number of cohabiting couples and one-person households. Family structures have also been changed by lower fertility rates, higher life expectancy, migration and, especially in Africa, HIV/AIDS. The UN therefore urges its members to take these changes into account when developing social policies.

In November 2004, the government of Qatar organised a conference in Doha, ostensibly to celebrate the tenth anniversary of the UN's Year of the Family. In reality, it brought together some of the world's most conservative religious forces. Besides Yusuf al-Qaradawi, the supervisor of IslamOnline, those attending included Cardinal Alfonso Trujillo, who campaigns against condoms on behalf of the Catholic church, similarly-minded Christians from several countries, Richard Wilkins, the Istanbul miracle-worker (together with other representatives of the Mormon church) and Mahathir Mohamad, the dictatorial former prime minister of Malaysia who sacked and jailed his deputy for alleged homosexuality. Opening the conference, Sheikha Mousa bint Nasser al-Misnad, the wife of Qatar's ruler, announced that the well-being of the family was in peril and warned against trying to 'redefine the concept of family in a manner contrary to religious precepts'.

In preparation for its family conference, the government of Qatar appointed the World Family Policy Center to arrange a series of preliminary meetings in Mexico City, Sweden, Geneva, Kuala Lumpur, Manila and Strasbourg 'to collect the best scholarship on the current state of marriage and family life' and make recommendations. The conference website[86] gave few clues about the organisation that had been assigned to this important task beyond saying it was based in Utah – though the World Family Policy Center is actually an offshoot of Brigham Young University, run by the Church of Jesus Christ of Latter-Day Saints (the Mormons).

IslamOnline gave extensive coverage to the Doha conference without mentioning the Mormon connection. Its website also has a special section called 'The Family Under Attack' where it makes common cause with various Catholic groups and United Families International, an American organisation which preaches sexual abstinence to the AIDS-hit countries of Africa and blames condoms and sex education for the spread of HIV.

The government of Qatar followed up its Doha conference by submitting a conservative resolution on the family to the UN General Assembly. Behind the scenes, Wilkins was working miracles once again, organising an email campaign to persuade UN delegations to accept it. 'Even though it was over the weekend, with only one day's notice, you responded by sending more than 70,000 emails,' the Mormon magazine, *Meridian*, informed its readers.[87]

The resolution was approved by the General Assembly without a vote, much to the dismay of the European countries and several others. The EU, Norway, Switzerland, Canada, Australia, Iceland, Liechtenstein and New Zealand all dissociated themselves. New Zealand's representative pointed out that it was highly unusual for the General Assembly to pass resolutions based on conferences (such as that in Qatar) to which not all member states had been invited. The debate was being used, he said, to attack a long-standing international consensus on the diversity of family structures and the advancement of women and children's rights. It was also seeking to promote one model of the family at the expense of others.

*Meridian* magazine, meanwhile, was jubilant. 'For the first time at the UN, we had the anti-family powers scrambling by surprising them,' it said.

# SIX

# Sex and Sensibility

HALF-A-CENTURY ago there was general agreement among Muslims, Christians and Jews that homosexuality was bad. Since then, significant bodies of opinion in Judaism and Christianity, though not in Islam, have moved towards a more tolerant view. Among the first religious groups to challenge the prevailing attitude, back in 1963, were the Quakers[1] who suggested that what matters in a relationship is not the gender or sexual orientation of the people involved, but the feelings they have for each other:

> Surely it is the nature and quality of a relationship that matters: one must not judge it by its outward appearance but by its inner worth. Homosexual affection can be as selfless as heterosexual affection, and therefore we cannot see that it is in some way morally worse.
>
> Homosexual affection may of course be an emotion which some find aesthetically disgusting, but one cannot base Christian morality on a capacity for disgust. Neither are

we happy with the thought that all homosexual behaviour is sinful: motive and circumstances degrade or ennoble any act ...

... An act which expresses true affection between two individuals and gives pleasure to them both, does not seem to us to be sinful by reason alone of the fact that it is homosexual. The same criteria seem to us to apply whether a relationship is heterosexual or homosexual.[2]

Substantial parts of the Christian church have since adopted a similar view. In Judaism, the first moves towards institutional acceptance of gay Jews came in the 1970s when the Union of American Hebrew Congregations and the Central Conference of American Rabbis adopted resolutions favouring civil rights for gay people (in 1975 and 1977 respectively).[3] This is not to suggest that Jews and Christians as a whole have now come to terms with homosexuality; some have, but the battles continue to rage. In Poland, a strongly Catholic country, the mayor of Warsaw banned the city's gay pride march in June 2005 for the second year running. It went ahead regardless, with more than 2,000 people taking part – though they were pelted with eggs and stones by supporters of the Catholic-nationalist Polish Families League.[4] In Jerusalem a couple of weeks later, the ultra-Orthodox mayor banned a similar march, though his decision was promptly overturned by an Israeli court. As the parade took place a Jewish religious extremist attacked three marchers with a knife and reportedly told the police he had come 'to kill in the name of God'.[5] Despite such instances of fanaticism, however, opinion in both faiths covers a broad range from outright hostility to complete acceptance, with many shades in between.

As a result, it is no longer possible to speak of the 'Christian' or 'Jewish' view of homosexuality.[6]

An intriguing question is why these changes have occurred in Christianity and Judaism but not in Islam, especially since all three religions are closely related. Christianity grew out of Judaism, and Islam draws on both these earlier traditions: Jews, Christians and Muslims are all – as Muslims say – 'people of the Book'. Some suggest the difference can be explained by Muslim scripture. The Qur'an, Khalid Duran writes, 'is very explicit in its condemnation of homosexuality, leaving scarcely any loophole for a theological accommodation of homosexuals in Islam'.[7] That is a questionable assertion, even if the vast majority of Muslims agree with it. The vast majority of Christians would have said the same about the Bible only a few decades ago, though many have since changed their minds. While it is true that Muslim scholars usually *interpret* the Qur'an in ways that seek to close as many loopholes as possible, their interpretations are not only shaped by what the Qur'an actually says but by prevailing social and cultural values. This is well-illustrated in Egypt and Lebanon – Muslim countries with large Christian minorities – where church leaders generally adopt a similar position on homosexuality to their Muslim counterparts. An attack delivered in 1990 by Pope Shenouda III, head of the Coptic Orthodox Church in Egypt, for instance, is virtually indistinguishable from the statements made by Egyptian Muslim clerics. 'What rights are there for homosexuals?' Pope Shenouda asked. 'Their only right is to be led to repentance. But to live in such defilement of the body, in such dishonour of the body, in such abomination and sin, and then ask for their so-called human rights [is] unthinkable.'[8]

One important historical difference between Muslim

and Christian countries has been in the spread of secularism. Separation of church from state has undoubtedly had a huge impact on Christianity, allowing official doctrine to be questioned and permitting a diversity of views. Judaism, meanwhile, is in a similar position: it has not been a state religion since ancient times and modern Israel, despite its Jewish character, is officially secular. In the Muslim world, however, with a few exceptions such as Turkey, secularism has not taken hold.[9]

Changes in Christian attitudes towards homosexuality can also be viewed as part of an historical progression, stimulated by a concern for social justice and respect for all human beings, that possibly has its roots in the anti-slavery campaigns of the late eighteenth and early nineteenth centuries but can certainly be traced back through the battles for racial equality and women's rights in the twentieth century. Comparable social pressures in the Muslim world have generally been weak or absent. The ineffectiveness of feminist movements within Islam is a particularly important factor; in Christianity the battles fought by feminists did much to prepare the way for recognition of homosexuality. More generally, at a time when Christian thinkers have been exploring new horizons, Islam has been swept by strong regressive currents that invoke 'traditional' values as a defence against perceived threats from outside.

Although Christian arguments about homosexuality generate much heat, homosexuality is not the real issue; it is a test case in a wider battle. The real issue, as described by sociologist James Hunter, is a conflict between two opposing 'moral visions of the human good and the proper ordering of society' which he characterises as orthodox and progressive.[10]

This is the fundamental religious debate of today and it cuts across old sectarian boundaries:

> Progressive Protestants, Roman Catholics, and Jews now have much more in common with one another – theologically, ethically, and politically – about such contested issues as sexuality than they have in common with any of their more conventional orthodox colleagues from within their particular traditions ... Church debates over homosexuality divide Methodists from Methodists, Roman Catholics from Roman Catholics, Jews from Jews, and so forth ... One of the most contested areas of conflict is over the meaning and place of sexuality, as well as over the connections between sexual justice and spirituality.[11]

So far, Muslims have been shielded from these arguments by the lack of any serious challenge internally from a progressive Islamic trend. For Muslims whose sexuality brings them into conflict with religious orthodoxy, this has several negative effects. In many parts of the world gay Jews and Christians who seek to reconcile faith and sexuality can find fellow-believers who are supportive rather than judgmental. This is not to belittle the mental anguish that many Christians and Jews still experience in confronting their sexuality, but for Muslims it is far more difficult: they can expect little or no help from other believers and may, in effect, find themselves rejected by a faith which refuses to let them leave. The most they can hope for, if not to be totally shunned and condemned, is to be told to change their ways and marry, or to spend their lives in celibacy. The question this raises is whether the true spirit of Islam (or any other religion for that matter) is served by depriving people of loving, caring relationships, cemented by the sharing of physical pleasures, simply because they are attracted to members of their own sex.

Many gay people, of course, would agree with those Islamic scholars who say that religion and homosexuality are fundamentally incompatible; as a result, instead of fearing the wrath of God as the scholars demand, they have chosen to have nothing further to do with religion. In secular societies that is a choice they are free to make, but in some Muslim countries renouncing Islam is as serious an offence as sodomy; in Saudi Arabia both are punishable – at least in theory – with death. Although that is an extreme case, elsewhere the social pressures to pray five times a day, to attend the mosque on Fridays, to fast during Ramadan and comply with other religious observances can be considerable. Within families, coming out as a non-believer can be no less traumatic than coming out as gay or lesbian. One ex-Muslim, now living in the United States, said he had avoided telling his parents in Pakistan that he was both gay and an atheist – though of the two he thought confessing his atheism would be worse. 'Even if I'm leading an immoral life and sleeping with boys, there's hope. But with this [atheism], I'm giving God the finger. It would hurt them that their son is going to hell,' he said.[12]

In secular societies debates about religion and sexuality may arouse general curiosity but they are of real concern only to believers. In Muslim countries the relevance of religious teaching stretches far wider. The constitutions of almost all Arab states enshrine Islam as the official religion and even where there is no attempt to apply the *shari'a* systematically, the opinions of

Islamic scholars cannot be discounted when formulating laws and government policies. Increasingly, Muslim countries also deploy 'Islamic' arguments to block human rights legislation and reverse liberal social policies at an international level.[13] In these circumstances the teachings of Muslim scholars legitimately become a matter for scrutiny and debate by others beyond the boundaries of Islam.

\* \* \*

JEWISH, Christian and Muslim condemnations of homosexuality have traditionally been justified by reference to the story of the prophet Lot (or Lut as he is known in the Qur'an).[14] The biblical version is recorded in the Book of Genesis where God resolves to punish the people of Sodom and Gomorrah if the complaints that He has heard about their misbehaviour are found to be true:

(20)  Then the Lord said, 'Because the outcry against Sodom and Gomorrah is great and their sin is very grave,

(21)  I will go down to see whether they have done altogether according to the outcry which has come to me; and if not, I will know.'[15]

The nature of their sin is not stated here but references elsewhere in the books of the prophets imply that the Sodomites, whatever their sexual behaviour, were the archetype of a sinful people. The book of Ezekiel, for example, says:

Behold, this was the iniquity of thy sister Sodom, pride, fulness of bread, and abundance of idleness was in her and in her daughters, neither did she strengthen the hand of the poor and needy.[16]

The story in Genesis continues with the arrival of two angels in Sodom. Lot welcomes them into his house and feeds them:

(4)     But before they [the angels] lay down [to sleep], the men of the city, the men of Sodom, both young and old, all the people to the last man, surrounded the house;

(5)     and they called to Lot, 'Where are the men who came to you tonight? Bring them out to us, that we may know them.'

(6)     Lot went out of the door to the men, shut the door after him,

(7)     and said, 'I beg you, my brothers, do not act so wickedly.

(8)     Behold, I have two daughters who have not known man; let me bring them out to you, and do to them as you please; only do nothing to these men, for they have come under the shelter of my roof.'

(9)     But they said, 'Stand back!' And they said, 'This fellow came to sojourn, and he would play the judge! Now we will deal worse with you than with them.' Then they pressed hard against the man Lot, and drew near to break the door.

(10)    But the men put forth their hands and brought Lot

into the house to them, and shut the door.

(11)    And they struck with blindness the men who were at
the door of the house, both small and great, so that
they wearied themselves groping for the door.[17]

The verb to 'know' in Verse five is usually considered a euphemism
for sexual relations, indicating that the men of the city intended
to gang-rape the two male angels.[18] Lot responds by offering his
virgin daughters instead. The gender of the persons involved
here is immaterial: the point is that the angels are Lot's guests
and, under the rules of hospitality applicable at the time, he has
a duty to protect them at any price. 'Do nothing to these men,'
he says, 'for they have come under the shelter of my roof' (Verse
8).

Although this episode introduced the word 'sodomy' into
the English language, the story recounted in Genesis does not
describe homosexuality as usually practised. It is not consensual
sex between males that brings the wrath of God upon Sodom;
God is already angry at the people's multiple wrong-doing and
the threat to Lot's guests merely provides confirmation of their
sinfulness and seals their fate. Everyone in the city is punished
along with the would-be rapists – women and children as well
as the menfolk. Lot's wife is punished too as she escapes with
her husband and daughters – turned into a pillar of salt because
she disobeys God's command and looks back to witness the
destruction.

As with the Bible, readers of the Qur'an have tended to focus
on sexual aspects of the Lot/Lut story, to the exclusion of much
else. The Qur'an, like the Bible, speaks of a variety of sins. Setting
aside for a moment the question of any sexual misbehaviour, we

are told that Lot's people 'cut the road' (presumably highway robbery) and committed 'wickedness' in their meetings. More generally, they were guilty of evil deeds and 'abomination' ... 'such as no creature ever did before'. They were wanton, senseless, froward, corrupt; they were wrong-doers and evil-living, and rejected warnings. All these terms are used to describe them in the Qur'an. Some of the words – 'abomination', 'wanton', etc – can be read (both in English and Arabic) with sexual connotations but an important study by Amreen Jamal, examining the use of the same words elsewhere in the Qur'an, shows that attributing a sexual meaning to them is not necessarily justified.[19]

The Qur'an presents Lot as one of a series of prophets whose message was rejected by his people. Some of these prophets are drawn from the Jewish tradition (Lot, Noah, Moses) and others from the Arabian tradition, but in each case the moral point is the same: the people rejected their prophets and God punished them:

(12)   The folk of Noah denied (the truth) before them, and (so did) the dwellers at Ar-Rass and (the tribe of) Thamud,

(13)   And (the tribe of) A'ad, and Pharaoh, and the brethren of Lot,

(14)   And the dwellers in the wood, and the folk of Tubb'a: every one denied their messengers, therefor My threat took effect.[20]

Unlike the biblical account, however, the Qur'anic version of the Lot story is fragmented. Lot is mentioned in fourteen of the 112 suras (chapters)[21] and it is necessary to reassemble these scattered elements in order to see the sequence of events more clearly. As in the biblical version, the fate of Lot's people is already sealed by the time the heavenly messengers arrive:

(58)   They said: We have been sent unto a guilty folk,

(59)   (All) save the family of Lot. Them we shall deliver every one,

(60)   Except his wife ... [22]

Lot is initially concerned for the safety of his guests: 'he was troubled upon their account, for he could not protect them' (29:33). In *Surat al-Hijr* (15), the story continues:

(67)   And the people of the city came, rejoicing at the news (of new arrivals).

(68)   He said: Lo! they are my guests. Affront me not!

(69)   And keep your duty to Allah, and shame me not!

(70)   They said: Have we not forbidden you from (entertaining) anyone?

(71)   He said: Here are my daughters, if ye must be doing (so).

*Surat al-Hud* (11) describes it slightly differently:

(78)   And his people came unto him, running towards him – and before then they used to commit abominations. He said: O my people! Here are my daughters! They are purer for you. Beware of Allah, and degrade me not in (the person of) my guests. Is there not among you any upright man?

(79) They said: Well thou knowest that we have no right to thy daughters, and well thou knowest what we want.

(80) He said: Would that I had strength to resist you or had some strong support (among you)!

*Surat al-Qamar* (54) mentions the incident in a single verse:

(37) They even asked of him his guests for an ill purpose. Then We blinded their eyes (and said): Taste now My punishment after My warnings!

The intention of the townsfolk towards Lot's guests is not fully spelled out in these passages. Lot has clearly made himself unpopular and has apparently been denied the right to receive visitors: 'Have we not forbidden you from (entertaining) anyone?' (15: 70). The townsfolk therefore try separate Lot and his guests. The sentence: 'They even asked of him his guests for an ill purpose' (54: 37) in Pickthall's version is a loose translation. The translations by Yusufali ('And they even sought to snatch away his guests from him') and Shakir ('And certainly they endeavoured to turn him from his guests') seem closer to the original Arabic.[23] In terms of the rules of hospitality, this is a serious matter for Lot, who has a duty to protect his guests: 'Affront me not!', 'Shame me not!', he says (15: 68–69).

Although the idea that the townsfolk intended to abuse the messengers sexually is not made explicit, Lot's offer of his daughters – 'They are purer for you' (11: 78) – certainly points in that direction, though the response of the townsfolk is oddly moralistic – 'Well thou knowest that we have no right to thy daughters' (11: 79). They add: 'Well thou knowest what we want' – a tantalisingly cryptic remark that is not elaborated in the text.

Separately, in other suras, there are the verses in which Lot is recorded as saying to the townsfolk:

Will ye commit abomination (*al-faahisha*) such as no creature ever did before you? Lo! ye come with lust (*shahwatan*) unto men instead of (*min duun*) women. Nay, but ye are wanton (*musrifuun*) folk. (7: 80–81)

What! Of all creatures do ye come unto the males, and leave the wives your Lord created for you? Nay, but ye are froward (*'aaduun*) folk. (26: 165–166)

Will ye commit abomination (*al-faahisha*) knowingly? Must ye needs lust (*shahwatan*) after men instead of women? Nay, but ye are folk who act senselessly (*tajhaluun*) (27: 53–54)

Lo! ye commit lewdness (*al-faahisha*) such as no creature did before you. For come ye not in unto males ... ? (29: 28–29)

These verses, needless to say, are often treated as the basis for a generalised condemnation of homosexuality, though there is really not enough evidence to justify such a conclusion. The remarks appear in isolation from the rest of the Lot story, so it is difficult to place them chronologically in the sequence of events or to be sure of their actual context. One possibility is that Lot uttered the words in response to the townsfolk's threat to his guests – in which case the context, as in the biblical version, is an attempt at non-consensual sex that bears little relevance to homosexuality as normally practised. Another possibility is that the remarks refer to previous events that we know nothing about. One suggestion, for example, is that the men of the town were in the habit of sexually assaulting the victims of their robberies but, again, that is speculation.[24] Further complicating the picture, while Suras 7 and 27 talk generally about lust for men 'instead of women', Sura 26 talks more specifically about men forsaking their *wives* for other men – in which case the important issue would be adultery, regardless of the gender of the sexual partners. For all these reasons, it is unwise to claim that the verses condemn homosexuality in the form that it is usually known today. It is also difficult to imagine that the phrase 'lewdness such as no creature did before' (Sura 29) really means the people of Lot were the first ever to engage in same-sex acts – though there are many who interpret it that way:

> Before the people of Sodom, never did this evil even enter the mind of mankind, let alone practising it. The Umayyad Khalifah 'Abdul Malik said that if this episode of the homosexuals was not mentioned in the Qur'an, he would not have conceded the reality of this crime since it was unthinkable that man will descend to such a degenerate level and debase himself in a type of act which is not indulged in by even the overwhelming majority of lowly beasts.[25]

The Lot story is also reconstructed in popularised versions which embellish the sexual aspects way beyond anything that can be justified by the Qur'anic text:

> These sodomites even indulged in their homosexual orgies

publicly. Their wickedness had attained the level where the mere sight of a handsome young man made them so agitated that they pounced upon him as famished people would fall on food ...

The Qur'an has depicted the scene when the angels of punishment [visited] Lot (*alayhis salaam*) as his guests in the guise of handsome young men. [Lot] did not recognise them in the first instance. But he knew the shameless habit of his people. He was extremely distressed and he apprehended that his people would certainly demand unnatural and shameful sexual activity. His apprehension was correct. They could not sit silently at the news of such 'boys' of excellent beauty. These sodomites recklessly rushed to the home of Lot (*alayhis salaam*) to gratify their unnatural desires. Lot (*alayhis salaam*) found himself in a difficult situation. He prompted them to legally satisfy their sexual appetite with women, even offering his daughter in lawful marriage to the most gentle of them ...[26]

Even apparently serious scholars such as Ahmad Kutty, of the Islamic Institute in Toronto, who provides *fatwas* for IslamOnline, manage to draw sweeping conclusions based on flimsy evidence, such as 'homosexuality is the most heinous sin because of which Allah destroyed an entire nation.'[27] Nowhere does the Qur'an state that homosexuality is the most heinous sin, or that it was the specific reason for punishing the people of Lot.

These simplistic and highly questionable interpretations of the Lot story generally pass unchallenged. But, as can be seen from the discussion of the Qur'anic text above, the story is far less clear-cut, and the business of interpreting it more complex, than many assume. The biblical version, of course, was regarded in much the same way until quite recently when reappraisals by John Boswell[28] and others questioned the popular assumptions.

The Lot/Lut story, as generally perceived, is a prime example of interpreting scriptural passages in a narrow, legalistic way. What probably began as a Jewish folk tale[29] has been transformed into a legal precedent to the extent that Islamic scholars can recommend stoning to death as the punishment for sodomy on the grounds that it replicates God's punishment of Sodom by stones raining from Heaven. The story has a moral purpose, certainly, but – unlike some other passages in the Bible and the Qur'an – it is not delivered in prescriptive terms. Those who favour legalistic interpretations also tend to focus on the bits that suit their case while ignoring others. In the Biblical and Qur'anic versions of the story, Lot/Lut offers his daughters to the mob – a shocking way to behave by modern standards, but nobody treats it as a general licence to do such things today. In the book of Genesis, a curious but rarely-mentioned sexual episode follows the destruction of Sodom. The righteous Lot goes to live in a cave with his two daughters but he has no wife and no male heir. The daughters decide to resolve this problem by getting their father drunk then having sex with him. This happens on two consecutive nights and in due course both daughters bear him a son.[30] It is interesting that those who so readily interpret the earlier part of Lot's story as God's condemnation of homosexuality seem less eager to interpret its denouement as signalling divine approval for incest while under the influence of drink.

In the Qur'an, Lot is mentioned repeatedly in conjunction

with other prophets who were rejected by their people – Noah, Abraham, Salih, Hud, etc. All these stories serve a similar purpose and form part of a theme: 'Their situations are different, but their ethical message is the same to each community. Through different means, each community finds ways of rejecting their Prophet, and the means are often violent.'[31] The tales can also be viewed in the historical context of the early Muslims' struggle to establish themselves in the face of rejection and repudiation. From among this collection of tales, the Lot story – uniquely – has been singled out by scholars for legalistic treatment. Scott Siraj al-Haqq Kugle, in his essay on sexuality, diversity and ethics in Islam, considers how another of the stories from the series might look if treated in the same way:

> Allah sent Salih to the people of Thamud as their Prophet ... the people of Thamud were wealthy, powerful, and arrogant ... Salih announced to his people that a certain camel was made sacred and should be allowed to wander freely, eat and drink on anyone's land, and be respected by all. The camel stood symbolically for the weak and vulnerable members of society ...
>
> The people of Thamud rejected Salih as their Prophet and ridiculed his exhortations to live up to an ethic of care and justice. When he urged them to protect the consecrated camel, the arrogant nobles of their community hamstrung her, tied her up, and slaughtered her. As a consequence, their city with all its inhabitants was destroyed by Allah (with an earthquake and choking clouds from what appears to be a volcanic eruption). Why did they kill the camel? To repudiate their Prophet, lower his dignity in the eyes of their

fellows, and reject the belief in the One God which was the
foundation of his ethical message.

Nobody would take seriously a commentator who
presents the people of Thamud as being obsessed by a hatred
of camels or a perverted lust for camel blood that corrupted
their innermost dispositions. Nobody would take seriously
a jurist who argued that slaughtering another's camel is a
capital crime, based on the example of the people of Thamud
who were destroyed after killing a camel. Nobody would
argue that anyone who slaughters an animal that does not
belong to him should be punished by asphyxiation, in a
rough human approximation of how Allah razed the people
of Thamud by a volcanic eruption. Anyone suggesting these
interpretations would be laughed out of the mosque.[32]

\* \* \*

WHEN scholars talk about the 'fixed principles' of Islam or
begin a sentence with the words 'Islam says ...', it is a sure sign
that some particularly dogmatic statement is about to follow.
The point of these phrases is to claim a monopoly on rectitude:
to assert that the speaker's view is the only one permitted and
that anyone who disputes it cannot be a good Muslim. Another
way of avoiding debate is to argue that even when religious
precepts seem inexplicable or irrelevant to a given situation
any attempt to question them is a challenge to the superior
wisdom of God. Addressing the case of a gay man who insists

that his sexual activities are not hurting anybody, the Muslim organisation Straightway says:

> There is good reasoning behind every command or prohibition. On the other hand, we do not necessarily know what the reasoning is! Sometimes we can take a good guess, but we cannot be sure. Only Allah truly knows what the benefits or harms of any action are for this life or the next. While it may seem that what we do causes no harm, perhaps it is more harmful than we can even imagine.[33]

A reasonable answer to this line of argument is that God has endowed us with intelligence and common sense, and expects us to use it. One extraordinary and horrific example of following supposedly divine rules without applying common sense occurred in 2002 when fire broke out at a girls' school in Mecca. Saudi religious police were on hand to ensure that those trying to escape were properly attired in headscarves and black *abayas*. Eyewitness accounts told of girls being forced back into the burning building to retrieve their head-coverings. Several who went back died in the blaze – the price of enforcing fixed principles.[34]

The occasions when ethical questions pose a simple choice between good and evil tend to be a luxury. Often it is necessary to weigh the benefits of various courses of action and consider whether any harm is likely to result from each. This is what the religious police failed to do in the Mecca school fire, and it is what Islamic scholars fail to do when arguing against homosexuality. They urge gay men to seek a 'cure' (even though it is unlikely to succeed and could be harmful), and tell them to find a wife as soon as possible. In the rush to condemn homosexuality and declare it a 'crime' against the rights of women,[35] they are happy to disregard the consequences – and the immorality – of the solutions they recommend. The popular cleric, Yusuf al-Qaradawi, describes homosexuality as a crime against women, but if pressurising gay men into marriages that they do not want, and may be totally unsuited for, is not a crime against the rights of women, it is hard to know what is. Furthermore, is it more likely that such unwanted marriages will strengthen the institution of marriage, as the scholars presume, or weaken it?

At the root of religious debate about sexuality is the willingness, or otherwise, of believers to adapt to changing circumstances and new understandings of human behaviour. Sexual diversity is a concept not discussed in the Qur'an (or the Bible, for that matter) – from which some conclude that it does not exist or cannot be allowed. Linked to this is an absolutist view which treats rules of behaviour as applicable at all times and in all situations, whether the issue is about correct use of the right hand, maintaining proper standards of dress in the event of a fire, or sex.

The Qur'an regulates sexual relations between men and women in some detail and, as Kugle notes, assumes a heterosexual norm among its listeners. But he continues:

This does not automatically mean that the Qur'an forbids homosexuality or condemns homosexuals – it means only that the Qur'an assumes that sexual desire between men and women is the norm and that addressing and regulating this desire is the basis for establishing a moral society.

Heterosexuality is certainly a numerical norm. In any society, homosexuals are a numerical minority and are discursively located at the margins of ethical regulations ... However, despite being a numerical minority, homosexual women and men are also present in society and numerically persistent. In every historically documented society there is evidence of homosexual desire and activity and there are persons characterised by such desire and activities.[36]

There are several reasons to suppose that the Qur'anic view of sexuality merely addresses the usual case, and provides rules specifically for that, rather than excluding all other possibilities. For example, there is some evidence that the Prophet was aware of sexual diversity (if not by that name) and was not noticeably troubled by it. People of ambiguous gender and sexuality did exist in Medina during the Prophet's lifetime, often working as popular performers.[37] Also, in a list of men who were allowed to see the women of a household unveiled – husbands, brothers, etc – the Qur'an includes the special category of 'servants who are not in need of women'.[38] Whatever the reason for their lack of need for women (eunuchs, perhaps, or the very elderly), they are mentioned in a matter-of-fact way that implies acceptance of the idea that some people have different sexual desires from others.

The rule about using the right hand for clean purposes and the left for unclean purposes (discussed in Chapter 5) is another case of addressing the norm rather than the exceptions. Imam al-Nawawi, a famous scholar who lived in the thirteenth century CE, described the use of right and left hands for their assigned purposes as 'a fixed rule' in Islamic law, but he also recognised that not everyone could be expected to observe it. 'If one has an excuse for not eating and drinking with his right hand, such as sickness or an injury, then this is not blameworthy,' he said.[39]

Sometimes the need for exceptions is obvious, sometimes less so. For people with physical disabilities – paralysis, amputation of an arm, etc – it is clear that the rule cannot apply and so scholars make the necessary allowances. For people who are merely left-handed, however, the reason for their behaviour is not immediately apparent. Though many Muslims now accept that left-handedness is innate behaviour and accommodate it, others still regard is as perversity or wilfulness. As in the case of left-handedness, there is no obvious physical reason why some people should be sexually attracted to others of their own gender. Scholars therefore assume it must be a personal choice, and interpret the rules accordingly.

Despite the intolerance often found in Muslim societies today, Kugle observes that the Qur'an 'positively assesses natural diversity in creation and in human societies'.[40] In contrast to the biblical story of Babel, where God scatters the people and makes them speak mutually incomprehensible languages as a punishment, the Qur'an welcomes their differences:

> We created you different tribes and nations so that you may come to know one another and acknowledge that the most honourable among you are those that stay the most conscious of Allah.[41]

> From among Allah's signs is the creation of the heavens and the earth and the difference of your tongues and the variation of your colours.[42]

Kugle continues:

With the Qur'an's vivid portrayal of diversity at so many levels of the natural and human world, it would be logical to assume that this diversity of creation plays out on the level of sexuality as well. It is also plausible to assert that, if some Muslims find it necessary to deny that sexual diversity is part of the natural created world, then the burden of proof rests on their shoulders to illustrate their denial from the Qur'anic discourse itself.[43]

The fact that sexual diversity is not addressed more explicitly by scripture can be viewed positively or negatively. For many Muslims it has become a pretext for closing doors and preventing further discussion. For many Christians and Jews, on the other hand, it has opened doors to creative approaches that are guided more by ethical principles than fixed rules. The focus is on the nature of relationships and the context in which sexual acts take place: whether they are purely for gratification or an expression of real love.

Recognising that contemporary scientific theory does not view homosexuality as willed behaviour or as a disease, Rabbi Lewis Eron suggests that traditional Jewish attitudes to same-sex acts are no longer adequate and asks whether Judaism can justifiably prevent gay people from expressing their feelings sexually:

Jewish sources reject celibacy. Legitimate sexual activity is encouraged. Sexual expression is not restricted to procreation within Judaism. Sexual relations within a marriage are a legitimate source of pleasure and strengthen the love of the couple for each other. Offering celibacy to gay people as the sole option, therefore, seems to run counter to Jewish understandings of the role of sex in human life.[44]

From a slightly different angle, Rosemary Haughton, a Roman Catholic theologian, contrasts official church doctrine with the reality at ground level. Working among the down-and-out, she observed the close friendships that developed between destitute women, and sometimes between men too:

> In some cases the relationship is, or may become, overtly sexual. It is natural for intimacy and friendship to be experienced physically, and some kinds of physical endearment seem acceptable, but at a certain point they don't seem acceptable any more.
>
> ... Is it really possible, in terms of moral theology, to draw a line? Of course we have always done so, but if we do, why do we? What is behind the thinking that assumes that any kind of genital contact creates a morally totally different situation from other kinds of physical intimacy? (Whether or not we *approve* of certain kinds of intimacy is not the point.) We need to ask these questions, and if not to answer them at least to be willing to look at the quality of the relationships ... It is in the giving and receiving of life and love that we discern the presence of God. At what point and on what grounds does God suddenly cease to be present?[45]

Christians and Jews may differ among themselves about the answers to these questions, but Muslims have scarcely begun to ask the questions, let alone attempt to answer them.

# SEVEN

# Paths to Reform

AHMED AL-ENEZI and Shahir al-Roubli were executed for murder at Arar in northern Saudi Arabia, close to the border with Iraq. Little is known about the two men except that they were lovers. When another man found out about their relationship and threatened to make it public, they killed him. Announcing their executions, a brief statement from the Saudi interior ministry said the couple had run over Malik Khan, a Pakistani citizen, with their car. They had then beaten him on the head with stones and set fire to his body, 'fearing they would be exposed after the victim witnessed them in a shameful situation'.[1]

One murder, two executions: three unnecessary deaths. Were it not for the Saudi law against homosexuality, with its extraordinarily severe penalties, all three men would still be alive and, most probably, doing no harm to anyone. Whether Malik Khan thought it was his religious duty to report the two male lovers to the authorities, or whether he had spotted an opportunity to extort money from them, is unclear. The balance of probability is that it was the latter, since anti-homosexuality laws, wherever they exist, provide a licence for extortionists.

The case of Ahmed al-Enezi and Shahir al-Roubli is one answer to those who deny that homosexuality is a problem in the Middle East: if only outsiders would refrain from complaining, they say, people who wish to indulge in same-sex activity would be able get on with it discreetly, others would be able to pretend that it does not happen, and everyone would be happy. But plainly there *is* a problem, not only because of the law but because of the attitudes that prevail in the region. The question is whether change is possible and, if so, how it might come about.

Before attempting to answer that, it is necessary to consider the nature of same-sex activity in Arab-Islamic countries, since there are disputes about it. On one side of the argument are those who maintain that gay, lesbian, bisexual and transgendered people exist everywhere, in all cultures. On the other side are those who say they do not. In Muslim countries, Jeffrey Weeks writes, there is 'no concept of "the homosexual", except where it has been imported from the West, no notion of homosexuality, and no gay way of life'.[2] While it may appear that there are irreconcilable differences here, both views are probably correct up to a point. Male same-sex activity, Weeks says, is allowed or at least condoned under certain conditions but:

> Those adult men who do not fit readily into prevailing notions of true manhood (that is, local men who are effeminate, or just want to lead an exclusively gay life, or Westerners themselves) are often looked down upon and despised.[3]

Joseph Massad of Columbia University also views the concept of homosexuality (and, indeed, heterosexuality) as a foreign import. Complaining that promotion of gay rights in Arab and Muslim countries is an imperialist-style 'missionary' project orchestrated by what he calls the 'Gay International', Massad writes:

> By inciting discourse about homosexuals where none existed before, the Gay International is in fact *heterosexualising* a world that is being forced to be fixed by a Western binary [i.e. 'gay' or 'straight']. Because most non-Western civilisations, including Muslim Arab civilisation, have not subscribed historically to these categories, their imposition is producing less than liberatory outcomes: men who are considered the passive or receptive parties in male-male sexual contacts are forced to have one object choice and identify as homosexual or gay, just as men who are the 'active' partners are also forced to limit their sexual aim to one object choice, women or men. Most 'active' partners see themselves as part of a societal norm, so heterosexuality becomes compulsory given that the alternative, as presented by the Gay International, means becoming marked outside the norm – with all the attendant risks and disadvantages of such a marking.[4]

The issue here is partly one of concepts but also of terminology. For a start, the Arabic language has no generally-accepted equivalent of the word 'gay'. The term for 'homosexuality' (*al-mithliyya al-jinsiyya* – literally: 'sexual same-ness') is a fairly recent introduction, and the same applies to Arabic terms for 'heterosexuality' and 'sexual orientation'. Another new word, *mithli* (derived from 'same') is sometimes used for 'gay' or 'homosexual', but is not in general currency. These linguistic gaps are often cited to support the argument that the concepts they refer to do not really exist in Arab society. An alternative explanation is that the concepts do exist but the Arabic language had no need for terminology to describe them until recently. Discussing the case of lesbianism, for example, Iman al-Ghafari of Tishreen University in Syria, writes:

> In the Arab world ... the lesbian identity doesn't seem to exist, not because there are no lesbians, but because practices which might be termed lesbian in Western culture are left nameless in the Arab culture. Taking into consideration that the word 'lesbian' [*suhaaqiyya*] is rarely used in Arabic and, once used, it is charged with negative connotations, most lesbians avoid any public assertion of their identities. Besides, it is quite easy for Arab lesbians to deprive their emotional and physical intimacies of their lesbian connotations because it is common in a conservative Arab culture that advocates separation between the sexes to find intimate relations among members of the same sex, without having to call such relations homosexual.[5]

In the context of these linguistic arguments, it is worth noting that 'homosexuality' and 'gay' (with sexual connotations) are comparatively recent additions to the English language. 'Homosexuality' is an adaptation of *Homosexualität* – a German word that first appeared in print in 1869.[6] The first undisputed use of 'gay' implying homosexuality came in 1929, in Noel Coward's musical comedy, *Bitter Sweet*, where four overdressed 'dandies' from the 1890s sing:

Pretty boys, witty boys,
You may sneer
At our disintegration.
Haughty boys, naughty boys,
Dear, dear, dear!

Swooning with affectation ...
And as we are the reason
For the 'Nineties' being gay,
We all wear a green carnation.

'Green carnation' alludes to the gay playwright, Oscar Wilde, who liked to wear one in his buttonhole.[7]

Despite the lack of generic terminology, however, Arabic does have an ample number of words identifying people who are disposed towards specific types of homosexual activity. *Khawal*[8] and *khanith/mukhannath* refer to effeminate men. There is also *luti*, derived from the name of the prophet Lot, of Sodom and Gomorrah fame, which is roughly equivalent to 'sodomite'. Others include *ma'bun* (a passive sodomite), *mu'ayir* (a passive male prostitute) and *dabb* (an active sodomite who rapes victims in their sleep).[9] A lack of suitable vocabulary has proved no barrier to the spread of jokes that depict various towns in the Middle East as having rampantly homosexual inhabitants. One of these places is Idlib in Syria. Why Idlib was singled out is unclear but the jokes have probably been around for generations. Similar jokes can be found in Iran referring to Qazvin – a town whose reputation may well date back more than 600 years to the time when Obeid e Zakani, a bawdy poet and satirist, lived there.

In the Arab media, 'gay' and 'homosexual' are normally represented by the heavily-loaded *shaadh* ('queer', 'pervert', 'deviant') though some of the more serious newspapers have begun to accept *mithli* as a neutral alternative. The widespread use of '*shaadh*' raises an interesting question, however. If Arab sexuality is as undefined as some suggest, what is the social norm that the 'deviant' *shaadh* is thought to be flouting? Is it heterosexuality or something else?

Arab society has traditionally been more concerned with sexual acts and roles than with sexual identities. If a man assumes the active role in anal intercourse with another man, his action is not necessarily regarded as shameful or as indicating sexual orientation. He is merely performing the role that men normally perform in intercourse with women. The fact that he does this with a man rather than a woman may even be interpreted as a sign of heightened masculinity, since sex with another man is popularly thought to require greater strength or sexual prowess. Assuming the passive position, on the other hand, is considered demeaning and a betrayal of manhood, since in this case the man replicates the role of a woman. The element of 'shame', therefore, rests on an assumption that women are inferior to men. There is also a widespread belief that those who take the passive role cannot be doing it for pleasure – hence the tendency of the Egyptian police to regard such men as prostitutes.[10] As in the West, popular Arab perceptions of male same-sex activity focus almost exclusively on anal intercourse, ignoring a variety of other possibilities, and participants are assumed to play fixed roles – either active or passive, but not both. In contrast to the West, however, there is also a striking absence of any notion that same-sex contacts might extend beyond physical gratification to a gay lifestyle or to loving, caring relationships. In the view of many Arabs, therefore, the significant distinction is not between heterosexual and homosexual but between penetrator and penetrated: men are the penetrators (of women and sometimes other men) while women are the penetrated – in which case the 'deviance' of the *shaadh* is that he behaves as a woman.[11]

Popular though this penetrator/penetrated model may be, it is not recognised by religion or the law. In Arab countries where same-sex acts are illegal, both parties – active as well as passive – are held culpable. Conventional Islamic teaching, meanwhile, assumes the existence of heterosexuality (if not homosexuality) and promotes it strongly, urging everyone to marry at the earliest opportunity and have children. In the belief that men are uncontrollably attracted to women it also goes to great lengths to keep the sexes apart except where they are related by blood or marriage. It is rather odd, therefore, to accuse gay rights campaigners of inadvertently 'heterosexualising' the Arab world when the law and religion – far more powerful influences – are already trying so hard to do just that.

Despite the claim that international gay and lesbian campaigners seek to re-define same-sex contacts between Arabs according to their own concepts, there are clearly some who don't. Massad quotes Robert Bray, an officer of the International Lesbian and Gay Association as saying: 'Cultural differences make the definition and the shading of homosexuality different among peoples ... But I see the real question as one of sexual freedom; and sexual freedom transcends cultures.'

Recognising that same-sex emotions and activities do not necessarily come with an identity attached, Massad adopts the phrase 'practitioners of same-sex contact'. This has merits but also limited usefulness. It covers a multitude of shades, from those who have occasional same-sex contacts to those who have nothing else. By lumping them all together it sidesteps the question of whether any of these 'practitioners' have a right to identify themselves as gay, lesbian, etc, if they so wish. Massad simply dismisses such people as unimportant victims of Western influence. Were it not for the meddling foreigners, he implies, all 'practitioners' would be able to practise their same-sex contacts untroubled by the authorities, social pressures or any questions about their sexuality. The fact remains, though, that in most Arab countries 'practitioners of same-sex contact' are not free to do so. Apart from the social pressures that prevent them from being open about it, they are breaking the law, regardless of whether they consider themselves gay or not.

Massad does not deny that gay and lesbian Arabs exist, but he says:

Although the advent of colonialism and Western capital in the Arab world has transformed most aspects of daily life, efforts to impose a European heterosexual regime on Arab men have succeeded only among the upper classes and the increasingly Westernised middle classes. It is among members of these wealthier segments of society that the Gay International has found native informants. Although members of these classes who engage in same-sex relations have more recently adopted a Western identity (as part of a more general, class-wide adoption of everything Western), they remain a minuscule minority among those men who engage in same-sex relations and who do not identify as 'gay' or express a need for gay politics ... there is no evidence of gay movements anywhere in the Arab world or even of gay group activity outside of small groups of men in metropolitan areas such as Cairo and Beirut.[12]

This is a broad-brush picture and the references to 'upper classes' and 'wealthier segments of society', while true up to a point, need to be treated with caution. A random selection of newspaper and magazine articles about gay Arabs reveals a wide range of occupations: several students, a man working for an advertising company, a restaurant owner, a bank employee, a doctor, an actor, a restaurant worker and a gardener.[13] It is certainly true that Arabs who identify as gay or lesbian tend to live in big cities, but for a variety of reasons – such as migration from small towns where they find life oppressive – the same applies in many other countries, including those in the West. Talk of a 'class-wide adoption of everything Western' is also an exaggeration; Arabs adopt – and often adapt – whatever aspects they like but reject much else. A recent survey, for instance, found that even among those who favour American products and culture, there was overwhelming opposition to American foreign policy.[14] Arab Westernisation, too, is often of a superficial kind. Among gay and lesbian youngsters in Egypt, for example, it can amount to little more than frequenting fashionable cafés – those offering cappuccino and fruit juice from menus printed in English rather than the sawdust-floored places that serve traditional Egyptian tea. Even in the gay clubs of Beirut, Western techno beats have limited appeal; it is when Arab music comes on in the early hours of the morning that the dance floor really springs to life.

The main problem with Massad's argument, though, is his eagerness to portray Western cultural influences in conspiratorial terms when in reality they are almost entirely the natural result of increased contact. Since the early 1990s, Arab exposure to Western culture has increased enormously through satellite television, foreign travel and – more recently – the Internet. Western sexual behaviour arouses much curiosity, both among those who see it as decadence and those who are simply intrigued. It is not unreasonable to suggest that widely-circulated stories about the sex lives of international celebrities (such as the arrest of the singer, George Michael), and Western debate about gay marriages, are likely to have more influence on Arab ideas of sexuality than the supposed missionary efforts of the 'Gay International'. So far, the effects are most apparent among the educated urban youth. Egyptians are becoming more aware of their own sexuality, though the process is slow. According to Josette Abdalla, a psychologist at American University in Cairo: 'This is in part the result of more exposure to mass media, Western influences and more access to papers, satellite dishes and TV.'[15]

In an interview with the *Daily Star* newspaper, Brigitte Khoury, a clinical psychologist at the American University of Beirut, agreed that youngsters were being influenced by Western ideas but felt this often left them confused. 'Young people in Lebanon are faced with a mixed message,' she said. 'They are bombarded with images and values of the West which they try to emulate, but their more traditional society forbids the liberated sexuality stereotypically associated with the West.'[16] A mother quoted by the paper echoed this: 'Lebanese kids are aping the so-called sexual liberation of Western kids. But [whereas] a sexually active Western adolescent would be better prepared and informed, his or her Lebanese counterparts are left to their own devices.'[17] One ex-student quoted by the *Daily Star* even claimed that gayness had acquired a social cachet at his university in Lebanon: other students wanted to befriend him when they found out he was gay, he said – though he suggested they were only happy to be seen with him because his sexuality was not too obvious. He added: 'At least seventy percent of the men at my university had slept with another man. I don't think it's because they couldn't find girlfriends. It's because it was fashionable.'[18]

Supporters of 'cultural authenticity', in order to defend their position, have no option but to declare this a foreign conspiracy. 'One of the more compelling issues to emerge out of the gay movement in the last two decades,' Massad writes, 'is the universalisation of "gay rights". This project has appropriated the prevailing US discourse on human rights in order to launch itself on an international scale.' The inspiration, he says, came partly from 'the white Western women's movement, which had sought to universalise its issues through imposing its own colonial feminism on the women's movements in the non-Western world'. He also notes that the International Lesbian and Gay Association (ILGA) 'was founded in 1978 at the height of the Carter administration's human rights campaign against the Soviet Union and Third World enemies'. All branches of the human rights community, he says, continue to be guided by an 'orientalist impulse, borrowed from predominant representations of the Arab and Muslim worlds in the United States and Europe'.[19]

There are plenty of reasons other than an 'orientalist impulse' why gay rights activists might pay special attention to Muslim countries, however. Massad gives no hint that discrimination and abuses in Arab countries have anything to do with it, even though punishments for same-sex acts tend to be heavier there (on paper, if not always in practice) and the only countries in the world where the death penalty still applies justify it on the basis of Islamic law. The portrayal of Western campaigners as interfering busybodies might have more credibility if gay and lesbian Arabs were in a position to organise themselves in their own countries. On the whole, they are not. Consequently agitation from abroad, often with secret collaboration from anonymous people inside the country, has become a well-established practice.

The debate is often presented as a choice between cultural authenticity on the one hand and the adoption of all things Western on the other. In fact, neither is a realistic proposition. Exposure to foreign ideas and influences cannot be prevented, but nor are Arabs incapable of making critical judgements about them. Equally, Arab culture cannot be treated as a fossil; it is a culture in which real people lead real lives and it must be allowed to evolve to meet their needs. The issue, then, is not whether concepts such as 'gay' and 'sexual orientation' are foreign imports but whether they serve a useful purpose. For Arabs who grow up disturbed by an inexplicable attraction towards members of their own sex, they can provide a framework for understanding. For families – puzzled, troubled and uninformed by their own society – they offer a sensible alternative to regarding sons and daughters as sinful or mad.

\* \* \*

AS FAR as conscious efforts to promote change are concerned, there are huge differences between Arab countries in terms of what can realistically be achieved, at least in the short term. The essential first step, according to Ghassan Makarem, an activist in the Lebanese organisation, Helem, is 'to try to have some critical mass'.[20] Initially this requires a local network of gay men and lesbians that not only serves a social function, but allows them to talk about the issues that concern them, and eventually to organise. On their own, though, such networks can be extremely vulnerable, as their suppression in Egypt and Saudi Arabia has demonstrated. Gay and lesbian networks are not unique in this respect; on the whole, their treatment reflects government attitudes towards civil society movements in general.

Helem has survived in Beirut partly by not confining its attention to gay and lesbian activists alone; it has deliberately sought allies among others who work on sexual and reproductive rights, human rights, and so on, as well as sympathetic professionals such as lawyers, doctors and teachers. 'When we did this it was not that we were particularly accepted by Lebanese society but we were able to create a space that protects itself by being involved with other groups, by having people from other organisations, and by being visible.' Makarem said: 'Visibility was one of the main components of our strategy. We worked with human rights organisations on reviewing the penal code, for instance, and with women's organisations. We were actually quite aggressive with them on sexuality, telling them it had to be on their agenda. They didn't take that very well, but we made some good contacts with people in those organisations who were not very happy with their existing policies.' In the meantime, Helem was also developing contacts internationally.

'Change cannot happen purely locally, especially when you're talking about taboos such as this,' he continued. 'Connecting with the world through this kind of network is healthy, but you cannot just decide "I am going to create a network". It doesn't go as smoothly as you expect.'

Egypt, at the time of the Queen Boat arrests in 2001, also had gay networks, but they were primarily for socialising and had not established broader connections, either locally or internationally. Thus a trial that in different circumstances might have sparked a campaign for reform actually had the opposite effect: existing local networks either collapsed or were driven deeper underground. Part of the explanation for this lies in the different character of Egyptian civil society organisations compared to those in Lebanon. 'Lebanon and Egypt both have strong civil societies,' Makarem said, 'but Egyptian civil society is still part of the whole tradition of services and charities. In Lebanon you have a diversity of opinions in civil society and you have a liberal progressive current that's very small, not very vocal, but at the same time it's everywhere in anything that falls into the civil society domain. You have these currents in Lebanon that in Egypt are not as apparent. The progressive forces in Egyptian civil society are more or less traditional leftists from the 1970s and 1980s who are homophobic, sexist, etc. They come from a tradition that hasn't yet opened up to women or sexuality. This is not a minor difference, because when we started talking about Helem and about gay and lesbian rights in Beirut we could find allies in civil society who were willing to be a little bit vocal about it. I'm not saying everyone decided to support us but you could find people in women's organisations and youth groups and some human rights organisations who were willing to support the work that we were doing. This did not happen in Egypt.'

While international human rights organisations took up the Queen Boat case, Egyptian human rights groups did not, fearing that support for such a controversial cause would damage their credibility in relation to other matters such as unfair trials and political prisoners. Some, though, in line with the popular consensus, went further and denied that sexual orientation has any relevance to human rights. One activist from Egypt who dared to raise the issue was publicly denounced by a fellow human rights campaigner as the spokesperson for 'Egyptian perverts'.[21]

Another important factor behind the Queen Boat case in Egypt was the authorities' use of religion as a tool to fight Islamist militancy. Homosexuality was one area where the government could demonstrate their religious credentials and seize the moral high ground (as they saw it) without adverse political consequences. Similar examples can be found in other Arab countries, though in multi-confessional Lebanon it is more difficult to play that card. 'You have a situation in Egypt where the government uses religiosity in order to fight what they call political Islam,' Makarem said, 'so the decision to attack the Queen Boat, on a political level, was a decision to defuse the mobilisation of Islamists on moral issues. This is a pattern that you can see in many countries. The government would become more moralistic than the 'moral right'. But every time this happens, there's a victim.'

Visibility brings people face to face with sexual diversity and forces them to confront it in the reality rather than in the abstract, but not everyone reacts in the same way. Sometimes the result is less hostility, sometimes more. For Helem in Lebanon, increased visibility forms part of a long-term strategy for advancement and protection. So far, it has mostly been a positive experience but that is probably because Lebanese society allows a space for such expression. 'There is a moment when you have to take a tactical decision and say "OK, let's get in the papers, be on TV, have a poster with our logo, have a website,"' Makarem said. This moved a step further in March 2005 with the launch of *Barra* ('*Out*'), the Arab world's first gay and lesbian magazine – a glossy production of twenty-four pages circulating in Beirut.

In Egypt and Saudi Arabia, on the other hand, even a slight increase in visibility is liable to bring a crackdown. This, of course, leads to the argument that the best policy for gay men and lesbians in many Arab countries is to keep quiet. In the absence of local support networks, that is undoubtedly sensible but in the longer term it will do nothing to better their lot. Experience with the development of sexual rights in other countries shows that it is only when people make a fuss, and have the necessary organisation to back it up, that conditions improve. Even so, Salim, an Egyptian activist, is sceptical about Helem's emphasis on visibility and its approach more generally: too many of its ideas have been copied from the West, he said. 'Their magazine, for God's sake, is called *Barra*! We need to identify and explore non-Western ways of being gay.'[22]

\* \* \*

THOUGH there is a tendency for those who seek change

in Arab societies to focus on a single issue that interests them particularly – human rights, democratisation, women's rights, press freedom, and so on – it does not take long to discover that seemingly different reform issues have many interconnections and that progress with one often depends on someone else making progress with another. This can be discouraging at first but once there is modest progress on several fronts further progress becomes easier and gathers pace.

To some extent 'reform' has become a dirty word because of strident American demands to bring 'freedom' to the Middle East.[23] Simplistic portrayals of Arab regimes in terms of the former Soviet Union are also unhelpful, since they mis-identify the problem. The regimes tend to be autocratic rather than totalitarian[24] and do allow a degree of freedom, though often it is the sort of freedom where those with the right connections and enough money can do whatever they want, regardless of the law or anything else. Similarly, talk of a 'clash of civilisations', and portrayals of Islam as a bloodthirsty anti-Western religion, not only misrepresent the Arabs and their predominant faith but hamper progress by focussing on confrontation rather than the building of constructive international relationships.

As a result of this, Arabs who seek reform have to contend with claims that they are merely agents for a domineering American foreign policy as exemplified by the invasion of Iraq and a less than even-handed approach to the Israeli-Palestinian conflict. Suspicions that the US wants Arab reform in order to further its own strategic interests, and those of its allies, were reinforced by an American working paper circulated to the G-8 group of industrialised countries ahead of their summit meeting in June 2004. The document's opening paragraph spoke of conditions in the Arab world 'that threaten the national interests of all G-8 members'. It continued: 'So long as the region's pool of politically and economically disenfranchised individuals grows, we will witness an increase in extremism, terrorism, international crime, and illegal migration.'[25]

It is important, therefore, to distinguish between reform conceived as a Western insurance policy against extremists, terrorists, criminals, migrants, etc, and reform that serves the interest of Arabs themselves. Among the numerous proposals for reform emanating from the Arab world,[26] several common themes emerge. The most significant of these is a perception that democracy, in the sense of free elections and its other trappings, is not sufficient and that real progress will only come if there is comprehensive political, economic and social reform. Politically, the need is for modern styles of government based on transparency and accountability that avoid interfering unnecessarily in the daily lives of citizens. Economically, many of the problems also derive from the way government operates: superfluous bureaucracy, corrupt officials and controls that obstruct the free flow of information are some obvious examples. Socially, reform proposals usually highlight education – the promotion of 'basic and high quality skills and critical inquisitive thinking', as one document put it[27] – as a key to both political and economic development. In the social sphere too, the stifling of creative activity by governments and Islamist organisations has led to calls for cultural reform, which in turn touches on the sensitive matter of religious reform.

Discussion of reform cannot proceed very far without raising fundamental questions about the nature of the Arab state, the role of government, and the function of the law. Views on these matters held by Arab regimes range from the archaic to the confused, and their confusion is nowhere more apparent than on issues of personal freedom. For example, are private sexual acts between consenting adults a matter of state security? The Egyptian authorities appear to think so. To what extent should governments – which in most cases are scarcely models of virtue in the field of corruption – be the guardians of personal morality? While eager to hunt down and imprison gay men, the Egyptian government showed itself incapable of controlling things that actually endanger the public, such as the terrible air pollution in Cairo, the buildings that regularly fall down on top of people, and accidents on the railways. Following one disastrous train fire in which hundreds died, the government's reaction was to increase fares in order to provide life insurance for passengers. In Morocco, Egypt and Lebanon, large amounts of police time have been wasted in recent years tracking down and arresting devotees of heavy metal music.[28] In 2003, in the midst of the most serious terrorist campaign in Saudi Arabia's history, the interior minister, Prince Nayef, turned his attention to protecting citizens from 'un-Islamic' influences by banning female dolls and teddy bears.[29] Mobile phones with cameras were also made illegal for fear they might be used for immoral purposes – and of course became extremely popular.[30]

Attempting to govern people's lives in this way also brings Arab legal systems into disrepute. It results in laws that cannot be enforced systematically but are applied from time to time at the discretion of the authorities – usually when they decide to make an example of someone or to send a signal to the public. This is made worse by a style of detective work that relies less on evidence than on confessions (an invitation to torture) and by

and 'good manners'. Clothing had to be neat and clean, with 'appropriate footwear'. Midriff blouses, spaghetti straps, halters, strapless or backless clothing, shorts and divided skirts were forbidden for the women. 'No underwear, including bra straps and boxer shorts, may show,' the code stipulated. Also banned were 'clothes or tattoos that show profanity, violence, sexually suggestive phrases or pictures, alcohol, tobacco, drugs ...'[32]

This public display of purity did nothing to dampen speculation on the Internet that three women in the show were smoking off-camera. One viewer claimed to have heard the accidental dropping of an ashtray and the click of a cigarette lighter. 'Hey – they are human. We all have our demons,' an online commentator wrote. 'I feel sorry and sad for these ladies. They are living a hypocritical lifestyle.'[33]

While almost everyone agreed that such shows made trashy but compulsive viewing, the moral debate took a predictable course: conservatives denounced them as indecent while liberals accused them of imposing an artificial lifestyle on participants. 'These kinds of programmes are in contradiction with our habits and with the principles of Islam,' Sheikh Mohammed Hamdi, a Lebanese cleric, fumed. 'We are seeing youngsters kissing and expressing emotions. This is indecent.' A writer in the Beirut *Daily Star* retorted: 'Why complain about what is happening on television when you can walk around the streets of Beirut ... and see youngsters expressing emotion and kissing all the time. So it's on television? So what?'[34]

It is the pressure to conform to some kind of imaginary standard, far more than a lack of democracy, that makes many young Arabs want to emigrate. Whether in the field of sexual relations or elsewhere, those who don't conform are expected to play the game and keep their non-conformity to themselves. Genuine reform, however – in whatever field – requires a degree of openness and transparency that is incompatible with these deep-rooted habits of pretence and denial, so the issue will have to be confronted eventually. Demands for gay rights are one call among many to do just that: an assertion of individuality and personal freedom, and a vow to abandon pretence. In the words of the song:

> I am what I am
> And what I am
> Needs no excuses.[35]

Adjusting to a new world of openness may be painful for many, but the old ways look increasingly unsustainable as foreign travel, satellite television and the Internet crack open Arab society's protective cocoon.

The demands for equality and an end to discrimination that are voiced by gay rights activists apply equally in the areas of gender, religion and ethnicity. Apart from the continuing opposition to women's rights in significant parts of the region, one major obstacle to equality is the great importance that Arab society attaches to ties of kinship (which means the immediate family almost everywhere but also extends, in the more traditional areas, to include clan and tribe too). The demands of kinship turn nepotism into a virtue and are therefore difficult to reconcile with the ideas of freedom from discrimination embodied in the Universal Declaration of Human Rights or, indeed, with modern business concepts such as equal opportunities in employment. A man who is able to provide work for a relative is expected to do so, and we have seen it at the highest level in the trend towards 'republican monarchies' where a president's son is groomed to succeed him.

The reluctance to accept sexual diversity is echoed, too, in the fields of religion and ethnicity. The A to Z of ethnic and religious groups in the Middle East embraces Alawites, Armenians, Assyrians, Baha'is, Berbers, Chaldeans, Copts, Druzes, Ibadis, Ismailis, Jews, Kurds, Maronites, Sahrawis, Tuareq, Turkmen, Yezidis and Zaidis (by no means an exhaustive list), and yet serious discussion of ethnic/religious diversity and its place in society is almost as big a taboo as discussion of sexual diversity. If the existence of non-Arab or non-Muslim groups is acknowledged at all, it is usually only to declare how harmoniously everyone gets along. The roots of this attitude lie partly in history. Most Arab states, in the form we know them today, were created during the last century and their boundaries were determined – sometimes quite arbitrarily – by imperial powers. Successive Arab governments have had to grapple with the resulting problems, attempting to weld various tribal, ethnic and religious groupings into nations. The special Arab concern with national unity is therefore understandable up to a point, though often it turns into a dangerous obsession. Another factor is the importance Arab societies attach to avoiding *fitna*, or social discord. This has its benefits, but the abhorrence of *fitna* can also become an excuse for not acknowledging problems. The result is a sort of make-believe harmony in which differences are kept out of sight as much as possible. Experience elsewhere in the world shows that in the long run this simply does not work: the real way to avoid *fitna* is to face up to differences honestly and openly before they lead to a crisis.[36] Perhaps, more than anything else, acknowledgment of diversity in all areas of life – not as a threat but as a source of richness – is an essential first step on the road to reform.

Overall, this represents a formidable challenge for would-be reformers but there may also be reason for hope. Arabs nowadays have just too much contact with the rest of the world to maintain an isolationist 'cultural purity' approach. Almost all the difficulties faced by gay and lesbian Arabs today have been faced at some time by others elsewhere. Other societies have managed to address them successfully and one day, perhaps, Arab societies will do so too.

# Notes

For the convenience of readers who wish to look up the websites mentioned below, these notes are also available online with clickable links at: www.al-bab. com/unspeakablelove.

*Chapter 1*
1. Interview in Egypt, April 2004. Names of interviewees in this chapter have been changed; in some cases they assigned themselves a nickname.
2. Interview in Egypt, 2001. Ahmed himself later fled to the United States where he applied for political asylum.
3. Interview in Lebanon, June 2004. He spoke at length about his treatment. Because of the threats to his life, various details of his story that would make him easily identifiable have been omitted.
4. For example, a letter from a Sudanese man to gaymiddleeast.com told of a friend whose brother threatened to kill him after seeing him kiss another man. Three days later he was found stabbed to death. http:// www.gaymiddleeast.com/news/article2.htm.
5. Jimenez, Marina: 'Gay Jordanian Now "Gloriously Free" in Canada', in *The Globe & Mail,* Toronto, 20 May 2004. http://www.globeandmail. com/servlet/ArticleNews/TPStory/LAC/20040520/GAY20/ TPNational/TopStories. The documentary, *Gloriously Free,* was made by Filmblanc, a Canadian production company.
6. 'Honour' killings of women are common in Jordan and are also regarded by many as family matters. If the killers are prosecuted they usually receive very short sentences.
7. Jimenez, 'Gay Jordanian'.
8. Interview in Egypt, April 2004. He said he chose the nickname Billy 'because I like Billy Holliday'.
9. A typical psychiatric session costs 100 Egyptian pounds. Two sessions a week, spread over six months, makes a total of 5,000 pounds. This would

be more than a year's wages for the average Egyptian, though incomes vary hugely and for a middle-class family it would be a smaller proportion of their annual income. According to one interviewee, free treatment is sometimes available through charities.

10. Aitkenhead, Decca: 'Going Straight', *The Guardian,* 3 April 2004. http://www.guardian.co.uk/weekend/story/0,3605,1183596,00.html. For further information about the concept of sexual orientation, and the debates about it, see http://en.wikipedia.org/wiki/Sexual_orientation.

11. The sources of information most frequently used by young Egyptians appear to be www.gay.com and www.planetout.com.

12. Interview in Egypt, April 2004.

13. Interview in Beirut, March 2005.

14. Interview in Egypt, April 2004. Adagio – also sometimes known as 'Bonbon' – had grown up with five sisters, which he suggested could be the reason for his homosexuality.

15. Interview, March 2005.

16. www.al-fatiha.org.

17. It is an old Arab custom, reflecting the importance of male lineage, for parents to be popularly known by the name of their first-born son: Umm Ali ('the mother of Ali'), Abu Ali ('the father of Ali'), etc.

18. Interview in Beirut, April 2005.

19. R v IAT *ex parte* Shah. House of Lords, 1999.

20. In 1994 the case of Toboso-Alfonso, 20 I&N Dec. 819 (Board of Immigration Appeals 1990), involving a gay Cuban refugee, was designated as a legal precedent.

21. Stonewall, 'Applying for Asylum as a Refugee'. http://www.stonewall-immigration.org.uk/Asylum.htm. For a summary of the British asylum rules see: http://www.ind.homeoffice.gov.uk/ind/en/home/laws___policy/immigration_rules/part_11.html.

22. Sanders, Clive: 'Gay Times Law', *Gay Times* website article, 14 April 2003. http://www.gaytimes.co.uk/gt/default.asp?topic=article&ID=9104&pub=2127.

23. Stonewall, 'Applying for Asylum'.

24. *ibid.*

25. Sapsted, David: 'Gay Killed Himself over Asylum Failure', *Daily Telegraph,* 20 April 2005. http://www.telegraph.co.uk/news/main.jhtml?xml=/news/2005/04/20/nsuic20.xml&sSheet=/news/2005/04/20/ixhome.html; Athwal, Harmit: 'Inquest finds Asylum Refusal was Motive for Gay Iranian's Suicide', Independent Race and Refugee Network, 20 April 2005. http://www.irr.org.uk/2005/april/ha000014.html.

26. Athwal, 'Inquest finds Asylum Refusal'.

27. Lesbian and Gay Immigration Rights Task Force: 'Gay Men from China,

Jordan, Lebanon, Pakistan, Romania, and Russia Win Asylum'. http://
www.lgirtf.org/newsletters/Summer96/SU3.html (no longer available).

28. Hansen, Kvore: 'Gay Asylum Seeker from Morocco not Allowed to
Stay'. *Aftenposten*, Norway, 15 June 2000. Reproduced at http://www.
globalgayz.com/norway-news.html.

29. 'Gay Algerian granted Asylum in France', Behind the Mask (website on
gay and lesbian affairs in Africa), undated article. http://www.mask.org.
za/SECTIONS/AfricaPerCountry/ABC/algeria/alg_2.html.

30. See Lesbian and Gay Immigration Rights Task Force website: www.lgirtf.
org. The US does not consider same-sex partners of American citizens
as 'spouses'. The 1996 Defense of Marriage Act defines marriage as a
union between a man and woman, with the result that same-sex unions
recognised by some individual states (such as Hawaii and Vermont) or
other countries (e.g. the Netherlands) are not recognised for immigration
purposes.

31. Stonewall,     'Evidence'.     http://www.stonewall-immigration.org.uk/
Evidence.htm

32. Eron, Lewis. 'Homosexuality and Judaism', in *Homosexuality and World
Religions*, Arlene Swidler, ed., Valley Forge, PA, 1993, pp. 103–134 .

33. According to one report, sodomy carries a jail sentence of three to ten
years. See Baron, Dan: 'Palestinian Gays Seek Safety in Israel', in *Cleveland
Jewish News,* 15 January 2004. http://www.clevelandjewishnews.
com/articles/2004/01/15/news/israel/nseek0116.txt (also available at
http://www.sodomylaws.org/world/israel/isnews005.htm).

34. Tayseer was not his real name.

35. Halevi, Yossi: 'Refugee Status', *The New Republic*, 19 August 2002. http://
www.tnr.com/doc.mhtml?i=20020819&s=halevi081902 (subscription
only). Also at http://www.jpef.net/sep02/Refugee%20status.pdf. Two
other accounts involving a man from Gaza of about the same age were
published by the BBC ('Palestinian Gays Flee to Israel', 22 October 2003
http://news.bbc.co.uk/go/pr/fr/-/1/hi/world/middle_east/3211772.
stm) and the London gay magazine, *QX* ('Tortured and Jailed by the
Palestinian Police', Issue 462, 10 December 2003, http://www.outrage.
org.uk/qx-palestine.html). Although the man was not identified,
similarities in the three stories suggest they may all refer to the same
person.

36. ' "Death threat" to Palestinian Gays'. BBC, 6 March 2003. http://news.
bbc.co.uk/1/hi/world/middle_east/2826963.stm.

37. 'Palestinian Gay Runaways Survive on Israeli Streets'. Reuters, 17
September 2003. Reproduced at http://www.sodomylaws.org/world/
palestine/psnews003.htm.

38. There are echoes here of Britain in the 1950s and 1960s when gay men

engaged in secret government work were regarded as a particular security risk. The fact that their sexual activities were illegal at the time and had to be concealed exposed them to the possibility of blackmail by Soviet agents.

39. Halevi, 'Refugee Status'.
40. Reuters, 17 September 2003, 'Palestinian Gay Runaways'.
41. Baron, 'Palestinian Gay Runaways'.
42. Reuters, 17 September 2003, *op. cit.*; Halevi, 'Refugee Status'.
43. Several deportations were reported in 2003. See, for example, BBC, 6 March 2003, 'Death Threat'.
44. Reuters, 17 September 2003, 'Palestinian Gay Runaways'.
45. 'Palestinian Gays Flee to Israel', BBC, 22 October 2003. http://news.bbc.co.uk/go/pr/fr/-/1/hi/world/middle_east/3211772.stm.

*Chapter 2*

1. The rainbow flag, now internationally recognized as a gay symbol, was designed by Gilbert Baker, a San Francisco artist, for a local parade in 1978. Its initial eight coloured stripes were later reduced to six and it gradually became popular worldwide. It is generally regarded as representing hope and diversity. Some also associate it with 'Over the Rainbow', the song from *The Wizard of Oz* film which has a strong gay following. See http://en.wikipedia.org/wiki/Rainbow_flag; http://www-2.cs.cmu.edu/afs/cs.cmu.edu/user/scotts/bulgarians/rainbow-flag.html and http://flagspot.net/flags/qq-rb.html. There is apparently no 'right way up' to hang the flag.
2. *As-Safir, An-Nahar, L'Orient le Jour* and the *Daily Star*.
3. 'Homosexuals Carried their Flag and Participated', *An-Nahar*, 16 March 2003, p.4. In popular Arab culture, black T-shirts tend to be associated with satanism, heavy metal music and/or homosexuality.
4. See http://www.helem.net/about.zn.
5. Sanderson, James: 'Postcard from Beirut'. http://www.gayguidetoronto.com/1_turnstile/feb_2004.html. Helem's website includes a 'Queer Lebanon Guide' (http://beirut.helem.net/index.htm).
6. 'Police storm gay nightclub in Beirut'. *Daily Star*, 31 March 2003
7. *ibid.*
8. Author's interview, June 2004. There have been similar campaigns against 'devil worship' in Morocco and Egypt directed against heavy metal bands and/or their fans (see Whitaker, Brian: 'Highway to Hell', *The Guardian*, 2 June 3003. http://www.guardian.co.uk/international/story/0,968945,00.html).
9. Singh-Bartlett, Warren: 'For Some Young Lebanese, Staying Means "Life Will be Over"; Increasing Numbers are Fleeing Homophobic

Persecution.' *Daily Star,* 16 October 2001.

10. 'Dunkin' Donuts Accused of Discriminating Against Gay Customers.' *Daily Star,* 25 July 2003.

11. There is also a joint Israeli-Palestinian community centre in Jerusalem called Open House www.gay.org.il. Two other organisations, the Egyptian Initiative for Personal Rights (EIPR) and Hurriyyat Khassa ('Private Freedoms') in Lebanon, deal with gay and lesbian rights among a range of issues affecting people's personal lives – 'domestic slavery, sexual equality, democracy inside the family, and the right not to belong to a religious sect' in the case of Hurriyat Khassa (interview with Nizar Saghieh of Hurriyat Khassa, June 2004). The right to be secular is a particular issue in Lebanon, where all citizens are obliged to register as adherents of a specific faith or sect. An additional organisation based in Israel is Aswat, for 'Palestinian gay women' www.aswatgroup.org.

12. http://www.helem.net/about.zn.

13. Human Rights Watch, *In a Time of Torture: The Assault on Justice in Egypt's Crackdown on Homosexual Conduct,* March 2004, p.1. Available online at: http://www.hrw.org/reports/2004/egypt0304/.

14. Dawoud, Khaled: '50 Egyptian Gays in Court for "fomenting strife".' *The Guardian,* 18 July 2001. http://www.guardian.co.uk/international/story/0,523249,00.html.

15. Whitaker, Brian: 'Homosexuality on Trial in Egypt.' *The Guardian,* 19 November 2001. http://www.guardian.co.uk/elsewhere/journalist/story/0,600791,00.html.

16. 'Egyptian Government Denies Gay Crackdown', 4 April 2003. Cited at www.sodomylaws.org/world/egypt/egnews211.htm.

17. Bahgat, Hossam: 'Explaining Egypt's Targeting of Gays.' *Middle East Report,* 23 July 2001. http://www.merip.org/mero/mero072301.html.

18. Interview conducted in Egypt, April 2004.

19. Interview conducted in Egypt, April 2004.

20. Ghafari, Iman al-: 'Is There a Lesbian Identity in the Arab Culture?' in *Al-Raida* (Lebanese American University, Beirut) vol. XX, no. 99, fall 2002/2003. pp 86–90.

21. 'Gay Time Story: To be Gay in Saudi Arabia.' http://www.gaymiddleeast.com/news/article13.htm.

22. *ibid.*

23. Dahir, Mubarak: 'OutUK from Saudi Arabia.' Undated article. http://www.outuk.com/index.html?http://www.outuk.com/content/features/saudiarabia/.

24. Bradley, John: 'Saudi Gays Flaunt new Freedoms: "Straights can't Kiss in Public or Hold Hands Like Us.",' *Independent,* 29 February 2004. http://news.independent.co.uk/world/middle_east/article70138.

ece. There is further discussion of this in Bradley's book *Saudi Arabia Exposed* (Palgrave Macmillan, NY 2005).

25. Dahir, *op cit.*

26. Bradley, *op cit.*

27. Dahir, *op cit.*

28. Article 37. http://www.oefre.unibe.ch/law/icl/sa00000_.html.

29. For a portrait of the household as the basic unit of government in a traditional Arab society see Mundy, Martha: *Domestic Government: Kinship, Community and Polity in North Yemen.* I B Tauris, London, 1995.

30. Hamad, Turki al-: *Adama.* Translated by Robin Bray. Saqi, London, 2003.

31. For further discussion of these cases see Chapter 4.

32. Dahir, 'OutUK'.

33. Bradley, 'Saudi Gays'.

34. 'Gay Time Story: To be Gay in Saudi Arabia,' http://www.gaymiddleeast.com/news/article13.htm.

35. Dahir, 'OutUK'.

36. The raid was first reported in *al-Jazirah,* a Saudi Arabic-language newspaper, on 27 February 2004. There were several subsequent reports on 1 March 2004: 'Arrested Chadian Says he was Rehearsing for his Legal Marriage', *Arab News*; 'At Least 50 Men Arrested After Saudi Religious Police Raid Alleged Gay Wedding', *Associated Press*; 'Saudi Arabia Arrests "Gay Wedding" Guests', *Reuters*.

37. http://www.alwifaq.net/news/index.php?Show=News&id=5102 (in Arabic). See 'Saudi Puts Gay Wedding Party on Trial.' Saudi Institute press release, 16 March 2005. http://209.197.233.93/content/view/235/39/. Saudi Institute: no longer available

38. 'Saudi Arabia: Men "Behaving like Women" Face Flogging.' Human Rights Watch press release, 7 April 2005.

39. Human Rights Watch, *In a Time of Torture: The Assault on Justice in Egypt's Crackdown on Homosexual Conduct*, March 2004, pp. 49–52; 65–68. Available online at: http://www.hrw.org/reports/2004/egypt0304/.

40. Dahir, 'OutUK'.

41. www.gaymiddleeast.com.

42. 'Censorship in Saudi Arabia: Access to gaymiddleeast.com Blocked Again.' 19 March 2004. http://www.gaymiddleeast.com/news/article30.htm

43. Human Rights Watch, 'In a Time of Torture', pp. 73–74. The Internet conversations, which were in English, appeared in the case file.

44. Human Rights Watch, 'In a Time of Torture', p. 74.

## Chapter 3

1. Discussion of Arab news media in this chapter excludes news broadcasts which are generally not available in archive form, unlike many Western channels. Anecdotal evidence is that state-run channels ignore homosexuality entirely (even when, as happened in the Egyptian "Queen Boat" case, newspapers covered the story extensively).

2. http://english.aljazeera.net/english/. The search covered approximately a twelve-month period since the website began operating in 2003.

3. Sonnini, C. S. : *Travels in Upper and Lower Egypt*, p. 161. Quoted by Hopwood, Derek: *Sexual encounters in the Middle East: the British, the French and the Arabs*. Reading, 1999, p. 175.

4. Sherley, Thomas: *A discourse of the Turks*. Quoted by Hopwood, *Sexual Encounters*, p.175.

5. Hopwood, *Sexual Encounters*, p. 175.

6. The term 'Sotadic' derives from the name of Sotades, a Greek poet of the third century BCE, who composed homoerotic verses. Although Burton insisted that the boundaries of this Sotadic Zone were not racial but geographical and climatic, Stephen Murray notes: 'The covert geographical specification seems to be "south of Christendom" ... which is to say more cultural than climatic. Burton's frequent forays into comparative religion bolster this interpretation of his zone.' (Murray, Stephen, 'Some Nineteenth Century Reports of Islamic Homosexualities', in Murray, Stephen and Roscoe, Will: *Islamic Homosexualities: Culture, History and Literature*. New York 1997, p. 212.

7. Quoted by Murray, pp. 212–214.

8. It was first published privately in 1886 as a 'Terminal Essay' at the end of his ten-volume translation of the *Arabian Nights*. Although some homosexuality figures in the *Arabian Nights* stories, there was no need for Burton to provide a lengthy survey of practices by way of explanation. It seems likely that he wanted to write about the subject and used the *Arabian Nights* as a pretext for doing so.

9. Murray, 'Islamic Homosexualities', pp. 216-217.

10. Said, Edward: *Orientalism*. London 1978.

11. Lagrange, Frédéric: 'Male Homosexuality in Modern Arabic Literature' in Ghoussoub, Mai and Sinclair-Webb, Emma: *Imagined Masculinities: Male Identity and Culture in the Modern Middle East*. London 2000, pp. 169–198. As this appears to be the only detailed study of homosexuality in modern Arabic literature, it is cited extensively in the discussion that follows.

12. Lagrange, 'Male Homosexuality', p. 187.

13. Ibrahim, Sun'allah. *Sharaf.* Dar al-Hilal, Cairo 1997. Cited by Lagrange, 'Male Homosexuality', p. 189.

14. Ghitani, Gamal al-. *Risalat al-basa'ir fi al-masa'ir*. Cairo 1991. Cited by Lagrange, 'Male Homosexuality', pp. 187–188.

15. Choukri, Mohamed, *For Bread Alone*. London 2006, pp. 78–79.

16. Cited by *al-Ahram Weekly* in a press review. http://weekly.ahram.org. eg/2003/659/pr1.htm. Golda Meir was Israeli Prime Minister at the time.

17. *Al-Musawwar*, 18 May 2001. Cited by Human Rights Watch, *op cit*, p 40.

18. *Al-Masa'*, 15 May 2001. Cited by Human Rights Watch, *op cit*, note 126, p 39.

19. The imagery of disease and infection may have been partly intended as an allusion to HIV/AIDS.

20. *al-Ahram al-Arabi*, 25 August 2001. Cited by Human Rights Watch, *op cit*, note 134, p 40.

21. Bowd, Gavin: 'New Labour, New Lovers?', *al-Ahram Weekly*, 19 November 1998. http://weekly.ahram.org.eg/1998/404/in2.htm.

22. There are a few notable exceptions to this, such as the *Jordan Times* campaign against 'honour' killing of women.

23. Bradley, John: 'Saudi Gays Flaunt New Freedoms', in *Independent*, 29 February 2004. http://news.independent.co.uk/world/middle_ east/article70138.ece. Such activities are said to be widespread in the kingdom's sexually-segregated schools system. Ibrahim bin Abdullah bin Ghaith, the head of the religious police, seemed reluctant to take the matter further. 'This perversion is found in all countries,' he told *Okaz*. 'The number [of homosexuals] here is small ...'

24. 'Journalists Convicted for Gay Report.' Al-Jazeera, 18 May 2002. http:// english.aljazeera.net/NR/exeres/6EC117CC-3078-4D78-9751- A9F824BAF3ED.htm; 'Court Sentence Bans Journalists from Writing'. *Yemen Times*, 20 May 2004.

25. *Al-Wafd*, 20 January 2002. Cited by Human Rights Watch, *op cit*, note 183, p 55.

26. 'Al-Osboa met his ex-wife and his neighbours: the text of the Beheira perverts organisation ringleader's confession', in *Al-Osboa*, 28 January 2002. Cited by Human Rights Watch, *op cit*, note 184, p .55.

27. Human Rights Watch, *op cit*, p. 60.

28. The main exception is Lebanon, where this sort of discussion has taken place in some newspapers and on at least one TV programme.

29. Liang, Lilian: 'Hiding Themselves in the Crowd.' Published at http:// www.metimes.com/issue99-33/eg/egypt_gay_underground.htm but no longer available.

30. 'Gay Muslims Come Out in San Francisco Parade', published at http:// www.metimes.com/2K1/issue2001-26/reg/gay_muslims_come.htm,

but no longer available.

31. 'The Manufacture of Perversion' in *Al-Ahram al-Arabi,* 22 August 2001. Cited by Human Rights Watch, *op cit,* note 391, pp. 107–8.

32. A man dressed as a woman, operating one of the rides at a fairground in Agadir, was pointed out to the author by a Moroccan who said 'They usually have one at these places.'

33. Katz, Mark: 'Assessing the Political Stability of Oman', in *Middle East Review of International Affairs,* Vol 8, No. 3. September 2004. http://meria.idc.ac.il/journal/2004/issue3/jv8n3a1.html.

34. Ammon, Richard: 'The Accidental Informant', March 2002. http://www.globalgayz.com/g-malaysia.html.

35. Mattress shown in Anwar trial, BBC, 15 December 1998. http://news.bbc.co.uk/1/hi/world/asia-pacific/235255.stm; 'Malaysia's Anwar Ibrahim Set Free', BBC, 2 September 2004. http://news.bbc.co.uk/2/hi/asia-pacific/3619790.stm.

36. Afary, Janet and Anderson, Kevin: *Foucault and the Iranian Revolution: Gender and the Seductions of Islam,* Chicago 2005, p. 161.

37. For an account of homosexuality in classical literature see: Rowson, Everett: 'Middle Eastern Literature: Arabic'. http://www.glbtq.com/literature/mid_e_lit_arabic.html.

38. Lagrange, 'Male Homosexuality', p 175.

39. *ibid.* pp. 174–175.

40. Cited by Lagrange, 'Male Homosexuality', p. 173. Tifashi's work, *Nuzhat al-Albab fi ma la Yujad fi Kitab,* was re-published in Arabic (London 1992), and a partial English translation, from a French translation, was published as *The Delight of Hearts or What You Will Not Find in Any Other Book* (San Francisco 1988).

41. Lagrange, 'Male Homosexuality', p. 174.

42. Lagrange ('Male Homosexuality', pp. 171–172) cites an exception to this in Yusuf Idris's short story, *Hadithat Sharaf* (*A Matter of Honour,* 1957): 'At night [Gharib] couldn't stand sleeping at home and would prefer the tall heap of hay in the village barn. He used to bury himself in it, fondling his thighs and his chest, talking with his friends about girls, of whom they knew nothing [ ... ] There was something strange in Gharib, absent in most men. Perhaps it was his excess of manliness, or something else ... A woman simply had to see his neck, or the string of his *saroual* when he was working to start choking as if she had seen a naked man.'

43. Mamdouh, Alia: 'Presence of the Absent Man' in Johnson-Davies, Denys: *Under the Naked Sky: Short Stories from the Arab World,* London 2001, pp. 223–233. Another of Mamdouh's works – *Mothballs* (*Habbat al-Naftalin*), Garnet, Reading, 1996 – includes a lesbian scene between the narrator's two aunts.

44. Abdulhamid, Ammar: *Menstruation*. London 2001, pp. 46–47.
45. *ibid*, p. 51.
46. *ibid*, p. 101.
47. Ghafari, Iman al-: 'Is There a Lesbian Identity in the Arab Culture?' in *Al-Raida*, Beirut 2002/2003, vol. XX, no. 99, pp. 86–90.
48. Shaykh, Hanan al-: *Misk al-Ghazal*, Beirut 1996 (second edition). Published in English as *Women of Sand and Myrrh*, Sydney 1990.
49. Ghafari, 'Is there a Lesbian Identity?'.
50. Mansour, Elham: *Ana Hiya Anti (I Am You)*. Beirut 2000.
51. Matar, Nabil: 'Homosexuality in the Early Novels of Nageeb Mahfouz', *Journal of Homosexuality*, vol. 26 (4), 1994, pp. 77–90. Matar's paper explores the historical development of Mahfouz's views on homosexuality through his novels.
52. Lagrange, 'Male Homosexuality', pp. 191–192. Quoted from an interview between Lagrange and Mahfouz, 8 August 1998.
53. *Moroccan Slave* can be read in English at: http://inside.bard.edu/academic/division/langlit/flcl/capstonecourse/writers/images/moroccanslave.pdf.
54. Aswani, Alaa al-: *The Yacoubian Building*. Cairo 2004. pp 74–75.
55. *Ibid,* p. 180.
56. The book has several passages that might appal a gay Western reader, such as 'that miserable, unpleasant, mysterious, gloomy look that always haunts the faces of homosexuals' (p. 37). Humphrey Davies, the translator of the English edition, pointed these out to Aswani, who was 'seriously concerned that he might alienate a Western audience with such language and ... stressed that he hadn't meant any disrespect or to hurt anyone's feelings.' He suggested that Davies should feel free to omit them from the translation, though Davies did not, thinking that the contradictions were important. In the Arabic version, Aswani also uses the loaded term, *shaadh* ('queer', 'deviant'), as opposed to the neutral *mithli* (see chapter 7). The explanation he gave to the translator for this was that *mithli* was unfamiliar to Egyptian readers. (Author's correspondence with Davies, May 2005.) Nevertheless, gay Egyptians have generally reacted positively to the book.
57. Aswani: *The Yacoubian Buildings*, pp. 133–134.
58. 'Alaa El Aswani', in *Egypt Today*, August 2004. http://www.egypttoday.com/article.aspx?ArticleID=1797.
59. 'Yusra Fights Corruption with Adel Imam'. Albawaba website, 30 November 2004 . http://www.albawaba.com/en/entertainment/178044
60. Barakat, Hoda: *The Stone of Laughter*, Reading 1994, pp. 13–14. Originally published in Arabic as *Hajar al-Dahik*, London 1990.
61. *Ibid*, p. 14.

62. *Ibid,* p. 127.

63. Qur'an XII (Yusuf), 23–28.

64. Barakat: 'Stone of Laughter', pp. 127–128.

65. Author's interview with Hoda Barakat in London, 13 November 2004.

66. Haddad, Mark. Interview in Arabic with Hoda Barakat, *Barra* magazine , issue 1, Beirut 2005.

67. 'Lebanese Group Comes out with Public Battle for Gay Rights'. Agence France Presse, 20 October 2004. http://www.dailystar.com.lb/article. asp?edition_id=1&categ_id=2&article_id=9412.

68. Dirk Bogarde (1921–1999) is regarded as one of the British cinema's greatest stars. He was a matinee idol in the 1950s. With *Victim*, he became one of the first actors to play a gay role without making the character a 'type'. Although this raised questions about his own sexuality, it established him as a serious actor. Among his many other roles was that of Gustav von Aschenbach who develops an infatuation for a beautiful boy in Visconti's 1971 film, *Death in Venice*. He lived for many years with his manager and friend, Tony Forwood. See: http://www.imdb. com/name/nm0001958/bio.

69. For details of the film, and viewers' comments on it, see Internet Movie Database: http://www.imdb.com/title/tt0055597/

70. Shafik, Viola: *Arab Cinema: History and Cultural Identity*, Cairo 1998, p. 10.

71. *Ibid,* p 15.

72. 'Arab Cinema: the Early Years'. Notes accompanying a season of Arab films shown by Channel Four television in Britain during the late 1980s. Reproduced at http://www.al-bab.com/arab/cinema/film1.htm.

73. Menicucci, Garay: 'Unlocking the Arab Celluloid Closet.' *MERIP*, issue 206. http://www.merip.org/mer/mer206/egyfilm.htm. Because it has not been possible to view all the films mentioned in this section, particularly the older ones, some of the descriptions of their content rely on Menicucci's article.

74. 'Yousri Nasrallah: "Je Suis Contre la Dictature Majoritaire".' Interview in French in *L'Humanité*, 5 December 2001. http://www.humanite.presse. fr/journal/2001-12-05/2001-12-05-254562.

75. Originally a term for male transvestite dancers. Today it is commonly applied to the passive partner in homosexual intercourse and is often used as an insult to cast aspersions on a man's masculinity.

76. Menicucci: 'Unlocking the Arab Celluloid Closet.'

77. Shafik: 'Arab Cinema', p. 34.

78. *Ibid,* p 34.

79. Chahine's use of a male-male relationship as a metaphor for warm Soviet-Egyptian relations provides an interesting contrast to the negative use of

such relationships as a metaphor for foreign exploitation.

80. 'Arab Cinema: Youssef Chahine.' Notes accompanying a season of Arab films shown by Channel Four television in Britain during the late 1980s. Reproduced at http://www.al-bab.com/arab/cinema/film2.htm.
81. Menicucci: 'Unlocking the Arab Celluloid Closet'.
82. Shafik: 'Arab Cinema', p. 186.
83. A reference to the Queen Boat case.
84. *L'Humanité*: *op cit.*

*Chapter 4*

1. http://www.un.org/Overview/rights.html. The Arab contribution to the document is often overlooked: one of the key figures involved in the drafting process was Charles Malik, a Lebanese Christian. See 'A Conversation With Habib Malik.' http://usinfo.state.gov/journals/itdhr/1098/ijdp/habib.htm.
2. 'The louder we will sing,' Amnesty International, 1999. http://web.amnesty.org/library/index/ENGACT790031999.
3. For full text of the Brazilian draft see http://www.thegully.com/essays/gaymundo/030422_un_res_lgbt_br.html. The ILGA supported the resolution but suggested it should refer to 'gender identity' as well as sexual orientation.
4. 'Commission on Human Rights Approves Measures on Promotion and Protection of Human Rights, Other Issues.' UN press release, 24 April 2003. http://www.unhchr.ch/huricane/huricane.nsf/view01/4C24CE534B31644BC1256D1300257B62?opendocument.
5. 'UN Rights Body Postpones Attempt to Tackle Gay Rights Amid Anger from Muslim Countries,' Associated Press, 25 April 2003. See also 'Muslim States Block UN Move on Sexual Orientation,' *Reuters*, 25 April 2003 and Osborn, Andrew: 'Muslim Alliance Derails UN's Gay Rights Resolution,' *The Guardian*, 25 April 2003. http://www.guardian.co.uk/international/story/0,3604,943116,00.html.
6. The Islamic Conference Organisation is the main international Muslim body operating at government level.
7. UN press release, *op cit.*
8. Those supporting the Pakistani move were: Algeria, Bahrain, Burkina Faso, Cameroon, China, Congo, Gabon, India, Kenya, Libyan Arab Jamahiriya, Malaysia, Pakistan, Saudi Arabia, Senegal, Sierra Leone, Sri Lanka, Sudan, Swaziland, Syria, Togo, Uganda and Zimbabwe. Those opposing it were: Armenia, Australia, Austria, Belgium, Brazil, Canada, Costa Rica, Croatia, France, Germany, Guatemala, Ireland, Japan, Mexico, Paraguay, Peru, Poland, Republic of Korea, Sweden, Ukraine, United Kingdom, United States, Uruguay and Venezuela. Six countries

abstained – Argentina, Chile, Cuba, Russian Federation, South Africa and Thailand – and two of the fifty-three-member commission were absent.

9. The countries listed by ILGA are Afghanistan, Iran, Mauritania, Pakistan, Sudan, Saudi Arabia and Yemen, plus possibly Chechnya and the United Arab Emirates. See: http://www.ilga.info/Information/Legal_survey/ Summary%20information/death_penalty_for_homosexual_act.htm.

10. In these countries there may nevertheless be strong social taboos or prosecutions under more general 'immorality' laws. The Arab countries not listed by ILGA are Comoros, Egypt, Iraq, Jordan, Palestine (Palestinian Authority) and Somalia.

11. Executions also took place in Afghanistan under the Taliban regime, though the current practice is unclear. In some of the other countries, the death penalty for same-sex offences appears not to be applied. Executions reported in Yemen in recent years have all been for murder, though reporting is erratic.

12. It is worth noting that in Arab countries with large Christian minorities, such as Egypt and Lebanon, the views of church leaders on homosexuality do not differ substantially from those of their Muslim compatriots.

13. The total in 1952 was made up of 670 prosecutions for sodomy; 3,087 for attempted sodomy or indecent assault; and 1,686 for gross indecency. See http://www.glbtq.com/social-sciences/wolfenden_report.html. The total for 1939 was 1,276. See http://www.sodomylaws.org/world/ united_kingdom/uknews24.htm.

14. 'The 1950s Great Purge.' http://myweb.lsbu.ac.uk/~stafflag/purge1950s. html. Peter Wildeblood later described his arrest and imprisonment in *Against the Law* (Weidenfeld & Nicholson, London 1955) Reprinted by Weidenfeld & Nicholson, with an introduction by Matthew Parris, in 1999.

15. Stewart, Graham: 'The Accidental Legacy of a Homophobic Humanitarian' in *The Times*, 2 October 2000. Reproduced at http:// www.sodomylaws.org/world/united_kingdom/uknews24.htm.

16. Parris, Matthew: 'Heroic in Perversity' in *The Times*, 20 November 1999. Reproduced at http://www.indegayforum.org/authors/parris/parris1. html. See also http://myweb.lsbu.ac.uk/~stafflag/wolfenden.html.

17. This was higher than the age of consent for heterosexual sex. The report also said legalisation should not apply to members of the armed forces and merchant navy.

18. Stewart, 'The Accidental Legacy'.

19. For a concise account of the Wolfenden report, and the circumstances surrounding it, see: http://www.glbtq.com/social-sciences/wolfenden_ report.html.

20. These four elements of Islamic jurisprudence (*fiqh*) – *fiqh al-kitab*, *fiqh al-sunna*, *qiyas* and *ijmaa* – were set out by the famous scholar Muhammad ibn Idris ash-Shafii (767–820). For a concise account of the development of Islamic law see: 'Islamic Jurisprudence and its Sources.' http://www.steinigung.org/artikel/islamic_jurisprudence.htm.

21. The Shi'a branch is dominant in Iran. Among the Arab countries, it is important in Iraq, Yemen, Lebanon and Bahrain.

22. Esposito, John (ed), *The Oxford History of Islam,* Oxford, 1999. p 95.

23. Kugle, Scott Siraj al-Hajj, 'Sexuality, Diversity, and Ethics in the Agenda of Progressive Muslims,' in Safi, Omid (ed.), *Progressive Muslims.* Oxford 2003. p. 220.

24. Kugle (*op cit,* p 221) cites two examples: 'Whomever you find doing the act of the people of Lut, kill the active and the passive participant' (rejected by al-Jassas on the grounds that one of its transmitters, Amr ibn Abi Amr, is weak and unreliable). 'The one practising the act of the people of Lut, stone the one on top and the one of the bottom, stone them both together' (rejected by al-Jassas on the grounds that one of its transmitters, Asim ibn Amr, is also weak and unreliable). Kugle adds: 'Despite these critiques, the *hadith* continue to circulate and are frequently put to rhetorical and even legal use.'

25. *Ibid*, note 68, p. 233.

26. Arguments equating anal sex between men with *zina* can be disputed. The act is physically different, as are its possible consequences. In *zina*, the lack of a contractual relationship is an important element because of concerns about the possibility of illegitimate children, problems in establishing parentage, inheritance rights, etc – issues that do not arise in the case of same-sex acts.

27. Tatchell, Peter: 'Islamic Fundamentalism in Britain.' http://www.petertatchell.net/religion/islamic.htm.

28. Sofer, Jehoeda: 'Sodomy in the Law of Muslim States' in Schmitt, A, and Sofer J: *Sexuality and Eroticism Among Males in Moslem Societies.* Binghamton, NY 1992.

29. This ambiguity is discussed by Sofer, *ibid*, p. 144.

30. http://www.sodomylaws.org. Slightly different information, under the heading 'Homosexual Rights Around the World' can be found at http://www.actwin.com/eatonohio/gay/world.htm.

31. See http://en.wikipedia.org/wiki/Gay_rights_in_Iraq.

32. 'Yemeni Villagers Shoot Dead Teenager After Rape' in *Agence France Presse*, 13 May 1999.

33. The absence of reports from the other countries that have the death penalty does not necessarily mean no executions have taken place. It is probable there have been none in the UAE and Yemen, though the

picture in Mauritania and Sudan is unclear. It is also possible that in Saudi Arabia the reported executions have not been the only ones.

34. 'Executions in Saudi Arabia.' Planet Out, 11 July 2000. Reproduced at http://www.sodomylaws.org/world/saudi_arabia/saudinews04.htm.

35. Krisberg, Kim: 'Saudis Beheaded for Sodomy' in *The Washington Blade*, 4 January 2002. Reproduced at http://www.sodomylaws.org/world/saudi_arabia/saudinews15.htm.

36. The province was also home to several of the September 11 hijackers. For further discussion of Asir province and the behaviour of its menfolk, see: Bradley, John R., *Saudi Arabia Exposed*, New York 2005. In particular, chapter 3, 'Flower Men, Tribal Sheiks.'

37. 'Iran: Two More Executions for Homosexual Conduct'. Press release from Human Rights Watch, New York, November 22, 2005. http://hrw.org/english/docs/2005/11/21/iran12072.htm.

38. *Ibid.*

39. 'Gay blackmailer hanged in Iran'. News24.com, April 30, 2005. http://www.news24.com/News24/World/News/0,,2-10-1462_1697953,00.html.

40. 'Iran: Two More Executions for Homosexual Conduct'. Press release from Human Rights Watch Press, New York, 22 November 2005. http://hrw.org/english/docs/2005/11/21/iran12072.htm.

41. *Ibid.*

42. 'Iran Executes Gay Teenagers', OutRage press release, 21 July 2005. http://www.outrage.org.uk/pressrelease.asp?ID=302.

43. 'Iran: End Juvenile Executions,' Human Rights Watch press release, 27 July 2005. http://hrw.org/english/docs/2005/07/27/iran11486.htm.

44. Wockner, Rex: 'Full Story Behind "Iran Gay Hangings" Mired in Controversy.' 365Gay.com, 3 August 2005. http://www.365gay.com/newscon05/08/080305iranFolo.htm.

45. 'Iran's Execution of Gays Part of Ethnic Repression,' British Ahwazi Friendship Society, 24 July 2005. http://www.ahwaz.org.uk/2005/07/irans-execution-of-gays-part-of-ethnic.html.

46. Raban, Jonathan: *Arabia Through the Looking Glass.* London 1980, p. 243.

47. Abu Nawas/Nuwas was a poet of the Abbasid period, famous for his penchant for young men.

48. Human Rights Watch, *op cit,* footnote 52, p. 24.

49. 'Saudi Youth Faces Death for Rape and Murder.' *Arab News*, 4 October 2003. The passage quoted here is an English-language version of the account published by *Okaz* in Arabic on the previous day.

50. 'Nine Saudi Transvestites Jailed.' Associated Press, 16 April 2000.

51. Human Rights Watch, *op cit.* The discussion of Egyptian law that follows

is drawn mainly from this report, pp. 129–43.

52. Originally promulgated in 1951 as Law no. 68/1951 on Combating Prostitution, it was reintroduced with minor changes during Egypt's ill-fated union with Syria (in order to apply to Syria as well as Egypt) and now known as Law 10/1961.

53. Appendix 21, minutes of session No. 34 of the House of Representatives, 26 June 1949, p. 2099. Cited by Human Rights Watch, *op cit,* p. 133.

54. Appendix 202, minutes of session No. 22 of the Senate, 2 April 1951, p. 1680. Cited by Human Rights Watch, *op cit,* p. 133.

55. Human Rights Watch, *op cit,* p. 133.

56. *Ibid.*

57. *Ibid.*

58. Appendix 202, minutes of session no. 22 of the Senate, 2 April 1951, p. 1681. Cited by Human Rights Watch, *op cit,* p 133.

59. Edwar Ghali al-Dahabi, al-Jaraa'im al-Jenseya, *Sexual Crimes,* Cairo1988. p. 183. Cited by Human Rights Watch, *op cit,* p. 135.

60. Article 9(c) of Law 10/1961.

61. Article 14 of Law 10/1961.

62. Egyptian Criminal Code, article 178.

63. Egyptian Criminal Code, article 278.

64. Egyptian Criminal Code, article 269 *bis.*

65. This particular account is from an arrest report by Muqaddam Ahmed Salem, filed at Qasr al-Nil Court of Misdemeanors, but Human Rights Watch (*op cit,* p. 140) says many other examples could be cited and adds: 'The anonymous third party is always immediately released, though he is the only witness to the "crime". All victims interviewed by Human Rights Watch called this incident a fiction.'

66. The Arabic phrase used in article 534 is: '*kul majaama'a 'ala khilaaf al-tabia'a.*' '*Mujaama'a*' comes from a verbal root which conveys notions of joining together. The third form of the verb, from which '*mujaama'a*' is derived, is defined in Hans Wehr's dictionary as meaning 'to have sexual intercourse'.

67. Author's interview, June 2004.

68. 'Two Lesbians Arrested for "unnatural" sex' in *Daily Star,* 23 August 2002.

69. 'Interpretation of Homosexuality in Lebanese Society.' http://www.helem.net/page.zn?id=1.html.

70. 'Law enforcement agents' practices.' Helem website. http://www.helem.net/page.zn?id=3.html.

71. *Ibid.*

72. Mirsad is an acronym for 'Multi-Initiative on Rights: Search, Assist, Defend'.

73. For more detailed accounts of the Batal-Mughraby case, see: 'Internet, Gay Rights Targeted,' Human Rights Watch, 23 September 2000; 'GayLebanon.com: a Miscarriage of Justice?' in *Daily Star,* 16 March 2001; 'Appeals Court Overturns Conviction of Defendants in GayLebanon Case,' in *Daily Star,* 19 July 2001.

74. 'Law enforcement practices'. Helem website. http://www.helem.net/page.zn?id=3.html.

75. Human Rights Watch, *op cit,* p.1.

76. 'New Raid on Homosexuals in Qatar.' ArabicNews website, 23 October 1997. http://www.arabicnews.com/ansub/Daily/Day/971023/1997102308.html. 'Bahrain Deporting 2,000 Gays from RP,' in *Manila Standard,* 11 July 2002. http://www.sodomylaws.org/world/bahrain/banews002.htm. 'Bahrain Cracks Down on Gay Migrant Workers,' in *Manila Times,* 11 July 2002. http://www.sodomylaws.org/world/bahrain/banews001.htm.

77. Berg, Charles: *Fear, Punishment, Anxiety and the Wolfenden Report.* London 1959. p. 16.

*Chapter 5*

1. The site listed the imams involved in answering questions as: Dr Dani Doueiri and team, Beirut, Lebanon; Dr Muhammed Musri, Islamic Center of Central Florida, Orlando; Dr Yahia Abdul Rahman, LaRiba Bank, California; Dr Ahmed H. Sakr, Foundation of Islamic Knowledge, California; Dr Muzammil Siddiqui, Islamic Society of Orange County, California. It states that answers merely reflect the opinions of the scholars and are not necessarily fatwas. See: http://www.islamicity.com/qa/about.shtml.

2. Question no. 2633; Question Date: 1/13/1998. Original spelling and grammar of the letter have been retained. http://www.islamicity.com/qa/action.lasso.asp?-db=services&-lay=Ask&-op=eq&number=2633&-format=detailpop.shtml&-find.

3. Question no. 1099 Question Date: 4/25/1997. http://www.islamicity.com/qa/action.lasso.asp?-db=services&-lay=Ask&-op=eq&number=1099&-format=detailpop.shtml&-find.

4. Question no. 2658 Question Date: 2/4/1998. http://www.islamicity.com/qa/action.lasso.asp?-db=services&-lay=Ask&-op=eq&number=2658&-format=detailpop.shtml&-find.

5. For examples see: Griffiths, Raza: 'Sodom and the Koran' in *Gay Times* (UK), May 2000. Reproduced at http://groups.yahoo.com/group/al-fatiha-news/message/45.

6. In the discussion that follows, 'IslamOnline' refers to www.islamonline.net which is owned by 'Al-Balagh Cultural Society for the Service of

Islam on the Internet', based in Doha, Qatar. There is a similarly-named
website, www.islamonline.com, which is owned by AJ Publishing in
Dubai. AJ Publishing also owns www.aljazeera.com, which is sometimes
confused with www.aljazeera.net, the website of the Qatar-based TV
channel, al-Jazeera.

7. 'Can I Attend a Homosexual "Wedding"?' http://www.islamonline.
net/fatwa/english/FatwaDisplay.asp?hFatwaID=101635.

8. 'How to Give up Homosexuality.' http://www.islamonline.net/fatwa/
english/FatwaDisplay.asp?hFatwaID=99505.

9. *Ibid.*

10. See http://www.islamonline.net/english/aboutus.shtml.

11. See http://www.msnbc.msn.com/id/6191955/.

12. The visit, and particularly Qaradawi's meeting with the 'gay-friendly'
mayor of London, was opposed by large sections of the British press,
together with various gay, Jewish, Hindu and Sikh organisations. See
http://www.londoncommunitycoalition.org/

13. For further background on Qaradawi, a fairly sympathetic account is
at http://encyclopedia.thefreedictionary.com/Yusuf+al-Qaradawi. A
more critical account, by the Anti-Defamation League is at http://www.
adl.org/main_Arab_World/al_Qaradawi_report_20041110.

14. Abbar, Farhat al-: 'Qaradawi Urges Gender Equality on Blood Money.'
IslamOnline, 24 December 2004. http://islamonline.net/English/
News/2004-12/24/article05.shtml.

15. See, for example, Whitaker, Brian: 'Legally Brutalised' in *The Guardian*,
30 November 2004. http://www.guardian.co.uk/elsewhere/journalist/
story/0,,1362957,00.html.

16. Qaradawi, Yusuf al-, 'The Lawful and the Prohibited in Islam.'
International Islamic Federation of Student Organisations, Kuwait
1984. Quoted by London Community Coalition, http://www.
londoncommunitycoalition.org/qaradawi-coalitiondocument.pdf, pp.
24–25.

17. 'Homosexuality is a Major Sin.' http://www.islamonline.net/fatwa/
english/FatwaDisplay.asp?hFatwaID=30519.

18. Awady, Nadia el-: 'Homosexuality in a Changing World: Are
We Being Misinformed?' http://islamonline.net/english/
Contemporary/2003/02/article01-0.shtml.

19. 'Islamic Manners in Dealing with Homosexuals.' Fatwa by Dr Muzammil
Siddiqi, former president of the Islamic Society of North America, 18
June 2003. http://www.islamonline.net/fatwa/english/FatwaDisplay.
asp?hFatwaID=2753.

20. 'Homosexuality and Lesbianism: Sexual Perversions.' http://www.
islamonline.net/fatwa/english/FatwaDisplay.asp?hFatwaID=100855.

21. 'Can I Attend a Homosexual "Wedding"?' http://www.islamonline. net/fatwa/english/FatwaDisplay.asp?hFatwaID=101635.

22. *Ibid.*

23. 'Death Fall as Punishment for Homosexuality.' http://www.islamonline. net/fatwa/english/FatwaDisplay.asp?hFatwaID=76474.

24. 'Homosexuality and Lesbianism: Sexual Perversions.' http://www. islamonline.net/fatwa/english/FatwaDisplay.asp?hFatwaID=100855.

25. 'Homosexuality is a Major Sin.' http://www.islamonline.net/fatwa/ english/FatwaDisplay.asp?hFatwaID=30519.

26. 'Homosexuality and Lesbianism: Sexual Perversions.' http://www. islamonline.net/fatwa/english/FatwaDisplay.asp?hFatwaID=100855.

27. 'Islamic Manners in Dealing with Homosexuals.' http://www. islamonline.net/fatwa/english/FatwaDisplay.asp?hFatwaID=2753.

28. 'Islam's Stance on Homosexual Organisations.' http://www.islamonline. net/fatwa/english/FatwaDisplay.asp?hFatwaID=72432.

29. 'How to Give up Homosexuality.' http://www.islamonline.net/fatwa/ english/FatwaDisplay.asp?hFatwaID=99505.

30. 'What We Offer.' http://www.narth.com/menus/goals.html. For a detailed article about homosexuality 'cures' in the United States, including Narth and its religious connections, see Aitkenhead, Decca: 'Going Straight,' *The Guardian,* 3 April 2004. http://www.guardian. co.uk/weekend/story/0,,1183596,00.html.

31. In a briefing paper, 'Just the Facts about Sexual Orientation & Youth: a Primer for Principals, Educators and School Personnel,' the American Psychiatric Association states: 'The most important fact about "reparative therapy", also sometimes known as "conversion" therapy, is that it is based on an understanding of homosexuality that has been rejected by all the major health and mental health professions. The American Academy of Pediatrics, the American Counseling Association, the American Psychiatric Association, the American Psychological Association, the National Association of School Psychologists, and the National Association of Social Workers, together representing more than 477,000 health and mental health professionals, have all taken the position that homosexuality is not a mental disorder and thus there is no need for a "cure".' http://www.apa.org/pi/lgbc/publications/justthefacts.html.

32. 'Answers to your questions about sexual orientation and homosexuality.' http://www.apa.org/pubinfo/answers.html#cantherapychange.

33. Awady, *op cit.*

34. 'Homosexuality-Related Research.' http://islamonline.net/english/ Contemporary/2003/02/article01-2.shtml.

35. 'The Muslim View of Homosexuality.' http://www.narth.com/docs/ muslim.html.

36. Whatever factors were involved in decisions by the American Psychological Association and the American Psychiatric Association to remove homosexuality from their lists of mental illnesses in the 1970s, it should be noted that the government-appointed Wolfenden Committee in Britain reached the same conclusion twenty years earlier – at a time when gay activism had scarcely begun. For more on Wolfenden, see Chapter 4.
37. For biographical details see http://63.175.194.25/words/munajed/munajid_eng.html.
38. 'Having the Habit of Eating with one's Left Hand.' Islam Q&A http://63.175.194.25/index.php?In=eng&ds=qa&lv=browse&QR=3020&dgn=4.html.
39. The following is typical of modern guidance given to parents who ask if they should discourage children from using their left hand: 'The short and emphatic answer is "No"! Handedness is determined by the brain, not the hand, and the most versatile hand is that which helps brain and hand work together for language and writing. Left-handedness is part of a person's makeup, not a trend or habit that can be quashed or discouraged. With consideration and encouragement, left-handers can learn to overcome many of the obstacles encountered through living in a right-handed world.' http://www.all4kidsuk.com/left_handed_children.help.shtml.
40. Psalm 118, verse 15–16.
41. Matthew 25, verse 41.
42. For more about left-handedness, see http://en.wikipedia.org/wiki/Left_handed. Also 'The Left-Handed Riddle.' *Health News,* April 1992. http://www.findarticles.com/p/articles/mi_m0857/is_n2_v10/ai_12206761. Superstitions about the left, from a variety of cultures, are described at: http://www.anythingleft-handed.co.uk/lefty_myths.html.
43. This was particularly important because the usual method of cleansing, with water or a stone rather than paper, could bring the hand into direct contact with faeces. Food was traditionally eaten from a shared plate, using the fingers rather than knives and forks – a practice that continues in some areas.
44. 'Left-Handedness.' http://www.islamicity.com/dialogue/Q325.HTM.
45. 'Wife Having a Relationship With Another Man.' http://www.islamonline.net/fatwa/english/FatwaDisplay.asp?hFatwaID=87322.
46. See chapter 4.
47. http://www.straightway.org.uk. It is a British-based organisation.
48. 'We are Being Misinformed.' http://straightway.sinfree.net/understanding/awady-comments.htm. The author's name, Mujahid Mustaqim, translates into English as 'Straight Struggler' and is almost

certainly a pseudonym. Pages on Straightway's website are headed 'The Straight Struggle', with quotations from the opening sura of the Qur'an (*al-Fatiha*): 'Guide us to the straight path.'

49. *Ibid.*

50. 'Submitted Questions & Comments.' http://straightway.sinfree.net/ feedback/quecom.htm.

51. 'Kissing Others: What is and is Not Allowed?' http://islamonline. net/fatwa/english/FatwaDisplay.asp?hFatwaID=105368 (no longer available).

52. 'Why Should I Marry?' http://www.inter-islam.org/Lifestyle/marry. htm#Mastb.

53. 'Solo Sex (Male and Female Masturbation).' http://www.alinaam.org.za/ library/solos.htm. (Alinaam is the website of a South African madrasa.) Also reproduced at http://straightway.sinfree.net/rulings/morality_ solo.htm.

54. 'Mastribution' [*sic*]. *Islamic Voice*, June 1998. http://www.islamicvoice. com/june.98/islamic.htm.

55. Presumably 'thick and dense' refers to seminal fluid rather than the actual sperm.

56. *Islamic Voice*, 'Masturbation'.

57. Qur'an XXIII (*al-Mu'minun*) 5–7. Pickthall's version. http://www.usc. edu/dept/MSA/quran/023.qmt.html.

58. 'Islamic Rulings on Homosexuality.' Reproduced at http://straightway. sinfree.net/rulings/fatwas4.htm.

59. 'Addiction to Porn and Masturbation: Islamic Remedy.' http://www. islamonline.net/fatwa/english/FatwaDisplay.asp?hFatwaID=104514.

60. 'Islam's Stance on Oral Sex.' http://www.islamonline.net/fatwa/english/ FatwaDisplay.asp?hFatwaID=31729.

61. 'Ask the Imam.' http://www.islam.tc/ask-imam/view.php?q=11873.

62. http://www.dawateislami.net/services/imam/view.asp?problemid=9& pageno=1&title=Divorce+(Talaq).

63. 'Is Anal Intercourse Permissible?' http://www.sistani.org/html/eng/ main/index.php?page=4&lang=eng&part=1.

64. Mufti Ebrahim Desai. http://www.islam.tc/ask-imam/view. php?q=11873.

65. Qur'an II (*al-Baqara*) 223. Pickthall's version. On the association between agricultural and sexual fertility, Prof Fred Halliday points out that the colloquial Portuguese term for 'vagina', *buseita,* appears to be derived from the Arabic for 'a little field' (correspondence with the author, August 2005).

66. 'Islamic Ruling on Anal Sex.' http://www.islamonline.net/fatwa/ english/FatwaDisplay.asp?hFatwaID=28770. There are others who

argue that this verse prohibits vaginal sex from the rear.

67. *Ibid.*

68. 'Men Wearing Silver Chains.' http://www.islamonline.net/fatwa/english/FatwaDisplay.asp?hFatwaID=115154.

69. For further discussion of transgender issues in an Islamic context see: 'Gender Identity and Islam.' http://www.safraproject.org/sgi-genderidentity.htm.

70. Quoted by IslamOnline. 'Having an Affair with a Hermaphrodite.' http://www.islamonline.net/fatwa/english/FatwaDisplay.asp?hFatwaID=61625.

71. 'Five Sisters Undergoing Sex Change.' *Arab News,* 16 June 2004.

72. The report did not say where the operation took place but named the doctor as Muhammad Hassan, a plastic surgeon. It was published in the *Middle East Times,* Issue 10, 2004, attributed to Agence France Presse. It is reproduced at http://www.gaymiddleeast.com/news/article17.htm.

73. Harrison, Frances: 'Iran's Sex-Change Operations.' BBC Newsnight, 6 January 2005. Reported on the BBC website, 5 January 2005. http://news.bbc.co.uk/go/pr/fr/-/1/hi/programmes/newsnight/4115535.stm.

74. Fathi, Nazila: 'As Repression Lifts, More Iranians Change Their Sex.' *New York Times,* 2 August 2004. http://query.nytimes.com/gst/abstract.html?res=F10711F834590C718CDDA10894DC404482.

75. Harrison, 'Iran's Sex-Change Operations.'

76. According to the Associated Press, Iran and Egypt are the only Muslim countries in the Middle East where people can officially change their gender with relative ease. Jordan, Lebanon and Syria also recognise gender changes, but it takes complicated and lengthy court proceedings. See: 'Kuwaiti Sex-Change Woman Fights a Lonely Battle Against Muslim Conservatism.' Associated Press, 4 November 2004.

77. Griffiths, *op cit.*

78. Made for television on a low budget in 1985, *My Beautiful Laundrette* was so well received by critics at the Edinburgh Film Festival that it was later distributed internationally for cinemas. The writer, Hanif Kureishi, won an Oscar nomination for Best Screenplay. Details: Internet Movie Database http://www.imdb.com/title/tt0091578/. Review: Edinburgh University Film Society http://www.eufs.org.uk/films/my_beautiful_laundrette.html.

79. Whitaker, Brian: 'Saudi Textbooks "Demonise West".' *The Guardian,* 14 July 2004. http://www.guardian.co.uk/international/story/0,3604,1260676,00.html. Also see: 'Saudi School in Virginia Disparages Christianity and Judaism.' Saudi Institute, 13 July 2004. http://www.saudiinstitute.org/index.php?option=content&task=vi

ew&id=136. The claim in the textbook is contradicted by the Qur'an (II, 136): 'We believe in Allah, and the revelation given to us, and to Abraham, Ishmael, Isaac, Jacob, and the Tribes, and that given to Moses and Jesus, and that given to (all) Prophets from their Lord: we make no difference between one and another of them: and we bow to Allah.' The main author of the religious curriculum is Sheikh Saleh al-Fawazan, who believes slavery is justified in Islam, opposes the marriage of Arab women to non-Arab men (even if they are Muslims) and has issued a fatwa against watching television.

80. Interview in Griffiths, Raza, 'Sodom and the Koran'.

81. 'Muslims' implementing shari'ah in the West.' http://www.islamonline. net/fatwa/english/FatwaDisplay.asp?hFatwaID=72190.

82. Sheikh Ahmad Kutty is described as a senior lecturer and Islamic scholar at the Islamic Institute of Toronto, Ontario, Canada.

83. 'Socialisation with Non-Muslims: Permissible?' http://www.islamonline. net/fatwa/english/FatwaDisplay.asp?hFatwaID=100762.

84. Wilkins, Richard: 'The Worldwide Attack on Marriage – a Battle We Cannot Lose.' *Meridian* online magazine (undated). http://www. meridianmagazine.com/familywatch/041014attack.html. See also: 'The Miracle in Istanbul 1996 Stopped a Plan to Make Gay Marriage a "Human Right".' http://www.renewamerica.us/columns/mostert/040225.

85. Wilkins, Richard. 'Istanbul: Defending the Family.' Account in the history section of the WFPC website. http://www.worldfamilypolicy. org/history.htm.

86. http://www.dicf.org.qa/english/index.html.

87. 'Meridian Readers Made a Big Difference at the United Nations.' http:// www.meridianmagazine.com/familywatch/041208difference.html.

*Chapter 6*

1. The Quakers (http://www.quaker.org.uk/), also known as The Religious Society of Friends, are a small sect with about 210,000 members that began in Britain in the 1650s. They have no formalised ritual or doctrine. Though rooted in the Christian tradition, they do not regard the Bible as their only source of inspiration. For a brief description of their history and beliefs, see: http://www.bbc.co.uk/religion/religions/christianity/ subdivisions/quakers/index.shtml.

2. Friends Home Service Committee: *Towards a Quaker View of Sex.* London, revised edition, 1964. Extracts reproduced at http:// worldpolicy.org/globalrights/sexorient/1964-quaker.html. See also http://www.quaker.org.uk/Templates/Internal.asp?NodeID=90275. html.

3. Eron, John Lewis: 'Homosexuality and Judaism' in Swidler, Arlene (ed):

*Homosexuality and World Religions.* Trinity Press International, Valley
Forge, Pennsylvania, 1993. p.124.

4. 'Gay-Rights Supporters Rally in Polish Capital Despite Ban, Opposition
   Taunts,' *Associated Press*, 11 June 2005. 'Gay Marchers Ignore Ban
   in Warsaw,' BBC, 11 June 2005. http://news.bbc.co.uk/2/hi/
   europe/4084324.stm.

5. 'Jerusalem Gay March Ban Set Aside,' BBC, 26 June 2005. http://
   news.bbc.co.uk/2/hi/middle_east/4624843.stm. Man charged over
   Jerusalem attack BBC July 5, 2005. http://news.bbc.co.uk/2/hi/
   middle_east/4653655.stm.

6. Duran, Khalid, 'Homosexuality and Islam' in Swidler, p. 181.

7. 'Homosexuality and the Ordination of Women.' Two lectures given by
   His Holiness Pope Shenouda III on 26 November 1990. http://tasbeha.
   org/content/hh_books/ordofwom/index.html. For a summary of the
   Coptic Orthodox church's views on homosexuality see: http://www.
   religioustolerance.org/hom_copt.htm.

8. For an overview of current Christian and Jewish attitudes see http://
   en.wikipedia.org/wiki/Homosexuality_and_Christianity and http://
   en.wikipedia.org/wiki/Homosexuality_and_Judaism.

9. It is perhaps no coincidence that among the Muslim countries secular
   Turkey has some of the most liberal policies on homosexuality.

10. Hunter, James Davison: *Culture Wars: The Struggle to Define America.*
    New York 1991. p. 106.

11. Ellison, Marvin: 'Homosexuality and Protestantism' in Swidler,
    'Homosexuality', pp. 170–171.

12. Dietrich, Heidi 'To be Gay and Muslim.' http://www.alternet.org/
    story/12817.html.

13. For more on successful Muslim efforts to block discussion of sexual
    orientation at the UN see Chapter 4. Another example is the debate about
    the UN's definition of 'the family' – see Whitaker, Brian: 'Fundamental
    Union,' Guardian Unlimited, 25 January 2005. http://www.guardian.
    co.uk/elsewhere/journalist/story/0,7792,1398055,00.html.

14. Besides the Lot story, there are a number of other scriptural issues in
    Judaism and Christianity. They are not discussed here because they
    are of limited relevance to Islamic views of homosexuality. For more
    information about the various Christian arguments, see http://www.
    religioustolerance.org/homosexu.htm. For the development of Jewish
    ideas on homosexuality see: Eron, 'Homosexuality and Judaism', pp.
    103–134.

15. Genesis 18: 20–21. The Revised Standard version is quoted here because
    its meaning is clearer. The King James Version says: 'And the Lord said,
    Because the cry of Sodom and Gomorrah is great, and because their sin

is very grievous; I will go down now, and see whether they have done altogether according to the cry of it, which is come unto me; and if not, I will know.'

16. Ezekiel 16: 48–49. For further discussion of this from a Jewish viewpoint, see Eron, 'Homosexuality and Judaism', pp. 103–134.

17. Genesis 19: 4–11. Revised Standard Version.

18. The interpretation of 'know' in this passage is sometimes disputed. However, the story makes little sense if it simply implies 'to get to know' or 'become acquainted with'. Its meaning in this context seems clear, especially in view of the way 'know' is used again in Verse 8.

19. Jamal, Amreen: 'The story of Lot and the Qur'an's Perception of the Morality of Same-Sex Sexuality.' *Journal of Homosexuality*, vol 41(1) 2001.

20. Qur'an 50 (*Qaf*).

21. The relevant verses in the Qur'an are: 6 (*al-Anaam*): 85–87; 7 (*al-Araf*): 78–82; 11 (*al-Hud*): 73 and 79–84; 15 (*al-Hijr*): 58–77; 21 (*al-Anbiya*): 70–75; 22 (*al-Hajj*): 43–44; 26 (*al-Shuara*): 160–176; 27 (*al-Naml*): 55–59; 29 (*al-Ankabut*): 25–34; 37 (*al-Saffat*): 133–138; 38 (*Sad*): 11–14; 50 (*Qaf*): 12–13; 54 (*al-Qamar*): 33–40 and 66 (*al-Tahrim*): 10.

22. Qur'an 15 (*al-Hijr*).

23. The Arabic says: '*wa laqad raawaduhu 'an daifihi*.' The verb here is the third form of *raada* which, according to Hans Wehr's dictionary, in combination with the preposition '*an*, means 'to seek to alienate or lure away.' According to Wehr, when used without the preposition and with a direct object, the verb means 'to attempt to seduce.'

24. Kugle, *op cit,* quotes a reconstruction of the Lot story by the twelfth-century *Stories of the Prophets* by al-Kisa'i (p. 210).

25. http://www.alinaam.org.za/library/homos.htm. On the question of homosexuality among animals, modern research suggests it is quite widespread. See: http://en.wikipedia.org/wiki/Non-human_animal_sexuality.

26. *Ibid*

27. 'Can I Attend a Homosexual "Wedding"?' http://www.islamonline.net/fatwa/english/FatwaDisplay.asp?hFatwaID=101635.

28. Boswell, John: *Christianity, Social Tolerance and Homosexuality.* Chicago 1980.

29. Armstrong, Karen: 'Not-So-Holy Matrimony' in *The Guardian,* 30 June 2003. http://www.guardian.co.uk/comment/story/0,,987573,00.html.

30. Genesis 19: 30–38.

31. Kugle, *op cit.* p 223.

32. *Ibid*.

33. 'Submitted Questions & Comments.' http://straightway.sinfree.net/

feedback/quecom.htm.

34. Human Rights Watch: 'Religious Police Role in School Fire Criticised.' Press release, 15 March 2002. http://hrw.org/press/2002/03/saudischool.htm; 'Saudi Police "Stopped" Fire Rescue.' BBC, 15 March 2002. http://news.bbc.co.uk/1/hi/world/middle_east/1874471.stm.

35. 'Homosexuality is a Major Sin.' http://www.islamonline.net/fatwa/english/FatwaDisplay.asp?hFatwaID=30519.

36. Kugle, *op cit.* p 200-201.

37. Rowson, Everett: 'The Effeminates of Early Medina' in Comstock and Henking (eds): *Que(e)rying Religion: a Critical Anthology.* New York 1997. Cited by Kugle, *op cit.* p. 197.

38. Qur'an 24:31 (*al-Nur*), Shakir's version. This is translated by others as 'male servants free of physical needs' (Yusuf Ali) and 'male attendants who lack vigour' (Pickthall). From the context, this clearly indicates men who were not heterosexually active.

39. 'The Significance of Doing Things With Right Hands.' http://www.islamonline.net/fatwa/english/FatwaDisplay.asp?hFatwaID=58534.

40. Kugle, *op cit.* p. 194.

41. Qur'an 49: 13 (*al-Hujurat*).

42. Qur'an 30:22 (*al-Rum*).

43. Kugle, *op cit.* p. 194.

44. Eron, 'Homosexuality and Judaism'.

45. Haughton, Rosemary: 'The Meaning of Marriage in Women's New Consciousness' in Roberts, William (ed): *Commitment to Partnership: Explorations of the Theology of Marriage,* New York 1987. Quoted by Carmody, Denise and John: 'Homosexuality and Roman Catholicism' in Swidler, *op cit.* pp.145–146.

*Chapter 7*

1. 'Saudi Executes Gay Lovers for Killing Pakistani.' Reuters, 13 March 2003.

2. Foreword to Schmitt, Arno, and Jehoeda, Sofer: *Sexuality and Eroticism Among Males in Moslem Societies.* New York 1992. Page *x*.

3. *Ibid.*

4. Massad, Joseph: 'Re-orienting Desire: the Gay International and the Arab World,' Public Culture 14 (2), pp. 361–385. For a précis see: http://www.uchicago.edu/research/jnl-pub-cult/backissues/pc37/massad.html.

5. Ghafari, Iman al-: 'Is There a Lesbian Identity in the Arab Culture?' in *Al-Raida* (Lebanese American University, Beirut) Vol XX, no 99, Fall 2002/2003. pp 86–90.

6. http://en.wikipedia.org/wiki/Homosexuality.

7. http://en.wikipedia.org/wiki/Gay.

8. *Khawal* was originally a term for male transvestite dancers who, in the nineteenth century, were regarded as a respectable substitute for female dancers. Today the word is often used as an insult to cast aspersions on a man's masculinity.

9. Lagrange, *op cit.* pp. 169–198.

10. *In a Time of Torture: The Assault on Justice in Egypt's Crackdown on Homosexual Conduct.* Report by Human Rights Watch, March 2004. http://www.hrw.org/reports/2004/egypt0304/.

11. This is not necessarily the reality, however. A gay interviewee in Cairo insisted that a lot of married Egyptian men favour the passive role when having sex with other men.

12. Massad, 'Reorienting Desire', p. 372.

13. 'The Trials and Tribulations of Lebanon's Young Gays' in *Daily Star,* 26 October 1998. 'Gays and Lesbians Face Uphill Battle for Acceptance' in *Daily Star,* 9 July 2003. 'Hiding Themselves in the Crowd' in *Middle East Times,* August 1999. http://www.metimes.com/issue99-33/eg/ egypt_gay_underground.htm. 'Refugee Status' in *The New Republic,* 19 August 2002. http://www.tnr.com/doc.mhtml?i=20020819&s=halevi 081902.

14. For example: 'Impressions of America 2004.' Survey by Zogby International for the Arab American Institute. http://www.aaiusa.org/ PDF/Impressions_of_America04.pdf.

15. 'Hiding Themselves in the Crowd.' *Middle East Times,* August 1999. http://www.metimes.com/issue99-33/eg/egypt_gay_underground. htm.

16. Khayyat, Munira: 'Sex: Revolution or Revulsion.' *Daily Star,* 15 April 1999.

17. *Ibid.*

18. Singh-Bartlett, Warren: 'The Trials and Tribulations of Lebanon's Young Gays.' *Daily Star,* 26 October 1998.

19. Massad, *op cit,* pp 361-362

20. Interview in Beirut, March 2005.

21. Letter from al-Fatiha, published on Behind the Mask website. http:// www.mask.org.za/SECTIONS/AfricaPerCountry/ABC/egypt/ egypt_032.htm.

22. Interview in Cairo, May 2005.

23. See, for example, the address by President George Bush to the National Endowment for Democracy, 6 November 2003. Available at http:// www.whitehouse.gov/news/releases/2003/11/20031106-2.html     and http://www.al-bab.com/arab/docs/reform/bush2003.htm.

24. Gwertzman, Bernard: 'Bush Mistakes Arab Autocracies for Soviet

Totalitarianism.' Interview with Daniel Brumberg, associate professor at Georgetown University. Council on Foreign Relations, 7 November 2003. http://www.cfr.org/publication.php?id=6516.

25. For the full text of the document see: http://www.al-bab.com/arab/docs/international/gmep2004.htm. For a discussion of its contents see 'Beware Instant Democracy,' by Brian Whitaker. Guardian Unlimited, 15 March 2004. http://www.guardian.co.uk/elsewhere/journalist/story/0,7792,1169776,00.html.

26. For example: The Alexandria Statement, March 2004. http://www.al-bab.com/arab/docs/reform/alex2004.htm; Saudi National Reform Document, January 2003 http://www.al-bab.com/arab/docs/saudi/reform2003.htm; 'Three Middle Eastern Imperatives: Freedom, Democracy and Justice' – statement by forty civil society groups, Daily Star, 25 September 2004 http://www.dailystar.com.lb/article.asp?edition_id=10&categ_id=5&article_id=8698; The Sana'a Declaration, January 2004 (refers to Africa and Asia as well as the Arab countries) http://www.al-bab.com/arab/docs/reform/sanaa2004.htm.

27. 'Three Middle Eastern Imperatives: Freedom, Democracy and Justice' – statement by forty civil society groups, Daily Star, 25 September 2004 http://www.dailystar.com.lb/article.asp?edition_id=10&categ_id=5&article_id=8698.

28. Whitaker, Brian: 'Highway to Hell.' Guardian Unlimited, 2 June 2003. http://www.guardian.co.uk/international/story/0,,968945,00.html.

29. Whitaker, Brian: 'Saudi Ban on Female Doll Imports.' The Guardian, 18 December 2003. http://www.guardian.co.uk/international/story/0,,1109191,00.html.

30. 'Camera Phones.' Arab News, 14 July 2004.

31. The basic format of the programme, which has been adapted for many countries, is to confine a group of young people in a house where their interactions are constantly filmed. Viewers then decide which ones should leave and the last person remaining in the house is declared the winner.

32. 'House Rules.' http://www.hawasawa.com/eng/houserules.html. See also: Whitaker, Brian: 'Reality TV Grips and Enrages Arab World,' The Guardian, 2 March 2004. http://www.guardian.co.uk/international/story/0,,1159995,00.html.

33. 'Hawa Sawa: Puffing the Smoke.' http://aicha.blogdrive.com/.

34. 'Let's Ban Reality Television, But Not For Morality's Sake,' Daily Star, 5 March 2004.

35. The song, 'I am what I am,' was written by Jerry Herman for the musical La Cage aux Folles which opened in New York in 1983. It came to be regarded as a gay anthem. http://gayinfo.tripod.com/lyrics.html.

36. One Arab organisation which does address diversity issues, and argues that diversity can bring positive benefits, is the Syrian-based Tharwa Project (http://www.tharwaproject.com) which uses the slogan '*al-Ikhtilaf Tharwa*' – 'Difference is Wealth'.

# Bibliography

*Books (non-fiction)*

Afary, Janet and Anderson, Kevin: *Foucault and the Iranian revolution: Gender and the Seductions of Islamism,* University of Chicago Press, Chicago, 2005.

Berg, Charles: *Fear, Punishment, Anxiety and the Wolfenden Report.* George Allen & Unwin, London, 1959.

Boswell, John: *Christianity, Social Tolerance and Homosexuality.* University of Chicago Press, 1980.

Esposito, John, ed.: *The Oxford History of Islam,* Oxford, 1999.

Ghoussoub, Mai and Sinclair-Webb, Emma. *Imagined Masculinities: Male Identity and Culture in the Modern Middle East.* Saqi Books, London, 2006.

Hopwood, Derek: *Sexual Encounters in the Middle East: the British, the French and the Arabs.* Ithaca Press, Reading, 1999.

Human Rights Watch: *In a Time of Torture: The Assault on Justice in Egypt's Crackdown on Homosexual Conduct.* Human Rights Watch, New York, 2004.

Hunter, James Davison: *Culture Wars: The Struggle to Define America.* Basic Books, New York, 1991.

Murray, Stephen and Roscoe, Will: *Islamic Homosexualities: Culture, History and Literature.* New York University Press, New York, 1997.

Raban, Jonathan: *Arabia Through the Looking Glass.* Fontana/Collins, Glasgow, 1982 (fourth edition).

Safi, Omid, ed.: *Progressive Muslims.* Oneworld, Oxford, 2003.

Said, Edward: *Orientalism.* Routledge, London, 1978.

Schmitt, Arno, and Jehoeda Sofer. 1992. *Sexuality and Eroticism Among Males in Moslem Societies.* Harrington Park Press, Binghamton, NY, 1992.

Shafik, Viola: *Arab Cinema: History and Cultural Identity*. American University in Cairo Press, 1998.

Swidler, Arlene, ed.: *Homosexuality and World Religions*. Trinity Press International, Valley Forge, Pennsylvania, 1993.

Tifashi, Ahmad al-, ed.: *The Delight of Hearts or What You Will Not Find in Any Other Book*. Gay Sunshine Press, San Francisco, 1988. (Published in Arabic as Jum'a Jamal, ed.: *Nuzhat al-albab fi ma la yujad fi kitab*. Riyad el-Rayyes Books, London, 1992.)

*Chapters in Books*

Bradley, John: 'The Segregation of the Sexes' in Bradley, John: *Saudi Arabia Exposed*. Palgrave Macmillan, New York, 2005.

Carmody, Denise and John. 1993. 'Homosexuality and Roman Catholicism' in Swidler, Arlene (ed): *Homosexuality and World Religions*. Trinity Press International, Valley Forge, Pennsylvania, 1993.

Duran, Khalid: 'Homosexuality and Islam' in Swidler, Arlene, ed.: *Homosexuality and World Religions*. Trinity Press International, Valley Forge, Pennsylvania, 1993.

Ellison, Marvin: 'Homosexuality and Protestantism' in Swidler, Arlene, ed.: *Homosexuality and World Religions*. Trinity Press International, Valley Forge, Pennsylvania, 1993.

Eron, John Lewis: 'Homosexuality and Judaism' in Swidler, Arlene, ed: *Homosexuality and World Religions*. Trinity Press International, Valley Forge, Pennsylvania, 1993.

Kugle, Scott Siraj al-Haqq. 'Sexuality, diversity, and ethics in the agenda of progressive Muslims', in Safi, Omid, ed.: *Progressive Muslims*. Oneworld, Oxford, 2003.

Lagrange, Frédéric: 'Male Homosexuality in Modern Arabic Literature' in Ghoussoub, Mai and Sinclair-Webb, Emma: *Imagined Masculinities: Male Identity and Culture in the Modern Middle East*. Saqi Books, London, 2006.

Murray, Stephen: 'Some nineteenth century reports of Islamic homosexualities' in Murray, Stephen and Roscoe, Will: *Islamic Homosexualities: Culture, History and Literature*. New York University Press, New York, 1997.

Rowson, Everett: 'The effeminates of early Medina' in Comstock and Henking (eds): *Que(e)rying religion: a critical anthology*. Continuum, New York, 1997.

Sofer, Jehoeda: 'Sodomy in the law of Muslim states'. in Schmitt, A, and Sofer J, eds: *Sexuality and eroticism among males in Moslem societies*. Harrington Park Press, Binghamton, NY, 1992.

## Journal Articles

Bahgat, Hossam: 'Explaining Egypt's targeting of gays,' in *Middle East Report* (*MERIP*), July 23, 2001. http://www.merip.org/mero/mero072301. html.

Ghafari, Iman al-: 'Is there a lesbian identity in the Arab culture?' in *Al-Raida*. Lebanese American University, Beirut, vol. XX, no. 99, Fall 2002/2003. pp. 86–90.

Jamal, Amreen: 'The story of Lot and the Qur'an's perception of the morality of same-sex sexuality.' *Journal of Homosexuality*, vol. 41 (1), 2001.

Massad, Joseph: 'Re-orienting Desire: the Gay International and the Arab world', in *Public Culture 14* (2), pp. 361–85.

Matar, Nabil: 'Homosexuality in the early novels of Nageeb Mahfouz', *Journal of Homosexuality*, vol. 26 (4), 1994, pp. 77–90.

Menicucci, Garay: 'Unlocking the Arab celluloid closet'. *Middle East Report* (*MERIP*), Issue 206, Spring 1998. http://www.merip.org/mer/mer206/ egyfilm.htm.

## Fiction

Abdulhamid, Ammar: *Menstruation*. Saqi Books, London, 2001.

Alameddine, Rabih: *Koolaids*. Picador, New York, 1998.

Aswani, Alaa al-: *The Yacoubian Building*. Translated by Humphrey Davies. American University in Cairo Press, Cairo. 2004. (Originally published in Arabic as *Imarat Ya'qubian*. Maktaba Madbuli, Cairo, 2002.)

Barakat, Hoda: *The Stone of Laughter*. Translated by Sophie Bennett. Garnet Publishing, Reading, UK, 1994. (Originally published in Arabic as *Hajar al-Dahik*. Riad el-Rayyes Books, London, 1990.)

Choukri, Mohamed; Bowles, Paul (translator). *For Bread Alone*. Saqi Books, London, 2006.

Ghitani, Gamal al-. 'Hadha ma gara lil-shabb al-ladhi asbaha funduqiyyan' ('This is what happened to the boy who worked in a hotel') in *Risalat al-basa'ir fi al-masa'ir*. Maktaba Madbuli, Cairo, 1991.

Hamad, Turki al-: *Adama*. Translated by Robin Bray. Saqi Books, London, 2003.

Ibrahim, Sun'allah. *Sharaf*. Dar al-Hilal, Cairo, 1997.

Mahfouz, Naguib: *Midaq Alley* ('Zuqaq al-Midaq'). Anchor Books, New York, 1992.

Mansour, Elham: *Ana Hiya Anti* ('I Am You'). Riad el-Rayyes, Beirut, 2000.

Mamdouh, Alia: 'Presence of the absent man' in *Under the Naked Sky: short stories from the Arab world* selected and translated by Denys Johnson-Davies, Saqi Books, London, 2001.

Mamdouh, Alia: *Mothballs* ('Habbat al-Naftalin'), Garnet, Reading, UK, 1996.

Taia, Abdellah: *Moroccan Slave*. Can be read in English at: http://inside. bard.edu/academic/division/langlit/flcl/capstonecourse/writers/ images/moroccanslave.pdf.

Shaykh, Hanan al-: *Misk al-ghazal*. Dar al-Adab, Beirut, 1996 (second edition). Published in English as *Women of Sand and Myrrh*, translated by Catherine Cobham. Allen & Unwin, Sydney, 1990.

## *Films*

*Alexandria Once Again* ('Iskindiriyya Kaman wi Kaman', 1989). Directed by Youssef Chahine

*Alexandria, Why?* ('Iskindiriyya Leeh?', 1978). Directed by Youssef Chahine

*An Egyptian Fairy Tale* ('Hadduta Misriyya', 1982). Directed by Youssef Chahine

*Bezness* (1992). Directed by Nouri Bouzid

*Man of Ashes* ('Rih al-Sadd', 1986). Directed by Nouri Bouzid

*Mercedes* (1993). Directed by Yousri Nasrallah

*My Beautiful Laundrette* (1985). Directed by Stephen Frears.

*The Malatili Bath* ('Hamam al-Malatili', 1973). Directed by Salah Abu Saif

*The Nile and its People* ('al-Nass wal Nil', 1972). Directed by Youssef Chahine

*Victim* (1961). Directed by Basil Dearden

## *Gay, Lesbian and Related Websites*

Al-Fatiha Foundation (www.al-fatiha.org). An international organisation for Muslims who are lesbian, gay, bisexual, transgendered, or questioning their sexual orientation.

Algerigay (www.ffaid.org/algerigay). For gay Algerians (in French)

Aswat (www.aswatgroup.org). Israel-based organisation for 'Palestinian gay women'.

Behind the Mask (www.mask.org.za). A website on gay and lesbian affairs in Africa, including North Africa.

Bint el Nas (www.bintelnas.org). For 'women who identify as gay, lesbian, bisexual, transgender, and/or queer'.

Egyptian Initiative for Personal Rights (www.eipr.org). An organisation set up to defend personal rights and freedoms, including sexual rights.

Gay and Lesbian Arabic Society (www.glas.org). US-based organisation which aims 'to promote positive images of gays and lesbians in Arab communities worldwide, in addition to combating negative portrayals of Arabs within the gay and lesbian community'.

GayArab.org (www.gayarab.org). 'An oasis for the gay Arab.'

GayEgypt.com (www.gayegypt.com). A guide to gay life (and persecution) in Egypt.

Gay Middle East (www.gaymiddleeast.com). Country-by-country information, with recent gay-related news reports.

Gay Morocco (http://gaymorocco.tripod.com). An information exchange.

Helem (www.helem.net). Gay, lesbian, bisexual and transgender rights organisation. Its main goal at present is the abolition of article 534 of the Lebanese Penal Code which punishes 'unnatural sexual intercourse'.

Huriyah (www.huriyahmag.com). 'A queer Muslim magazine.'

Imaan (www.imaan.org.uk). A British-based support group 'for Muslim lesbians, gays, bisexuals, and transgendered people, as well as those questioning their sexuality or gender identity, and their family, friends and supporters'.

International Gay and Lesbian Human Rights Commission (www.iglhrc.org). Website documenting abuse and discrimination on the basis of sexual orientation around the world.

International Lesbian and Gay Association (www.ilga.org). A worldwide federation of national and local groups seeking equal rights for lesbians, gay men, bisexuals and transgendered people everywhere.

Kelma (www.kelma.org). Website for gay Arabs in France and North Africa.

Lesbian and Gay Immigration Rights Task Force (www.lgirtf.org). US-based organisation.

Muslim Wakeup (www.muslimwakeup.com). Web magazine for progressive Muslims which often discusses gender and sexuality.

Queer Arabs Blog (www.queerarab.blogspot.com). 'Rantings of angry sarcastic bitchy queer Arab Americans.'

Queer Jihad (www.well.com/user/queerjhd). A website that 'condemns all forms of terrorism, including prejudice and discrimination'.

Safra Project (www.safraproject.org). Project working on 'issues relating to lesbian, bisexual and/or transgender women who identify as Muslim religiously and/or culturally'.

Sodomy Laws (www.sodomylaws.org). Country-by-country guide to laws that criminalise 'non-reproductive, non-commercial, consensual sex between adults in private'.

Yoesuf Foundation (www.yoesuf.nl/engels). Dutch-based centre for information and education on Islam and sexual diversity.

# Index